THE WESTERN SOVIETS

GW00683981

Bookmarks

THE WESTERN SOVIETS WORKERS' ★COUNCILS VERSUS PARLIAMENT 1915·1920 DONNY GLUCKSTEIN

Published November 1985
by Bookmarks, 265 Seven Sisters Road, Finsbury Park, London N4 2DE, England.

ISBN 0 906224 22 5

Printed by A Wheaton and Company, Exeter.
Typeset by Kate Macpherson, Clevedon.
Design by Roger Huddle.

Bookmarks is linked to the Socialist Workers Party, one of a group of socialist
organisations linked internationally:

AUSTRALIA: **International Socialists**, GPO Box 1473N, Melbourne 3001.
BRITAIN: **Socialist Workers Party**, PO Box 82, London E2.
CANADA: **International Socialists**, PO Box 339, Station E, Toronto, Ontario.
DENMARK: **Internationale Socialister**, Morten Borupsgade 18, kld, 8000
    Arhus C.
IRELAND: **Socialist Workers Movement**, c/o 41 Herberton Park, Rialto, Dublin 8.
NORWAY: **Internasjonale Sosialister**, Postboks 2510 Majorstua, 0302 Oslo 3.
UNITED STATES: **International Socialist Organization**, PO Box 16085,
    Chicago, Illinois 60616.
WEST GERMANY: **Sozialistische Arbeiter Gruppe**, Wolfgangstrasse 81,
    D–6000 Frankfurt 1.

This book is published with the aid of the **Bookmarks Publishing Co-operative**.
Many socialists have a few savings put aside, probably in a bank or savings bank.
While it's there, this money is being re-loaned by the bank to some business or other
to further the aims of capitalism. We believe it is better loaned to a socialist venture
to further the struggle of socialism. That's how the co-operative works: in return for
a loan, repayable at a month's notice, members receive free copies of books
published by Bookmarks, plus other advantages. The co-operative has about 125
members at present, from as far apart as East London and Australia, Canada and
Norway.
    Like to know more? Write to the **Bookmarks Publishing Co-operative**, 265
Seven Sisters Road, Finsbury Park, London N4 2DE, England.

CONTENTS

Acknowledgement
Many people have helped in the writing and preparation of
this book. Particular thanks are due to Alex Callinicos, Tony Cliff,
Pete Goodwin, Chris Harman, Dave Hill, David Kirby, James
Hinton, Peter Marsden, Harry McShane, Penny Packham and
Gwyn Williams.

Dedication
To Rhian and Owen

INTRODUCTION

CAPITALISM is again in crisis. In the 1960s and 1970s apologists for the system argued that the Marxist prediction of economic breakdown and inevitable class war had been disproved by events, and that change could come through the conventional channels of parliamentary democracy. But the abject failure of such methods to undermine the roots of exploitation, or even defend workers from mass unemployment and the erosion of basic welfare provision, has again put the question of revolutionary change on the agenda, if only in the long term.

Nevertheless, although many workers regard parliament with distrust and cynicism, few see any alternative to the ballot box except East European-style Stalinist rule. Yet history has shown the *workers' council* to be a genuine alternative to both systems, an alternative which is still very relevant today. It was not thought up by some talented social planner. The workers and peasants of Russia in 1905 and 1917, like those of Germany in 1918, Hungary in 1956 or Chile in 1972, were not following a blueprint. They were creating a mass democracy which could solve the capitalist crisis in the interests of the majority. Historically, workers' power organised through councils (or *soviets* as the Russians called them) has been the greatest challenge to the state power of capitalism. Now, when the system is once more decaying, the tradition of workers' councils must be recovered from the obscurity into which it has been driven by its opponents — reactionaries, reformists and Stalinists alike.

This book does not attempt the monumental task of surveying *all* the examples of council activity to date. Beginning with a brief survey of the Russian experience, it concentrates on other examples of relevance to revolutionary socialists who operate in conditions of parliamentary rule and mass reformism. Three centres of council activity — each in a different country — Britain, Germany and Italy — are considered in detail.

This book does not pretend to neutrality. Marxists do not believe that the writing of history, any more than any other intellectual pursuit within class society, can claim to stand above the fundamental social division between exploiters and exploited. What follows takes as its starting point the need for a revolutionary overthrow of capitalism, which can be achieved only by the working class through its own activity and organisation. The workers' council is one of the tools of this process. If this book can bring to the labour movement today, and to the building of a revolutionary party, some understanding of past struggles it will have amply served its purpose.

In the period during and just after the First World War, Europe saw a great flowering of revolutionary activity in response to the crisis of imperialism and to the Bolshevik revolution. A comparison of countries as different as Russia, Italy, Britain and Germany is useful because it allows general lessons to be drawn. Purely national studies tend to be coloured by local traditions. Thus in Britain histories of this period are often dominated by trade union questions and shy away from politics. German writing, in contrast, is obsessed with the political process but hardly considers changes at workplace level, and so on. Obviously the limited focus of the nationally-based studies will find some reflection in the pages that follow, but the aim here is to show how workers' movements were part of a class struggle that transcended national frontiers. International comparisons are all the more valid for this particular period because the World War ironed out many of the differences between working-class struggles across Europe.

Workers' council movements did not take shape at the level of official public politics. As Gramsci put it, one has to 'look underground, in the obscurity of the factory and of the consciousness of the countless multitudes that capitalism subjects to its laws . . . where the relations are those of oppressor and oppressed, of exploiter and exploited; where for the worker liberty does not exist, democracy does not exist.'[1]

There are inevitable problems for the historian here. The ruling class employs a small army of civil servants, secretaries and publicists to record and disseminate its debates and decisions. As organs of an oppressed class, the workers' councils never had a **Hansard** in which they could commit their proceedings to paper.

Lacking paid functionaries, and operating in the midst of a turbulent class struggle, rank-and-file activists rarely found an adequate written expression for their ideas. Councils and shop stewards' organisations lacked even that regular organisation that workers' parties possessed in which people were chosen to take minutes, record conference decisions and so on. For these reasons it is quite unusual to find information on such matters as the meeting places of the rank-and-file militants and council executives, or the regularity of their sessions, or even the levels of attendance and breadth of representation. Sometimes this lack of precise detail makes the councils seem insubstantial, but the lack of documentary evidence is compensated for by evidence of workers' self-activity. For in the end workers' councils were above all organs designed for action.

To uncover the molecular process of rank-and-file struggle in individual factories and industries it has been necessary to limit the scope of this study to Glasgow, Berlin and Turin. To grasp the full implications of their struggles, these places must be seen as part of a much wider movement whose starting point was in Russia and especially in its capital, Petrograd.

Chapter One

SOVIETS AND REVOLUTION IN PETROGRAD

WESTERN Europe's workers' councils were part of a much broader working-class revolt whose immediate cause was the terrible bloodbath of the 1914–18 war. This conflict, which cost 13 million lives and left 36 million wounded, was the result of capitalist competition. It was but a short step from rivalry in the market place to imperialist war on the battlefields.

Writing from her prison cell in 1915, Rosa Luxemburg argued that 'bourgeois society faces a dilemma; either a transition to Socialism or a return to barbarism . . . we face the choice: either the victory of imperialism and the decline of all culture . . . annihilation, devastation, degeneration, a yawning graveyard — or the victory of Socialism — the victory of the international working class consciously assaulting imperialism and its method.'[1]

By the end of the war socialists were not the only ones who felt the capitalist world crumbling before them. Lloyd George warned statesmen assembled at the Paris Peace Conference that 'Europe is in a revolutionary mood. The whole of the existing social, political and economic order is being called into question by the mass of people from one end of Europe to the other.'[2] Even in Britain, the most stable of European states, secret government reports at the end of 1918 spoke of the 'spread of the bacillus of Bolshevism' adding there was a 'very widespread feeling among the working class that Thrones have become anachronisms, and that the Soviet may still prove to be the best form of Government for a democracy. This feeling does not seem confined to revolutionaries.'[3]

In these years militancy took on an extraordinary breadth and variety, extending from Dublin's Easter Rising of 1916 to the Russian revolution, from general strikes in Seattle to riots in Amritsar. In the post-war period the great Empires of central Europe — Austro-Hungary and Germany — dissolved before waves of workers' revolt. In France strikes reached a peak when dockers, sailors, miners and engineers struck in sympathy with railwaymen. Soviet Republics appeared in Russia, Hungary and Bavaria, while workers' councils were a powerful force in the rest of Europe.

In 1919, at the peak of the crisis, Zinoviev, president of the newly-formed Communist (Third) International, predicted that: 'Nobody will be surprised if, when these lines come to be printed, we have not three but six or even more Soviet republics. Old Europe is rushing towards revolution at breakneck speed.'[4]

Undoubtedly the single most important event of this remarkable epoch was the Russian revolution of 1917. In that year workers overthrew the Tsar and, after a brief transition period, seized power. The first successful workers' revolution was an inspiration to socialists everywhere. It showed the potential for a new sort of state based on soviets, on workers' councils, as well as the importance of the revolutionary party. The French revolution of 1789 had been the yardstick against which the bourgeois revolutions of the nineteenth century were all measured. These saw their own development through the eyes of the French experience. Each had its Convention, its Jacobins, even its own Napoleon. The October 1917 revolution in Russia serves Marxists in the same way and revolutionary movements elsewhere must be judged against this first and best example.

Lenin on the soviet state

The workers' council, in the form of the soviet, reached its highest expression, both practically and in theory, in Russia. Lenin made a particularly important contribution in both spheres. When he wrote the pamphlet **State and Revolution** in August 1917 he was able to draw on the example of the Paris Commune, 'the teaching of Marx' and the rich experience of two Russian revolutions — those of 1905 and February 1917.

Lenin begins this pamphlet by showing that the state 'is a product and a manifestation of the irreconcilability of class antagonisms'.[5] Thus in capitalist society, where a minority controls the wealth of society and exploits the majority, a special apparatus of repression — the state — is used to maintain class rule. This apparatus 'consists of special bodies of armed men having prisons etc at their command,' states Lenin.[6]

From this Lenin concludes that the 'liberation of the oppressed class is impossible *without the destruction* of the apparatus of state power created by the ruling class.'[7] This inevitably involves a revolution in which the oppressed class creates its own authority by which to challenge and defeat its enemy. Engels put it succinctly when he said:

> A revolution is certainly the most authoritarian thing there is; it is the act whereby one part of the population imposes its will upon the other part by means of rifles, bayonets and cannon . . . and if the victorious party does not want to have fought in vain, it must maintain this rule by means of the terror which its arms inspire in the reactionaries.[8]

The Marxist theory of the state is however no hymn of praise to state authority. Quite the contrary. In **State and Revolution** Lenin shows that after the victory of the working class and with the eventual disappearance of classes under communism, the state will 'wither away'. Once this repressive apparatus goes '*only* then . . . *it becomes possible to speak of freedom*' in a real sense.[9] However between the assault on capitalism and a classless society there must be a period of transition. During that time:

> suppression is *still* necessary, but it is now the suppression of the exploiting minority by the exploited majority . . . the 'state' is *still* necessary, but . . . it is no longer a state in the proper sense of the word; for the suppression of the minority of exploiters by the majority of the wage slaves of *yesterday* is comparatively so easy, simple and natural a task that it will entail far less bloodshed than the suppression of the risings of the slaves, serfs or wage-labourers, and it will cost mankind far less. And it is compatible with the extension of democracy to such an overwhelming majority of the population that the need for a *special* machine of suppression will begin to disappear.

The passage concludes by saying:

> *the people* can suppress the exploiters even with a very simple 'machine' . . . by the simple *organisation of the armed people* (such as the Soviets of Workers' and Soldiers' Deputies).[10]

It is clear from this that Lenin's concept of proletarian dictatorship had nothing in common with the Stalinist system which grew up in the late 1920s and under which the state bureaucracy, a tiny minority, dictated to the majority. For Lenin the key question was not constitutional trappings, nor the name the system of government gave itself (even though Stalin continued to talk of Soviets). What was important was whether the exploited class ruled over the exploiters, wage slaves over bosses. In Stalin's Russia, as in the West, the state served the purpose of a minority ruling class whose primary aim was the accumulation of capital, not the satisfaction of human need. That is why Russia from Stalin's time deserves the name 'state capitalist'. It has nothing to do with the workers' dictatorship described in Lenin's **State and Revolution**.[11]

Unfortunately Lenin was unable to expand on his arguments in **State and Revolution**. The pamphlet breaks off abruptly with only the chapter heading 'The experience of the Russian revolutions of 1905 and 1917' to indicate that an analysis of the Soviets was to follow. But as Lenin put it: 'It is more pleasant and useful to go through "the experience of the revolution" than to write about it.'[12] In later writings Lenin hinted at the practical contribution of Russia's revolutions to the Marxist theory of the state. He saw the Soviet Republic that emerged in 1917 as

> a new type of state that is transitional until the state disappears altogether . . . A bourgeois-democratic republic at best permits the organisation of the exploited masses, by declaring them free to organise, but actually has always placed countless obstacles in the way of their organisation, obstacles that were connected with the private ownership of the means of production in a way that made them irremovable. For the first time in history, Soviet power has not only greatly facilitated the organisation of the masses . . . but has made that organisation the essential permanent basis of the entire state apparatus . . .
>
> The more direct influence of the working masses on state structure and administration — ie a higher form of democracy — is also effected under the Soviet type of state, first by the electoral procedure and the possibility of holding elections more frequently, and also by conditions for re-election and for the recall of deputies . . . secondly, by making the economic industrial unit (factory) and not a territorial division the primary electoral unit, the nucleus of the state structure under Soviet power. This closer contact between the state apparatus and the masses of advanced proletarians that capitalism has united, in addition to effecting a higher level of democracy, also makes it possible to effect profound socialist reforms (such as) the creation of armed forces of workers and peasants which are much more closely connected with the working and exploited people.[13]

All previous states had been designed to preserve the property and rights of a narrow class of exploiters. The soviet state was therefore unique in basing itself on the exploited classes in their fight for emancipation.

The soviet and the direct democracy it embodied was no chance formation. As Marx had pointed out at the time of the Paris Commune: 'the working class cannot simply lay hold of the ready-made state machinery and wield it for its own purposes.'[14] A new machinery was needed because the old state, whatever its form, embodied capitalist interests. Although the surface appearance of capitalist states may vary from one country to another, the basis of bourgeois rule has always remained the same: the exclusion of the working masses from control both of the means of production (the factories and offices) and of the physical force of society (army, police and prisons). Capitalism uses its monopoly of productive wealth, and through foremen, the whip of unemployment and the like, disciplines and intimidates those who own little more than their ability to labour. The same wealth is used to buy and equip a second line of defence — the weapons and personnel forming the physical force of the state.

In carrying out this double task there is scope for superficial differences of style and method. Capitalist states may vary from fascist dictatorships such as Germany or Italy of the 1930s, or one-party state capitalisms such as Stalin's Russia or China today (where the open use of physical force is common), to bourgeois democracies such as those of the United States and Western Europe (where economic compulsion or the cooperation of labour bureaucrats is usually sufficient). In this latter case, far from the vote and other political rights giving power to the working majority, it actually makes the absolute power of the capitalist class even greater. As Lenin put it:

> the *more highly* democracy is developed, the *more* the bourgeois parliaments are subjected by the stock exchange and the bankers . . . Even in the most democratic bourgeois state the oppressed people at every step encounter the crying contradiction between the *formal* equality proclaimed by the 'democracy' of the capitalists and the thousands of *real* limitations and subterfuges which turn the proletarians into *wage-slaves*.[15]

When a tiny minority rule over many, the form of that rule can be flexible. A superficial democracy is merely one option among many.

For the working class the situation is quite different. To defeat capital it too needs a centralised state authority. However another consideration enters the picture, for the working class forms a majority in developed capitalism. And as Marx put it, 'the emancipation of the working class is the act of the working class itself'. This is not a statement of moral principle. To overthrow the massive and concentrated economic and political force of the bosses, the direct, active involvement of a substantial portion of the working class is an absolute necessity.

Such mass participation cannot be achieved by a small group of bureaucrats acting *for* the class, but only by the masses who are themselves organised for the seizure and retention of power. Such organisation must express the will of the masses as directly as possible and so minimise bureaucracy. It must also be freely shaped and directed by the majority and so be thoroughly democratic. Seen in this light it is clear that democratic control of power is not just an optional extra for workers. It is an essential element in the building of a workers' state. Without real democracy, such state organisation would lack the force of the mobilised masses. Without centralised authority, workers could not smash the resistance of capital.

For the working class, therefore, democracy and dictatorship are not in contradiction, but complementary. Workers' democracy and workers' dictatorship are embodied in the council state — the soviet republic. Elected at the point of production, its delegates are under the direct control of workers in the factories and offices. At the same time they unite the collective power of the class into a weapon of rule. For workers are not socially powerful by virtue of individual strengths but as collective producers of all wealth. The soviet concentrates strength at the point of production *and* lays claim to the summit of state power.

This differs at every point from bourgeois democracy. There the majority are distanced as much as possible from influence over the state. Elections happen only every few years. Constituency ballots are of no real advantage to workers, unlike factory elections, for in the latter case representatives can be checked on and recalled at any time should they stray from the wishes of those who choose them. Elections based on residence rather than the place of labour means workers do not take part in collective political debate — voters are more susceptible to the ideas of the capitalist-owned media and make decisions as individuals in isolated family units rather than as members of a class. Finally, whatever the election results and the composition of bourgeois parliaments, major decisions are always determined by capitalist economic interests and by an array of unelected civil servants, judges and police chiefs.

The soviet alternative to such sham democracy was not invented by Marx or Lenin, but grew directly out of the workers' own struggles, appearing first in 1905, in Russia.

1905

The 1905 revolution began when troops fired indiscriminately into a mass demonstration outside the Winter Palace in St Petersburg, then the Russian capital. At the high point of mass activity the Petersburg Soviet was formed. It lasted 50 days, from 13 October to 3 December, when its leaders were arrested. During this time it was, in Trotsky's words, 'the axis of all events, every thread ran towards it, every call to action emanated from it.'[16]

The Petersburg Soviet began life as a meeting of delegates to organise a political general strike. Originally proposed by the Menshevik wing of Russian socialism, the Soviet met the spontaneous demands of workers for mass organisation. Within three days it had assembled 226 delegates, chosen on the basis of one delegate per 500 workers in the factories. At this time there were no durable trade unions in Russia, while left-wing parties organised only a proportion of the working class and were closely restricted by police action. This meant the Soviet was undisputed as the mass collective organisation of Petersburg workers. As Trotsky wrote, its immediate popularity showed it had come into being

> as a response to an objective need — a need born of the course of events. It was an organisation which was authoritative and yet had no traditions, which could immediately involve a scattered mass of hundreds of thousands of people while having virtually no organisational machinery; which united the revolutionary currents within the proletariat; which was capable of initiative and spontaneous self-control — and most important of all, which could be brought out from underground within twenty-four hours.[17]

From the very beginning the Soviet was consciously political in character. Its first declaration called for use of 'the final, powerful weapon of the world workers' movement — the general strike'.[18] The strike which resulted paralysed the city for a week. It had no sooner ended than workers began spontaneously to demand the eight-hour day. The Soviet took up the call, but with only partial success.

Nevertheless, the close links workers saw between their struggle in the factories and the seizure of state power were underlined by the campaign. As one Soviet spokesman put it, the slogan '*Eight hours and a gun!* shall live in the heart of every Petersburg worker.'[19] The commitment of the masses to issues outside their immediate concern was put to the test when martial law was declared in Russian-occupied Poland and mutineers from the naval base of Kronstadt, near St Petersburg, were threatened with execution. In early November hundreds of thousands struck once more under Soviet leadership.

During these struggles the Soviet attempted to form its own militia and arm the workers, but this was possible only on a small scale. The Tsarist state was soon to recover its confidence, arresting the Soviet's leaders and breaking its organisation. An insurrection which broke out in Moscow was crushed soon afterwards and Russia entered a period of dark reaction.

The 1905 Soviet was unique in Russian history. Before this time there had been no well-established workers' organisations apart from the Social Democratic parties. These parties were organisations '*within the proletariat*', encompassing only the more advanced sections. The Soviet, in contrast, was an all-embracing organisation '*of the proletariat*'.[20] This distinction was important. A party is a *voluntary* organisation. Individuals choose to join it because they accept its politics. Though a revolutionary workers' party may be guided by a world-view which corresponds to the interests of the class, before a revolutionary upheaval it recruits only that minority which shares its ideals. The Soviet of 1905 was *non-voluntary*, being what Gramsci was to call a 'natural' workers' organisation, in that it was based on collective units, speaking in the name of all the workers in production, be they reformist or revolutionary.

Lenin was clearly aware of these differences from 1905 onwards, yet he saw both forms of organisation as important: 'The Soviet of Workers' Deputies or the party? I think that it is wrong to put the question in this way and that the decision must *certainly* be: *both* the Soviet of Workers' Deputies *and* the party.'[21] Lenin also glimpsed the limitations of the Soviet. It was capable of organising and reflecting the will of the working class. But the mass of workers cannot acquire a clear consciousness of their own class interest except during a period of revolution. In this the proletariat is different from the capitalists. By the time the latter overthrew feudalism they had, by means of their wealth, largely won an independent culture and ideology (through the free cities, universities and so on). The bourgeois revolutions of the 17th to 19th centuries were the final act of a much longer process during which capitalism had been constructed in the cracks of the feudal system.

In contrast to the capitalists, the working class is a direct object of exploitation. It is deprived of independent wealth and culture and subject to a virtual monopoly of ruling-class ideas through the media, education and the character of commodity production itself. The mass must acquire consciousness of its own interest by transforming itself through self-activity, which reaches its highest pitch during the revolution. At such times the Soviet, as a democratic body, may reflect this transformation, but it cannot direct it or lead it forward independently of the ideas already shared by a majority of workers.

Leadership must come from an organisation which enters the revolution *already conscious* of the final goal and able to offer a strategy that will guide workers towards this. Such is the party. With this distinction in mind, Lenin wrote: 'Soviets and similar mass institutions are not sufficient for organising the *immediate fighting force*, for *organising an uprising* in the narrowest sense of the word.'[22]

The crushing of the 1905 revolution pushed the soviet into the background, but it remained in the memory of Russian workers.

February 1917

When the First World War broke out Russia was still a predominantly rural society, the working class forming just 10 million of the 120 million population. Yet by 1917 the Russian capital, now renamed Petrograd, bore all the features of developed capitalism in an extreme form. Like Turin or Berlin, Petrograd had become a great industrial centre. Between 1890 and 1914 the number of factory workers had tripled, reaching 243,000. In the war another 150,000 were added so that by 1917 the city housed one eighth of the Russian working class.[23]

Most of the newcomers found work in the burgeoning munitions sector, the number of metalworkers rising by 135 per cent in just three years.[24] With two out of three Petrograd workers in this industry, engineering dominated the city, as it did in Glasgow or Berlin. And as in these cities, a small number of giant firms controlled the industry, massing together thousands of workers in each of their factories. Far outstripping even Berlin in this respect, Petrograd had in 1917 38 major plants which employed over 2,000 workers each.[25]

Inside these workplaces there were many craftsmen, but in contrast to the West they had been unable to form any sectional trade union organisation. This meant that the gulf between a skilled labour aristocracy and the semi- and unskilled workers, a marked feature of Western Europe, was almost absent in Petrograd.[26]

The wave of patriotic hysteria which engulfed Europe in 1914 was quick to recede in Russia. As inflation raged, it was not long before the strike movement that had been interrupted in 1914 re-emerged in full vigour. At its head stood Petrograd, with 72 per cent of all Russia's political strikes. It was noticeable that from the outset strikes over political issues outstripped economic disputes in the statistics.[27]

A further testimony to the substantial section of Petrograd workers who saw the connection between their immediate struggles and political action was the support received by the Bolsheviks in 1915. This party had been founded in 1903 by a split in the Russian Social Democratic and Labour Party. Led by Lenin, the Bolsheviks combined the most courageous workplace militancy with high revolutionary socialist principles. During the war they took the position that the defeat of Russia would be of benefit for the workers. Despite this extreme internationalist position the Bolsheviks won a majority in the 1915 elections to the War Industry Committees set up by the Tsarist government to stimulate munitions production. The other party to emerge from the split in 1903 was the Mensheviks. They represented the main reformist current in the Russian working class and many of their leaders supported the war.

The final reckoning with Tsarism came in the revolution of February 1917. This had two immediate sources, a strike against victimisation at the giant Putilov engineering works in Petrograd and the demand for bread, voiced principally by working-class women. On 23 February street demonstrations led to confrontation with the military in which substantial numbers of soldiers came over to the side of the workers. In the next five days Tsarism was

swept away and two new powers created: the Provisional Government (which represented Russian capitalism and inherited the
remnants of the old state) and the Soviet.

Although only formed on 27 February, the idea of a Petrograd
Soviet had been voiced by workers from the very beginning of the
revolution, some delegates apparently being chosen as early as 24
February.[28] The first practical steps to centralise these efforts were
made by right-wing Mensheviks released from prison by the
revolt.[29] They called for elections on the basis of one delegate per
1,000 workers, soldiers to be represented one per company. Within a week some 1,200 delegates were meeting in daily sessions.

The Soviet did not grow out of any neat structural concept.
According to Sukhanov, who witnessed its first meeting, the
chairman

> had neither a general plan of action nor control of the meeting itself,
> which proceeded noisily and quite chaotically. But this by no means pre-
> vented the Soviet from performing at this very first session its basic task,
> vital to the revolution — that of concentrating into one centre all the
> ideological and organisational strength of the Petersburg democracy,
> with undisputed authority and capacity for rapid and decisive action.[30]

An essential element which the 1905 Soviet lacked was army
support. This time it was different.

> Standing on stools, their rifles in their hands, agitated and stuttering,
> straining all their powers to give a connected account of the messages
> entrusted to them . . . one after another the soldiers' delegates told of
> what had been happening in their companies . . .
> The name of each of the magnificent regiments that had launched the
> revolution was met with a storm of applause.
> 'We had a meeting . . .' 'We've been told to say . . .' 'The officers hid
> . . .' 'To join the Soviet of Workers' Deputies . . .' 'They told us to
> say that we refuse to serve against the people anymore, we're going to
> join with our brother workers, all united to defend the people's cause
> . . . We would lay down our lives for that.' 'Our general meeting told
> us to greet you . . .' 'Long live the revolution!' the delegate would add
> in a voice already completely extinguished by the throbbing roar of
> the meeting.[31]

At a time when it was still uncertain how many of the seven million
Russian soldiers would abandon the Tsar, such physical backing
was vitally important.

Within hours the Petrograd Soviet of Workers' *and Soldiers'* Deputies had ventured beyond the 1905 limits to acquire the power of coercing the class enemy — the characteristic of a state. The 1905 Soviet had been primarily a committee which led political general strikes. As Trotsky had explained at the time: 'The revolutionary strength of such strikes consists in the fact that . . . they disorganise state power.'[32] In 1917 the Soviet went from disorganising the enemy to organising its *own* state power, not just in Petrograd but right across Russia. By 17 March 49 cities had soviets; five days later the number was 77 and by June 519.[33]

The control that the Petrograd Soviet was able to exercise within hours of its birth was tremendous. Against it stood the Provisional Government, which claimed to be the legitimate state authority. Its position was summed up by Guchkov, the War Minister, on 22 March:

> The Provisional Government possesses no real power and its orders are executed only in so far as this is permitted by the Soviet of Workers' and Soldiers' Deputies, which holds in its hands the most important elements of actual power, such as troops, railroads, postal and telegraph service. It is possible to say directly that the Provisional Government exists only while this is permitted by the Soviet of Workers' and Soldiers' Deputies.[34]

Despite this affirmation, the situation that prevailed between February and October was characterised by Marxists as one of 'dual power'. Trotsky explained the source of this condition:

> The political mechanism of revolution consists of the transfer of power from one class to another. The forcible overturn is usually accomplished in a brief time. But no historic class lifts itself from a subject position to a position of rulership suddenly in one night, even though a night of revolution . . . The historic preparation of a revolution brings about . . . a situation in which the class which is called to realise the new social system, although not yet master of the country, has actually concentrated in its hands a significant share of the state power, while the official apparatus is still in the hands of the old lords. That is the initial dual power in every revolution.[35]

In fighting for bread in February, the workers found themselves compelled to challenge the army and win over the rank and file to their side, binding them organisationally through the Soviet. But readiness to fight effectively for bread in no way implied a general willingness to smash the bourgeois state and consciously take power. Even in times of revolution 'the tradition of dead generations weighs like a nightmare on the brains of the living', to use Marx's phrase. Thus it was that in February the workers and peasants of Russia did not seek to monopolise power through the soviets nor wipe out what remained of the old state. The capitalists were permitted to organise their Provisional Government.

Still, 'dual power' was inherently unstable, as is any temporary equilibrium of forces in a continuing war. It did however create possibilities for a further deepening of the revolution and mass activity.

For a transfer of power from one class to another it is essential to crack the shell of the state's *physical* power, which protects and perpetuates the *social* relations of production within. But a social revolution does not mean simply transforming the state. There have been many instances this century (Eastern Europe after 1945 or China in 1948 for example) where apparently dramatic changes of state power have failed to transform class power, merely replacing one form of capitalist rule with another. A social revolution must penetrate to the very base of society — the power relations in production. Indeed this is what began to happen after February. The Tsar had gone but the revolution had failed to solve the fundamental causes of the crisis — the war, the land-hunger of the peasants and the brutal rule of capitalism in the factories. With workers to the fore, the masses began to improvise new institutions to solve these issues. An incredible flourishing of popular self-organisation was taking place, although different approaches were to be seen.

Some important sections, such as working-class women, tended to express their action by means of direct but de-centralised struggle. Their very lack of agitational experience left them without the inherent conservatism which inevitably burdened the more organised groups. The women had therefore gone forward to confront Tsarism when even revolutionaries such as the Bolsheviks had initially hesitated. However they were much less prominent when it came to shaping the movement and giving it coherent form. In Trotsky's **History of the Russian Revolution**, he shows how the Petrograd Soviet acted as a centre of self-activity, but also the degree of unevenness between different sections:

> The masses went over in droves to the socialists, whom they identified with the Soviet. Not only the workers and soldiers of the enormous

garrisons in the rear, but all the many-coloured small people of the towns — mechanics, street peddlers, petty officials, cab-drivers, janitors, servants of all kinds — feeling alien to the Provisional Government and its bureaux, were seeking a closer and more accessible authority . . .

Not all the toiling masses chose the Soviet; not all awakened at once; not every layer of the oppressed dared instantly believe that the revolution concerned them. In the consciousness of many only an undiscriminating hope was stirring. But all the active elements of the masses poured into the Soviet, and activity prevails in times of revolution . . . It was the sole genuine basis of the revolution.[36]

Sheltering under the armed protection of the Soviet a vast range of popular bodies appeared. There were district soviets (which mirrored the work of the central Soviet at local level and at points challenged it for authority), trade unions, a variety of militias and a host of committees — army committees, peasant committees, factory committees, housing committees, committees for administering and reducing queues — the list was endless, for the creative genius of the masses was unleashed.

Probably the most important of these institutions were those centred on the leading social force of the revolution — the working class. For while other sections of the masses were important, the key role, because of its internal cohesion and place in the productive process, fell to the industrial working class. The most important collective institutions outside the soviets were the factory committees. These were elected by mass meetings held at the factories. They were sometimes supplemented or replaced by shop stewards, who were elected in the different departments.

The practice of workplace organisation and election which underpinned both the soviet and factory committees dated back to the first efforts at collective organisation in the early years of the century. Continually suppressed, it always resurfaced when given the opportunity. Workplace organisation ran contrary to the trend to be seen in Britain, which proceeded from sectional organisation in narrowly-defined craft bodies. The Russian tradition reflected the conditions of mass production in which much of the industry there grew. Just as the experience of 1905 had united politics and economics in the slogan 'Eight hours and a gun', the 1917 offensive of the soviets against the old state was immediately matched by an offensive against capital in the factories.

A good example of this second front was the set of demands put by the Kersten Knitwear workers, many of whom were women:

1) the immediate removal of the head of the knitwear department as 'not corresponding to his appointment', 'he deals with the workers in a coarse manner'
2) the immediate introduction of the eight-hour day and a general raise of 50 per cent, pending a review of the wage rates
3) payment for the days of the revolution
4) wages to be paid every fortnight
5) defective goods to be sold to the workers at cost in limited quantities
6) overtime to be voluntary and paid at time and a half
7) the right to hold meetings without the permission or presence of foremen or representatives of the administration[37]

These demands were typical, ranging from the simple demand of the right to meet, to the most advanced — the right to determine who manages and the right to wages for the days of revolutionary strike action.

A purge of the old factory administration was a high priority for all workers. At the Putilov works the director and his aide were actually killed, another 40 managers being expelled at the same time.[38] A common sight in March was the 'carting out' of particularly obnoxious bosses and foremen in wheelbarrows. Wages were also a central concern of the factory committees and in the months up to July they were able at least to double average earnings in Petrograd.

The February revolution had destroyed the police force, some 40,000 rifles and revolvers being seized.[39] Two militia forces grew up in its stead. One was the civil militia, which tended to support the Provisional Government; the other was the workers' militia based mainly on units drawn directly from the factories. The Petrograd Cable Factory, for example, asked for 100 volunteer militiamen for every one thousand of its workers.[40] Wages for militia duties were extracted from the employers and volunteers served on a rota basis. The tradition of a police force organised outside of and *against* the majority thus received a serious blow.

Factory committee members, though concentrating on seemingly local issues, were usually elected on party lines. This reflected the deeply political character of much of the working class. The factory committees, like the soviets, were at first dominated by reformists, the Mensheviks and the Social Revolutionaries (SRs), a party with mass peasant support and some working-class following. Like their counterparts in the central Soviet the factory committee leaders did not conceive of the revolution as a challenge to capitalism, but only to undemocratic Tsarism. Their aim was not primarily 'workers' control' of all aspects of production and distribution, but a sort of dual power in the factories. Like the Soviet which claimed the right to inspect and oversee the work of the Provisional Government, the factory committees would keep watch on the factory management. But dual power in the factories was no more stable than dual power at government level.

The managements of state industries were the first to be displaced, owing to their direct links with Tsarism; but private capitalists who tried to cut back production or close down their enterprises soon followed. Of all the collective bodies created after February, the factory committees were closest of all to the rank-and-file workers, closer even than the district soviets or central Soviet where the influence of the relatively more backward 'peasants in uniform' — the army — was felt. They were therefore the first to register the many changes in the mood of the class.

The trade unions also enjoyed phenomenal growth after February. Before the revolution there had been just 14 tiny and ineffectual unions, 11 of which had been illegal. But within six months some 390,000 inhabitants of Petrograd had enrolled in a great variety of unions. The city had 'one of the highest levels of unionisation in the world.'[41] The unions, like the other collective organisations of the working class, fell under Menshevik-Social Revolutionary domination immediately following the revolution.

The various mass organisations, which in one way or another reflected the urgent demands of the people in action, were connected. The Soviet could not have developed into the full state power it became in October had it not been for the transformation of consciousness brought about by the various immediate struggles of workers, peasants and soldiers. These were given articulate form by section organisations such as factory committees or regimental committees. But such organisations could never have existed if the Soviet had not maintained the political freedom in which they operated.

The politics of the soviets

In membership the political parties were more restricted than mass institutions such as the soviets or factory committees. Unlike these bodies, which incorporated *all* the workers of a given city or factory, parties embraced only that section which shared broadly identical political ideas. They therefore had a unity of purpose and coherence that could not arise spontaneously in the collective organisations, and inevitably came to lead them. This was evident from the very first.

From February to August 1917 the Petrograd Soviet was dominated by a coalition of Mensheviks and SRs. Though they were not averse to using methods of bureaucratic manipulation, their influence in the meetings of the Soviet first grew from popular acceptance of their ideas. During March the Mensheviks and SRs had the support of almost the whole of the 2,800-strong plenary sessions of the Soviet. The chief opposition force, the Bolsheviks, had only around 65 delegates.[42]

The Menshevik-SR programme centred on the belief that the workers could not take power, and that the Russian bourgeoisie, as represented by the Provisional Government, must replace Tsarism. The Menshevik Tseretelli, who on his return from exile in Irkutsk became the political leader of the Soviet, summed up his programme very briefly:

> Of course you'll have to talk about the necessity of a compromise with the bourgeoisie. There can be no other road for revolution. It's true we have all the power, and that the [Provisional] Government would go if we lifted a finger, but that would mean disaster.[43]

Such a political outlook led the Executive Committee of the Soviet to try to hand back as much influence as possible to the Provisional Government. Its 'Instructions to all Soviets' stated:

> the Provisional Government must be regarded as the sole legal government for all Russia. All its decisions, unless protested by the soviet, must be carried out; all its government organs and comissars must be considered as legal authorities, unless they personally or politically endanger the cause of freedom.[44]

The Mensheviks and SRs disguised their programme with democratic phrases, insisting for example that only a Constituent Assembly elected by universal suffrage could represent the Russian people, while the soviets stood only for a minority. But in reality their policy meant subordinating the millions of peasants and workers to the rule of the tiny Russian bourgeoisie. It also meant accepting most of the political programme of that class, though each time this was cloaked with left phrases. For example, the Soviet leaders supported continuation of the war, but issued a statement calling for a negotiated peace. The Soviet supported maintenance of capitalism, but urged employers to treat their workers kindly. Though nominally supporting peasant ownership of the land, the SRs — a party which had a *mass* peasant membership — opposed the direct seizure of land, promising it would be delivered at some time in the future.

However, these general policies, which held sway in the Soviet's Executive Committee, continually conflicted with the immediate demands of the very people the Soviet claimed to represent. The most obvious instance of this was the famous Order No 1. This concerned the army and consisted of seven points, including the election of committees in all units; the right to accept no instructions that clashed with soviet authority; and the control of weapons to be in the hands of soldiers' committees. According to General Denikin, these simple measures 'gave the first and chief blow to the disintegration of the army.'[45] By this he meant the old army, in which a small group of upper-class officers held absolute power. This was now giving way to a new army responsive to the masses and their representative organisations.

A deep-seated hatred of the Tsarist officer caste had united all shades of opinion among the soldiers' delegates. They forced their will on the Soviet leadership, surrounding a member of the Executive Committee and dictating what he should write in Order No 1. But the Soviet Executive had very mixed feelings about this document, as one historian relates:

> On one hand, they had tried to avoid exclusive concentration of the insurgents' support for the Soviet, which might inevitably lead to the demand that the Soviet take power. On the other, they found it was necessary to dispel the intense anger and fear felt by the soldiers, which might trigger large-scale slaughter of officers.[46]

The same clash of views was manifested when it came to the burning issue of the eight-hour day. Many workers considered that the general strike which began with the revolution was not just about bringing down the Tsar, but should continue till the shorter working day was granted. However, Chkheidze, the Menshevik chairman of the Soviet, wanted disruption of munitions work to end right away. Although he won his resolution at the Soviet plenary, calling for a return to work from 7 March, it was resisted on the ground. The Petrograd Society of Factory and Mill Owners reported only 28 out of 111 factories were working on the day specified for a return.[47] Eventually the Soviet leadership was again forced by external pressure to respond to popular demands, negotiating the eight-hour day with the employers on 10 March.

The passing of Order No 1 and the campaign for the shorter working day pointed to a gap between the Soviet's Executive Committee and the mood of the masses. This gap reappeared whenever the Executive Committee under Menshevik-SR leadership took any action. Sukhanov, one of its members, wrote later that 'we devoted ourselves to our work almost without paying any attention to what was being done' in the plenary session of the Soviet.[48]

This Executive Committee was the *ad hoc* group of intellectuals which had organised the first meeting of workers' and soldiers' delegates. Its position had been confirmed by the first plenary meeting. As leading Mensheviks and SRs were co-opted on to it, the committee extended its organisation by creating over a dozen sub-commissions to deal with urgent problems. Later a special 'Bureau of the Executive Committee', with seven members, began to do much of the day-to-day decision-making.

The emergence of a group which by its actions showed itself to be divorced from the masses pointed to the dangers of bureaucracy even in a body as democratic as the Soviet. There was another disturbing feature. The 150,000-strong Petrograd garrison sent some 2,000 delegates to the Soviet, while the workers, who were twice as numerous as the soldiers, had only 800 representatives. In the early days this disproportion showed how workers were keen to win over the army and cement an alliance with the peasantry (for the soldiers were mainly 'peasants in uniform'). The individual peasant farmer lacked the collective experience and solidarity of the industrial worker and had, till conscription into the army, social horizons limited to the boundary of the fields he tilled. The preponderance of soldiers' delegates thus distorted the politics of the Petrograd Soviet, giving the more conservative elements a stronger voice than they might otherwise have possessed.

In formal terms all of these factors might seem to make the Soviet undemocratic. But democratic organisations are not created primarily by regulations but by the class content they embody and the real influence of the class that is represented. A powerless class has no democracy. For all the Soviet's imperfections — the result

of its improvised character and the lack of governing experience
and political understanding among the masses — it was still far
more democratic than parliaments chosen by even the most
scrupulously administered election. The implementing of Order
No 1 and the eight-hour day showed that as long as the masses held
elements of physical power in their hands, democracy was very
much alive.

This democracy, however, was constantly at risk of being
undermined from within the Soviet. As long as the leading group
were trying to bolster the power of the Provisional Government,
there was the danger that the Soviet would lose its real mass basis
and become a hollow shell, a talking shop, which like any bourgeois parliament would have the formal trappings of democracy
but no influence over the important decisions in society.

The Bolshevik party, though standing to the left in Soviet
debates, had been very confused during March. In Petrograd its
organisation in the metalworking district of Vyborg took an extreme
left position and a strongly anti-Provisional Government line. Con-
versely, Stalin and Kamenev, who controlled the party's central
organ **Pravda**, were much more conciliatory, both towards other
political parties and towards the Provisional Government. Lenin
resolved these differences on his return from exile during April.
He won the party to a clear position which cut right through the
illusions which had been sown by the ease of the February
revolution, that there might be peaceful progress through class
collaboration,

Lenin's starting point for an analysis of the 1917 soviets was
based not on what they claimed to be, but on a rigorous judgement
of the balance of class forces. As he put it in an article entitled 'The
Dual Power':

> The basic question of every revolution is that of state power. Unless
> this question is understood . . . there can be no intelligent participa-
> tion in the revolution, not to speak of guidance of the revolution.[49]

The importance of the Soviet's alternative authority was not its
institutional procedures:

> What is the political nature of this government? It is a revolutionary
> dictatorship, ie a power directly based on revolutionary seizure, on
> the direct initiative of the people from below, and *not on a law* enacted
> by a centralised state power.[50]

In his **April Theses** Lenin set out what he saw as the way forward. He later reiterated the argument, pointing out the danger of ignoring the Soviet, either by substituting the party for it as a state form, or the opposite — of merging the party with the Soviet and forgetting that the aim is state power.

> In the theses, I very definitely reduced the question to one of *a struggle for influence within* the Soviets of Workers', Agricultural Labourers', Peasants' and Soldiers' Deputies. To leave no shadow of doubt on this score I *twice* emphasised in the theses the need for patient and persistent 'explanatory' work 'adapted to the *practical* needs of the *masses*'. . . . Blanquism means the seizure of power by a minority, whereas the Soviets are *admittedly* the direct and immediate organisation of the *majority* of the people. Work confined to a struggle for influence *within* these Soviets cannot, simply *cannot*, stray into the swamp of Blanquism. Nor can it stray into the swamp of anarchism, for anarchism denies *the need for a state and state power* in the period of *transition*.[51]

Lenin was at pains to make it clear that the Bolshevik Party must work inside the soviets, not as part of the mish-mash of parties supporting the Provisional Government and disguising the rule of the capitalists, but for the seizure of full state power by the masses themselves. The slogan summing this up was 'All power to the Soviets'. The extreme clarity of Lenin's position, which gave no quarter to illusions in institutions or abstract claims to democracy, but based everything on a sober assessment of the realities of class struggle, was to be an invaluable guide to the party throughout the sharp twists and turns of the revolution.

Three demonstrations

Although the revolution stirred every section of the masses into life, the changes in the balance of social forces on the ground were not easy to measure. They were tested, however, by three political crises, explosions that were the result of the accumulating social tensions at the base of society and determined the future course of the struggle.

The interplay of politics and economics, of the politically advanced vanguard of the working class and its active but economically-oriented sections, forms the background to the three demonstrations of the 'April Days', 'June' and 'July Days'. At the time Lenin described them as follows:

In all three crises, the movement took the form of a *demonstration*. An anti-government demonstration — that would be the most exact formal description of events. But the fact of the matter is that it was not an ordinary demonstration; it was something considerably more than a demonstration, but less than a revolution. It was an outburst of revolution and counter-revolution *together*, a sharp, sometimes almost sudden elimination of the middle elements, while the proletarian and bourgeois elements made a stormy appearance.[52]

The first crisis, in April, arose when the Provisional Government's Foreign Minister, Miliukov, issued a note informing the Allies that all the current talk about peace should be ignored. The government's real intention, he said, was 'to bring the World War to a decisive victory.'[53] On 20 April mass demonstrations of workers and soldiers took to the streets in protest, to be met by sections of the right defending Miliukov's imperialist line. On the workers' side many Bolshevik slogans were prominent.

The Executive Committee of the Petrograd Soviet complained in their paper, **Izvestia**, that:

> The Soviet did not aspire to seize the power in its own hands, but nevertheless upon many banners carried by the partisans of the Soviet there were inscriptions demanding the overthrow of the government and the transfer of all power to the Soviet.[54]

The Mensheviks and SRs did not want confrontation in the streets to upset the delivery of power to the Provisional Government. They issued a ban on further street actions, which was respected because of the Soviet's continuing prestige and the Bolshevik policy of 'patiently explaining' their policies rather than immediate insurrection. The crisis ended when the Provisional Government issued a new note returning to its earlier phraseology and Miliukov, along with War Minister Guchkov, resigned his post.

Trotsky's explanation of the Soviet's role in these events stands equally for the crises that were to follow:

> This crying contradiction between the decisiveness of the mass offensive and the half-heartedness of its political reflection was not accidental. In a revolutionary epoch the oppressed masses turn more easily and quickly to direct action, than they learn to give their desires and demands a formal expression through their own representatives. The more abstract the system of representation the more it lags behind the rhythm of those events which determine the activity of the

masses. A Soviet representation, the least abstract of all, has immeasurable advantages in revolutionary conditions: . . .

But with all the advantages of their organic connection with the factories and regiments — that is, with the active masses — the soviets are nevertheless representative organs, and therefore not free from the qualifications and distortions of parliamentarism. The contradiction inherent in representation, even of the soviet form, lies in the fact that it is on the one hand necessary to the action of the masses, but on the other hand easily becomes a conservative obstacle to it. The practical way out of this contradiction is to renew the representation continually. But this operation, nowhere very simple, must in a revolution be the result of direct action, and therefore lag behind such action. At any rate, on the day after the April semi-insurrection . . . the same deputies were sitting in the Soviet as on the day before. Arriving once more in their accustomed seats they voted for the motions of their accustomed leaders.[55]

The 'April Days' accentuated the internal tensions present since February. On the one hand the Soviet leadership moved to the right: the Menshevik-SR leaders on the Executive Committee recognised that the Provisional Government survived only by the Soviet's intervention, so they agreed to take more direct responsibility for it, accepting six ministerial posts in a Coalition. On the other hand, the trend on the floor of the Soviet was in the opposite direction. The Bolsheviks began a successful campaign for the re-election of delegates which first bore fruit in the metalworking factories.[56] By May the engineering districts of Vyborg, Vasilievsky Island and Kolomna had left-wing majorities in their district soviets. Right-wing Menshevik support in particular had slumped.

One historian explains the change in these terms:

The virtual disappearance of the Menshevik-Defencists from the factories and the concomitant rise of the Bolsheviks, along with the only relative decline of SR influence, are explained by the fact that the shift to support for soviet power came largely, though not exclusively, from the more skilled sections of the working class. This was the Social-Democratic constituency, the main battleground of its two wings. And by the end of June the battle had been largely played out. On the other hand, the largely Bolshevik-SR struggle among the unskilled stratum was far from decided.[57]

The Bolshevik battle for the support of the unskilled was to be won principally through the party's stand on the economic crisis, which became acute later in the year. The politically-experienced sections came to the idea of soviet power more easily than those new to working-class struggle. The latter were to reach the same conclusions but through discovering by direct experience the inadequacy of sectional economic struggle.

June saw the next crisis. On the third of that month the first All-Russian Congress of Soviets met. It claimed an electorate of some 20 million people. The revolutionary wing, although far larger than in March, formed less than one fifth of the delegates. The Congress showed that the hold of the Menshevik-SR parties was also stronger in the provinces than in Petrograd, which for three months had been in the eye of the revolutionary storm. The delegates gave full support to the policy of compromise with the Provisional Government, but were soon faced with a difficult situation. The Bolshevik Party had wanted a demonstration on 10 June, the theme of which would be 'All power to the Soviets'. In addition, the first Congress of Petrograd factory committees had passed a resolution which said the only answer to economic dislocation was 'the transfer of power into the hands of the Soviet'.[58]

The question of dual power in the factories and the crisis in the state were linked together by the programme and the solution energetically expounded by the organised and disciplined Bolshevik Party.[59] The Bolsheviks were able to show an inner connection between the immediate experience of the workers in the factories and the political steps needed to secure even the minimum permanent gains. This battle was fought under the slogan of 'for workers' control'. Steven Smith has described the progression that was made from a desire to 'democratise' factory life to the concept of Soviet power:

> From being concerned essentially to *supervise* production, workers' control developed into an attempt to actively *intervene* in production . . . In the first period from March to April, workers' control was confined mainly to state enterprises. Factory committees everywhere attempted to establish some control of hiring and firing, as part of a broader drive to democratise factory relations. Employers were optimistic about the future and prepared to make concessions. In the second phase from May to June, most factory committees began to monitor supplies of raw materials and fuel and to check that their

factories were being run efficiently. It was in this period that the
Bolsheviks achieved political hegemony within the movement. In the
third phase from July to August, economic crisis erupted and class
struggle deepened . . . In the fourth period from September to October
. . . there was a severe economic and political crisis and class conflict
polarised . . . Factory committees became actively involved in the
battle to transfer power to the Soviets.[60]

The reaction of the Congress of Soviets to the demand for a
soviet government was to ban any public manifestation of the idea.
On this occasion the paradox of a demonstration calling for soviet
power marching in defiance of the Congress of Soviets itself was
avoided but not without difficulty. More than half the Congress
spent the night of 9 June on delegations to factories and regiments
arguing for the ban, but it was not their efforts that prevented the
demonstration, for as they reported next day:

> The delegates were met everywhere with extreme unfriendliness and
> allowed to pass only after lengthy disputes . . . Neither the Congress
> nor the Petersburg Soviet had the slightest authority. They were
> spoken of just like the Provisional Government: the Menshevik-SR
> majority had sold itself to the bourgeoisie and the imperialists . . .
> Only the Bolsheviks were trusted, and whether the demonstration
> took place or not depended solely on the Bolshevik Central
> Committee.[61]

It was the eagerness of the Bolshevik Party to avoid premature
confrontation that led to the demonstration of 10 June being
cancelled.

The Soviet leadership had no sooner avoided one embarrass-
ment than they created for themselves another by calling for a
march which would show the unity of 'democratic forces'. This
turned out to be a complete triumph for the Bolsheviks and 'a
stinging flick of the whip in the face of the Soviet majority'.[62] The
vast majority of the 400,000 people who marched on the 18 June
demonstration did not carry official Soviet placards but stood
behind the Bolshevik slogans 'All Power to the Soviets', and 'Down
with the Ten Capitalist Ministers'.

Further developments in the June crisis were nipped in the
bud by Kerensky who, as Minister of War, launched a new military
offensive. This action merely postponed the crisis for a week or
two. It resurfaced when the Provisional Government ordered

sections of the Petrograd garrison to the front to restore the army's flagging offensive. On 3 July, in protest against this order, the First Machine Gun Regiment decided to come out on the street bearing arms. It called upon the workers and soldiers of the capital for support. Gathering momentum, the movement even drew in sections of the Bolshevik Party, although this was against their current policy. The deepening of class antagonism hinted at in April and June meant that any large demonstration risked causing open warfare in the capital.

But Petrograd was not all of Russia. The masses in the capital were now far more radical than elsewhere. This advanced position was shown in the growth of the Bolshevik Party, which in May won a majority in the factory committees and a tenuous hold over the local trade unions. A number of regiments also loosely subscribed to Bolshevik ideas. But even in Petrograd revolutionary beliefs had not taken hold of the Soviet with its mixed composition and ossified Menshevik-SR majority. Only the workers' section had changed hands with re-elections, giving the Bolsheviks a majority late on the evening of 3 July.

In the face of the spontaneous outbreak of demonstrations Lenin had to consider three key factors — the situation in the Soviet, the sharpened class conflict and the risk of isolating Petrograd's revolutionary vanguard. He saw the situation in these terms:

> [The proletariat] must bury the illusion of the possibility of the peaceful transfer of power to the Soviets. Power is not transferred: it is taken with guns. The chain of events will be as follows: the bourgeoisie, recognising the strength of our organisation, taking account of the tremendous speed with which the masses are being involved, will not give us the opportunity of finally possessing them and will exercise all its strength in order to provoke these masses into a demonstration that would call forth repressions, that would break and divide them. Because of this we must concern ourselves with organisation in the most intensive way possible, giving them a definite slogan — the slogan of the impossibility of gaining power by peaceful means . . . if not in the coming weeks, then in any event in the near future.[63]

Despite the warnings of the Bolshevik central leadership, armed demonstrations filled the streets of Petrograd on 3 and 4 July. They were supported by a vast range of factories and military units. But the strategy of the movement was confused. The First

Machine Gun Regiment, for example, said they would follow
orders only when 'the government has been transferred into the
hands of the democracy represented by the All-Russian Soviet of
Workers', Soldiers' and Peasants' Deputies'. In the same resolution, however, they declared their readiness to used armed strength
to defy the Soviet:

> If the Soviet of Workers' and Soldiers' Deputies threatens this and
> other revolutionary regiments with forcible dissolution, in response
> we will likewise not stop at using armed strength to break up the
> Provisional Government and other organisations supporting it.[64]

Two other statements graphically illustrate the contradictions
of the 'July Days'. When Victor Chernov, the SR leader, tried to
calm the protestors, one person shouted: 'Take power, you son-of-
a-bitch, when it's given to you!'[65] Later a factory delegate, rifle in
hand, addressed the Soviet with these words: 'We demand the
departure of the ten capitalist ministers [from the Provisional
Government]. We trust the Soviet, but not those whom the Soviet
trusts.'[66]

Trotsky explained these attitudes well:

> The July demonstrators wanted to turn over the power to the soviets,
> but for this the soviets had to agree to take it. Even in the capital,
> however, where a majority of the workers and the active elements of
> the garrison were already for the Bolsheviks, a majority in the Soviet
> — owing to that law of inertia which applies to every representative
> system — still belonged to those petty bourgeois parties who regarded
> an attempt against the bourgeoisie as an attempt against themselves.
> The workers and soldiers felt clearly enough the contrast between
> their moods and the policy of the Soviet — that is, between their
> to-day and their yesterday. In coming out for a government of the
> soviets, they by no means gave their confidence to the compromisist
> majority in those soviets. But they did not know how to settle with this
> majority. To overthrow it by violence would have meant to dissolve
> the soviets instead of giving them power. Before they could find the
> path to a change of the personal composition of the soviets, the
> workers and soldiers tried to subject the soviets to their will by the
> method of direct action.[67]

The Bolshevik leaders, though opposed to the demonstrations,
felt compelled to take leadership of the movement, which at its
high point involved half a million people. They used their influence

to avoid further clashes. The July movement, as Lenin had predicted, was an opportunity for reaction to take revenge on an isolated Petrograd, although the situation would have been much worse had not the Bolsheviks organised and restrained the masses. The demonstrations brought down the wrath of the Menshevik-SR leaders, who outlawed the Bolshevik Party and invited right-wing officers and troops to take command of the streets. Many workers were disorientated by their failure to achieve any concrete gains and by the slander that Lenin was 'a German agent'. The leftward movement of the masses was temporarily halted.

The July Days showed very sharply the contrast between the soviets, the masses and the revolutionary party. The soviets, created in the first days of the revolution by the masses *as a whole*, had for that reason fallen into the hands of reformists opposed to exclusive soviet power and eager to block any attempts by workers and peasants to shape their own destiny. So the Petrograd Soviet soon lagged behind the workers of the city as they moved leftwards. These hundreds of thousands had not been hidebound by the soviet form, however, for they had taken on new struggles and formed new organisations — the factory committees, regimental committees and so on — that expressed their will on immediate issues.

The experiences of April and June showed how the masses had swung far to the left not only of the central Soviet, but also of the rest of the country. Their bursting on to the streets took them further than even Lenin and his supporters wished to go at the time, for they risked a crushing defeat at the hands of the right, who could count on the city remaining isolated. The Bolshevik revolutionary party was an independent force, although it was entrenched among both the masses and the Soviet. It united the most politically conscious elements of the working class and offered a Marxist analysis of events. It alone was able to prevent the disaster which would have overtaken an all-out insurrection in July.

Towards October

In Petrograd the Soviet was changing in character. For most workers and soldiers its primary purpose was as a centralised organisation of their collective will. In April and June the relations between the Soviet and the movement that created it had been strained. The July Days finally snapped the links, for at that time the Menshevik-SR leaders had sided with reactionary Tsarist officers such as General Kornilov, the military commander of Petrograd district, in attempting to crush the revolutionary left. The Soviet leaders now took over the running of the Provisional Government by taking a majority of seats in a new Coalition. At its head was Alexander Kerensky as 'Minister President'. He had joined the SRs after the February revolution and held posts as Minister of Justice, and of War and Marine, before assuming this new role.

It was evident that the dual power situation, in which the Soviet and the Provisional Government were alternative poles, had been changed by this new arrangement. Trotsky explains what had happened:

> The dual power was reconstructed, transformed, but it did not disappear. In the factories it was impossible as before to do anything against the will of the workers; the peasants retained enough power to prevent the landlord from enjoying his property rights; the commanders felt no confidence before the soldiers . . . It is absolutely indubitable that the Executive Committee had lost the lion's share of its importance. But it would be a mistake to imagine that the bourgeoisie had received all that the compromise leaders had lost. These leaders had lost not only to the right, but also the left — not only to the benefit of the military cliques, but also to the benefit of the factory and regimental committees. The power was decentralised, scattered . . .[68]

The Soviet had ceased to be capable of leading the class. It rarely met in plenary session any more. The higher organs of the Petrograd Soviet and the *Tsik*, the All-Russian Soviet Executive elected at the Congress of Soviets, all worked in complete isolation from the base. At one point Lenin suggested that factory committees take the key role of mass collective organisation, the question being not the name 'soviet' — but the character of being 'a power directly based on revolutionary seizure, on the direct initiative of the people from below.'[69] Lenin's new position did not amount to a renunciation of collective mass organisation. Looking towards the next phase of struggle he wrote: 'Soviets may appear in this new revolution, and indeed are bound to, but *not* the present Soviets.'[70]

As it turned out, the soviet system proved capable of regeneration from within. Once the shock of the July Days had passed, many Menshevik-SR leaders were recalled by the workers and soldiers who elected them for having welcomed the Tsar's generals back into the capital. A further powerful impetus to the renewal of the Soviet came from the unsuccessful right-wing coup of General Kornilov on 27–30 August when he planned, in alliance with several senior officers, to occupy Petrograd and smash the revolution. When news of Kornilov's actions reached the city, the Mensheviks and SRs found that to save their own skins they had to call on the initiative of the masses, an initiative they had tried to stifle.

The Bolsheviks welcomed this change. It gave an opportunity to strike back against the extreme right and expose the weakness of Kerensky and the Menshevik-SR leaders of the Soviet and of the Provisional Government. The Soviet Executive, in recognition of its decay and distance from the masses, now ceded its authority to a 'Soviet Committee of Struggle against the Counter-Revolution', in which the Bolsheviks played the major role. Simultaneously the district soviets, now under Bolshevik leadership, independently took over many of the functions hitherto fulfilled by the central Soviet. Factory committees, again under Bolshevik influence, organised armed militias and a Red Guard. The trade unions also played an important role in sabotaging Kornilov.

It was apparent at this moment of crisis that the Bolshevik programme of working-class power both helped create, and coincided with, the feeling of the Petrograd workers. The party's leadership of these mass institutions did not, as bourgeois historians suggest, come about by some trick or constitute a violation of Soviet democracy. it was the logical outcome of the situation. The party that believed in building a revolutionary dictatorship *from below* (in the sense, as Lenin had defined it, of the rule of the exploited over the exploiting minority), now came to lead the institutions in which this dictatorship could take shape.

The united action of Petrograd's workers and soldiers brought about the total failure of the Kornilov coup. Within three days it had collapsed, with Kornilov's troops either blocked by workers' action or mutinying. The damage done in July had been repaired. A sign of workers' renewed confidence in their own abilities was Bolshevik success in the Petrograd Soviet. On 1 September the party, carrying many rank-and-file Menshevik-SR delegates with them, won a motion for a government of workers and peasants by 279 to 115 votes.[71] The Moscow Soviet followed suit just four days later.

After Kornilov's failed coup there was a general revival of soviet organisation. New elections were held; plenaries became more frequent; executive committees were called to account and often replaced. In the Petrograd Soviet the new mood was confirmed by Trotsky's election as president.

This was just the last in a succession of victories which saw the Bolsheviks win control of several district *dumas* and *zemstvos* (local and county governments) but especially of directly working-class organisations.

> This was no accident: the trade unions, the factory committees, the economic and cultural assemblies of the working class, both permanent and transitory, were compelled by the whole situation, upon every private problem which might arise, to raise one and the same question: Who is the master of the house?[72]

Only the Bolsheviks provided a clear answer to the question. The party brought into harmony the different strands of the working class, and through them the mass institutions which now had caught up with the changing mood.

It had not been easy to arrive at this unified position. The way in which the different strands in the movement interacted and finally reached a common political strategy was illustrated at the Putilov works. Of its 36,000 or so workers 10,000 were from the countryside and new to industrial labour. They were known as 'black workers' (from the mud on their peasant boots) and had begun to organise for better wages in April 1917. The factory committee, which drew most of its members from the skilled section, tried to restrain the independent wage struggles of the 'black workers' in order to keep the factory workforce moving as one block. In June, hoping to avoid a spontaneous strike over wages, the factory committee sought better rates through union negotiation. Bolsheviks who wanted to avoid a premature uprising lent their support to the factory committee's tactic. On 21 June a meeting of several factory committees, the metal union and socialist parties passed a resolution which stated:

> We . . . propose that the Putilov workers restrain their justified displeasure at the conduct of the ministers who have delayed the solution of the conflict by every means. We believe it is necessary to prepare our forces for a speedy and general action . . . Even if the wage increases are now granted, the uninterrupted rise in the price of commodities and of accommodation will render this gain worthless. And so a decisive struggle is necessary to establish workers' control of

production and distribution, which, in turn, requires the transfer of power into the hands of the soviets.[73]

In July this holding operation broke down. The wage movement of Putilov workers helped fuel the mass demonstrations of that period. Once the July Days had passed without positive result, the scale of the industrial crisis in Petrograd brought even Putilov's unskilled workers to accept the Bolshevik strategy for a planned seizure of power.

> In the autumn the capital's workers faced a serious threat from the growing shortage of basic raw materials — the result of the dislocation caused by the war — and the deliberate withholding of resources by the employers, who now had the excuse they wanted to close or relocate factories. By September Russian industrial output was 40 per cent down on the beginning of the year.[74]

The workers' response was for the factory committees to take over the task of organising production. But this could only be a temporary solution. A Bolshevik resolution passed at the First All-Russian Factory Committee Conference in October explained why: 'The workers' control being implemented in the localities through the factory committees must be organised into a state-wide system, for only then will it achieve real, serious results.'[75]

The crisis in industry, the seizure of land by the peasants and chaos in the army all pointed in one direction — towards the need for soviet power. Even the strike tactic now appeared insufficient and it declined as a general means of struggle.[76]

But soviet power would not arise spontaneously. It had to be taken by insurrection. This was to be organised and led by the Bolsheviks and given legitimacy and state authority by the soviets. Opponents of the October revolution have suggested a cleavage between party, Soviet and the masses. The opposite was true. For the first time since February, the direction of all three reinforced each other. Such a favourable conjuncture of party, soviets and masses had to be made secure, and quickly. For it was threatened by counter-revolution and the approach of the German army to Petrograd. The Provisional Government was planning to surrender the city and action was urgently required.

The first step was taken by Lenin, who wrote a letter to the central committee of his party entitled 'The Bolsheviks must assume power'. The basis of his argument was that:

> The Bolsheviks, having obtained a majority in the Soviets of Workers'
> and Soldiers' Deputies of both capitals can and *must* take state power
> . . . The majority of people are *on our side* . . . There is an apparatus
> — the Soviets and the democratic organisations.[77]

With some resistance the party was won to the idea that it must
organise a new insurrection.

Such a stand implied, as Lenin had foretold in 1905, that the
soviets were unable to lead insurrection in 'the narrowest sense' of
the word. Though major soviets had Bolshevik majorities they
were still public forums in which the inevitably secret detailed
work of armed uprising could not be discussed. Also, while the
masses had been won *in general* to the slogan 'All Power to the
Soviets', the singleness of purpose and audacity required to make
the slogan a physical fact came only from the revolutionary party.

Some Bolsheviks argued that for formal reasons the insurrection should await the Second Congress of Soviets, which would be
called in late October. Here the party could hope to win a majority
of delegates. Lenin's reply to this was scathing:

> It would be naive to wait for a 'formal' majority for the Bolsheviks. No
> revolution ever waits for *that*. Kerensky and Co. are not waiting
> either, and are preparing to surrender Petrograd![78]

On 29 September he repeated the argument:

> To 'wait' for the Congress of Soviets would be utter idiocy, for it
> would mean losing *weeks* at a time when weeks and even days decide
> *everything*. It would mean faint-heartedly *renouncing* power, for . . . it
> will have become impossible to take power (both politically and
> technically, since the Cossacks would be mobilised for the day of the
> insurrection so foolishly 'appointed').[79]

A successful insurrection required the satisfaction of three
related needs. It had to offer a solution to the urgent crisis and
banish the constant threat of counter-revolution. Secondly the
technical/military tasks required to win had to be taken in hand.
Thirdly the maximum involvement of the Russian masses had to
be achieved, not in the narrow conspiratorial work, but in the
political leap which the seizure of power by one class from another
necessarily includes. To answer the demands of all three simultaneously required skills which Lenin called 'the art of insurrection'.[80]

The first concrete step towards the October rising was the creation of the Petrograd Military Revolutionary Committee.

> The one difficulty . . . not yet got over was that of reconciling an instrument of insurrection with an elective and openly functioning Soviet, upon whose benches, moreover, sat representatives of the hostile parties.[81]

The problem was solved when the Mensheviks suggested a committee to respond to Provisional Government plans for moving the garrison out of the capital. The committee was part of the Soviet machinery but restricted enough and of a political composition that allowed the Bolsheviks to pursue the organisation of insurrection. It took ten days between the proposal for a Military Revolutionary Committee, its adoption at a Soviet plenary, and its establishment, but as Trotsky said, 'the Soviet is not a party; its machinery is heavy'.[82]

The detail of the rising which this committee organised on 25 October and the handing of power to the Second Congress of Soviets cannot be dealt with here. But with the minimum of casualties the Provisional Government was overthrown. A straw poll of delegates to the Congress showed that 505 of the 667 soviets represented there believed all power should be taken by the soviets and this was done. Trotsky described the political mechanism of the revolution in these terms:

> The party set the soviets in motion, the soviets set in motion the workers, soldiers and to some extent the peasantry. What was gained in mass was lost in speed. If you represent this conducting apparatus as a system of cog-wheels — . . . you may say that the impatient attempt to connect the party wheel directly with the gigantic wheel of the masses — omitting the medium-sized wheel of the soviets — would have given rise to the danger of breaking the teeth of the party wheel, and nevertheless not setting sufficiently large masses in motion. The opposite danger was, however, no less real — the danger of letting slip a favourable situation as a result of inner friction in the soviet system.[83]

The October revolution demonstrated with absolute clarity both the importance of the soviet and its limitations:

> The organisation by means of which the proletariat can both overthrow the old power and replace it, is the soviets . . . However, the

soviets by themselves do not settle the question. They may serve
different goals according to the programme and leadership. The
soviets receive their programme from the party. Whereas the soviets
in revolutionary conditions — and apart from revolution they are
impossible — comprise the whole class with the exception of its
altogether backward, inert or demoralised strata, the revolutionary
party represents the brain of the class. *The problem of conquering the
power can be solved only by a definite combination of party with soviets
— or with other mass organisations more or less equivalent to*
soviets.[84]

The Russian revolution is an invaluable model of a successful
workers' uprising; indeed it is the *only* model we have. But Russia
was not seen as a model by most Marxists until 1917. Indeed it was
held to be an exceptional case, only the German movement being
worthy of emulation until then. However, since 1917 the Russian
example has been paramount, with every revolution having its
'February', its 'July Days' and looking forward to October. Such
parallels can be an aid to understanding, they can also obscure the
actual development of events — which never follows a set pattern
but is reshaped anew by human activity. There were enormous
differences between Russia and countries such as Britain or
Germany, then as now. The Russian working class lacked until
1917 things which workers in Western Europe took for granted:
the parliamentary system, powerful legal reformist parties, established trade unions with armies of full-time officials and so on. For
all that the Russians had one great advantage over the West. They
possessed a revolutionary party with mass support and a Marxist
leadership.

Despite the differences, the similarities during the years 1915–
1920 were equally remarkable — for in all the mass movements of
Europe workers were striving by revolutionary means towards the
common goal of socialism. And yet the contrast between Russia
and the West cannot be ignored. If we are to do more than passively
observe the Russian revolution we must understand how its lessons
can be *translated* for use in countries where political life is dominated by the apparatus of reformism: parliament, a mass reformist
social democratic or labour party, and an organised trade union
movement acting as intermediary between capital and labour —
conditions, in short, which face socialists in a large part of the
world today in the 1980s.

A vital aid to this translation is the historical legacy of Western Europe at the end of the First World War. Though ultimately unsuccessful, workers' councils — collective organisations equivalent to soviets — grew up in the face of mass reformism. Revolutionaries beginning as a tiny minority of the working class learned to confront the challenge of opportunity thus presented. The central part of this book is devoted to this experience.

Chapter Two

WESTERN IMPERIALISM IN CRISIS

TO UNDERSTAND the crisis that hit the hitherto stable capitalist countries of Western Europe we must go back to August 1914. The outbreak of hostilities forced ruling classes drastically to remould their power structures. Survival on the battlefield depended on enormous quantities of munitions. On 20 September 1918 the British Army, for example, fired 943,837 shells, weighing 40,000 tons altogether.[1] War on this scale demanded a national economy which worked as an efficient integrated production unit.

Britain led the way in this field, and set up a system of *state capitalism* in which the interests of the state and private business were combined. On the very first day of the war the railways were 'taken over' by the government. A Railway Executive Committee was appointed to run them, which consisted of the general managers of the main private lines and the President of the Board of Trade. Naturally the private owners were compensated for this shocking interference — their profits were guaranteed. Lives might be sacrificed for King and Country, but not profits!

The interpenetration of state and capital was repeated as one industry after another was incorporated into the machinery of war. By late 1918 the state controlled 90 per cent of imports, the use of most essential raw materials, and directly employed 3½ million people through the Ministry of Munitions.

As the state moved into economic life, so capitalists moved into the state. The all-powerful Ministry of Munitions under Lloyd George typified this process. In his words, it was 'from first to last a business-man organisation. Its most distinctive feature was the appointment . . . of successful businessmen to the chief executive posts.'[2]

The war imposed a curious symmetry on the policies of opposing states. Germany's leaders had not been prepared for a long war, but they soon realised the need for a drastic reorganisation of their resources. The government set up a special supply organisation — the Raw Materials Section. This was run by Walther Rathenau, the head of the AEG electrical company. It was not long before the fusion of state and business had penetrated to the deepest levels of German society. Under Rathenau's supervision, a system of giant corporations operating under government control ran most industrial production and distribution.[3] State action completed the process of capital concentration which normally took years to achieve.

In 1915 Italy sided with the British, French and Russians and joined the war. Here too the government looked to industrial expertise to reshape the economy. Turin's Industrial Employers League was called in to develop a system of government-controlled production which by 1918 encompassed 1,976 separate firms.

Everywhere economic life was distorted by the limitless demands of the military. The hunger for munitions drew millions of workers into metalworking while other industries stagnated. In Britain the numbers in engineering rose by 34 per cent to 2.4 million during the war; in Germany the increase was 44 per cent, bringing the munitions workforce to three million. Italy began the war with a miniscule armaments industry, but eventually had 905,000 people working on military contracts.

The sudden erection of state capitalist economies seemed at first a dramatic departure from the past, but in fact it represented an acceleration of tendencies present in the decades before 1914. As individual businesses struggled to compete with each other, they merged into ever larger units, and concentrated a growing number of workers in mass production. The logical completion of this process came in wartime, when whole countries became vast integrated factories under a state capitalist management. Production had once been the concern of a large number of small businesses with workers scattered over many plants. Now industry was organised through a large-scale, national effort. Individual bosses may have resented state encroachment, but as a class they benefitted from this opportunity to use the state to crack down on labour at home and crush commercial rivals abroad.

Such capitalist development contained a glaring contradiction which Engels had foreseen many years before. There was a conflict between *production of wealth*, achieved by the collective cooperation of millions, and the *private appropriation of that wealth* by a tiny group of capitalists. This reproduced itself as 'the antagonism between the organisation of production in the individual factory and the anarchy of production in society as a whole.'[4]

The wartime economies operated as great individual factories and the anarchy of capitalism was brutally expressed by war. The two contradictory forces of social production and war met in the munitions industry. It was here that the crisis was expressed with particular force, and that the workers' council movements began.

The ruling class attempted to solve its problems by the forced interpenetration of state and capital — of politics and economics. The workers' movement had to fight on the same ground as its adversary and match its weaponry. The workers' council — itself a fusion of economic and political struggle — was the result.

The labour movement under attack

A successful war effort abroad depended on working-class cooperation at home. At first the ruling classes had no problems, the hysterical patriotism of the first weeks of war had made sure of that. But it was obvious that the ravings of the press would lose their efficacy when workers confronted the grim realities of modern warfare. So the European states turned to a combination of persuasion and coercion to silence discontent and crush opposition.

The first prong of their attack was the taming of the traditional workers' leaders. This should not have been easy. The European labour movment had committed itself to resist imperialist war at the 1907 Congress of the Second International at Stuttgart, when all the major working-class parties had pledged themselves to 'do everything possible to prevent the outbreak of war.' If war should break out nevertheless, 'it is their duty to advocate its speedy end and to utilise the economic and political crisis brought about by war to rouse the various social strata and to hasten the overthrow of capitalist class rule.'[5]

On 4 August 1914 all these fine words were forgotten. The leaders of the British Labour Party and the German Social Democrats almost fell over themselves in the indecent haste with which they rushed to join the imperialist war. Italy's Socialist Party proved more resistant to chauvinism, but its slogan of 'neither support nor sabotage' meant that it would do nothing to interfere with the national war effort.

Trade union leaders embraced the imperialist cause as enthusiastically as their political counterparts. Even before 4 August the German Free Trade Unions promised to suspend strikes and wage campaigns 'in the national interest'. A few months later British trade union collaboration with the war was formalised in the Treasury Agreement, whereby all strikes which interfered with military production were outlawed in return for a hollow promise that limits would be imposed on profits. In Italy the metalworkers' leader summed up the general position when he declared: 'We were unable to prevent the war so it would be childish and ridiculous to think of resisting its consequences.'[6] This neat piece of logic allowed him to formally denounce the war but openly mobilise workers to sustain it.

The various labour and trade union leaders of Europe had declared a social truce for the duration of the war. They handed the working class, bound hand and foot, to the warmongers. Working-class institutions were not simply neutralised, but were incorporated into the apparatus of the state. Arthur Henderson, leader of the British Labour Party, was made chief industrial relations advisor to the Tory/Liberal coalition government. In Italy and Germany trade union officials sat next to military officers and employers on army conscription panels, and sent their members off to die in the trenches.

Abandoned by their traditional leaders, workers found themselves defenceless against a massive attack on civil rights. Emergency legislation such as Britain's Defence of the Realm Act and Germany's Law of Siege gave the police and military unprecedented powers. While the various parliaments limped on, their influence was negligible. Censorship and repression was now the total political programme of Europe's state machines.

The munitions industries were singled out for special attention because of their strategic importance. Britain's Munitions Act of July 1915 banned strikes by those on war work. It permitted the setting up of 'controlled' factories where all trade union practices were suspended. To prevent munitions workers going elsewhere for better pay and conditions, the law stated that anyone changing their job without the employer's permission could not be re-employed for six weeks.[7] Later conscription became another threat with which to discipline labour.

Germany learnt from the British example and introduced its own draconian law in December 1916. The 'Auxiliary Service Law' completed the process by which Germany was made into a unified war machine. All those not already working under military discipline (there were almost one million enlisted soldiers working in industry by 1917) were liable to forced 'patriotic Auxiliary Service' under government control. Here too the right to strike or change employer was severely restricted.

One apparent concession to labour was the encouragement of 'workers' committees . . . to promote a good understanding among the workers and between the workers and their employers.'[8] The government had been forced to accept such workplace labour representation because of its previous experience with Berlin's metalworkers, whose aggressive militancy had forced the establishment of special arbitration machinery — 'the War Board of the Metal Industry of Greater Berlin'. On this body there were three representatives each from management and unions, with a War Ministry official in the chair.

Italy's 'Industrial Mobilisation' system consisted of a network of committees similar to the Berlin War Board. Once again the appeal to patriotic duty had to be backed up by a battery of coercive powers. One third of workers in the war industries were conscripts who faced stiff military penalties if they stepped out of line. The threat of conscription was used to frighten the rest, and 'anti-social' behaviour such as arriving late or answering the foreman back were made criminal acts.

Although the various countries responded to the war in a similar way, the degree of its impact on workers' lives varied considerably. For example Britain called up between four and five million men between 1914 and 1918. Italy, with a smaller population, mobilised five and three-quarter million; and Germany a staggering 13 million soldiers.[9] Whereas Britain escaped the destruction of lives and property upon its territory, whole areas of the Continent of Europe were devastated.

One symptom of the economic stress of war was inflation. By 1918 the British cost of living had risen by 205 per cent over the pre-war level, that in Germany around 300 per cent, while the weak Italian economy saw a 400 per cent rise. In the struggle to keep pace with inflation, workers of different countries were not equally successful. It seems that British wage packets kept their value, while those in Germany, even in the better paid war industries, were behind — income dropping by 23 per cent in the war, as compared to Italy's steeper fall of 35 per cent. All this had an effect on public health. While the British suffered no decline, poor nutrition and harsh conditions led to serious deterioration in both Germany and Italy.[10] By 1918, for example, the death rate *behind the lines* in Turin had risen 49 per cent above its pre-war level, and its birth rate was down by 29 per cent.[11]

With relatively few men called up, the British trade unions actually grew during the war, but heavy military recruitment in Germany had a devastating effect on union membership. Here the capitulation of workers' leaders to imperialism was least expected, and its psychological effect all the more traumatic. By the middle of the war, demoralisation and mass conscription had halved the three million-strong membership of the Free Trade Unions.[12] In Italy too, the membership of the socialist-affiliated General Confederation of Labour slumped from a pre-war level of 335,000 to 230,000.[13]

Years of fighting, however, dampened workers' enthusiasm for 'King and Country'. As Rosa Luxemburg wrote:

> Gone is the first mad delirium. Gone are the patriotic street demonstrations, the chase after suspicious looking automobiles . . . Into the disillusioned atmosphere of pale daylight there rings a different chorus; the hoarse croak of the hawks and hyenas of the battlefield.[14]

Total war first brought terrific disorientation, and then a yearning, an intense thirst for justice on all planes of social life. This awakening hope left its mark in a post-war explosion of strike activity:

Average number of strikers per year[15]

	Britain	Germany	Italy
1911–14	881,000	311,000	239,000
1915–18	678,000	523.000	146,000
1919–21	2,108,000	1,085,000	987,000

Metalworkers take the lead

Practically without exception, the metalworking industry of each country was the first to initiate this revival of workers' militancy. What was perhaps more surprising, it was the privileged skilled workers who took the lead, transforming simple shopfloor unrest into the struggle for socialism through workers' councils. After all, metalworkers in general had a low strike record before the war and were often paid highest by employers and enjoyed better conditions than other sections.[16]

We have seen how the contradictions of social production and capitalist anarchy met in the munitions industry, but how did this operate on the practical level? The war, with its unquenchable thirst for weaponry, forced an expansion of the munitions industry, giving a new importance to the metalworker, and the skilled man in particular. As the leader of the Berlin turners put it, skilled men 'formed an organisationally solid and decisive group in the production process. They stood in a certain sense, at the heart of the large enterprise.'[17] And in an 'engineers' war' craftsmen knew that their skills were irreplaceable. The fact that they were far more valuable at their benches than serving as cannon fodder gave these men a sense of confidence — but not a sense of complacency.

For great changes were shaking up life in the factories. To achieve production targets in armaments, hours were pushed to the limit of endurance. At Fiat in Turin, employees worked a 75-hour week. Berlin turners had their hours raised from eight and a half to eleven a day. They now worked six days a week plus compulsory Sunday labour of between five and twelve hours.[18] Across the North Sea in Glasgow, engineers slaved equally long to produce munitions for use against German workers.

Workshop customs that had taken years to mature were outlawed under emergency legislation. Practices that had given the skilled man some control over his work environment were unceremoniously cast aside in the headlong rush to produce weapons.

This was most obvious when it came to the employment of women. Employers were keen to exploit this source of cheap labour for as one put it: 'What the war has clearly shown is not that women are paid too little, but that men had been *paid too much*.'[19] The general exclusion of women from enginering until the war, whatever the prejudice it showed, was a mark of the metalworkers' control of job security and wages. Their influx after 1914 illustrated the degree to which skilled workers' traditional defences had been breached. In Britain the number of women in government-controlled munitions plants grew by 390 per cent in just two years (compared with a modest male increase of 22 per cent).[20] According to one estimate, women formed 70 per cent of the Italian munitions labour force by 1917.[21] In Germany the overall number of women industrial workers rose by 46 per cent against a fall in male employment of 23 per cent.[22]

The introduction of new machinery adapted for use by un-skilled and semi-skilled labour completed the attack on the skilled engineer. Wartime capitalism was rapidly making the production process more *social* by involving ever-larger numbers and extend-ing the division of labour. This had begun even before 1914 and came from two sources. On the one hand factories employing many thousands of people were built for the purposes of mass produc-tion. Within these new factories tasks were split into simple operations that could be performed without the preparation of a long apprenticeship. On the other hand, employers drew upon new methods such as the 'scientific management' techniques pioneered by Frederick Taylor in America to help in this transformation. Where once a skilled man had chosen how to tackle a task, now the foreman, backed up by the time and motion expert, would instruct him how to perform it.

New machines went together with revised workshop pro-cedures and gave employers more direct control over metal-working operations than ever before. All the skill and initiative of the producer was removed. No longer could one craftsman follow an item from its beginning as raw metal, to its end as a machine, as had been the case in the nineteenth century. When a worker's pride in production was taken away, a sense of alienation filled the void that was left, but this did not have to lead to passive resignation. What was lost by the individual was gained by the collective. Products were now made by the cooperation of greater numbers of workers in larger factories, and this could bring a new sense of confidence and class consciousness.

Metalworking was not the only industry to have a high level of social production, but it alone provided the first leaders of the work-ers' council movements. For only this industry experienced both the anarchy of capitalist competition (expressed through demand for war munitions) *and* the sudden socialising of the work process.

The need for armaments gave skilled men a temporary bar-gaining power, but this of itself did not lead in the direction of workers' councils. Equally important was the special insight they gained into the contradictions of the capitalist system. They were offered a dual perspective: macroscopic (international war) and microscopic (capitalist attack at the point of production along with a more social labour process). It was this glimpse of the general features of the crisis that opened the way to the workers' council, for through it the crisis could be resolved.

The same broad vision was not available to soldiers. They too saw the awful reality of imperialism at close hand, and the legacy of war poets and writers shows how this led to extreme alienation. But it was a *non-class* experience, because it was cut off from the point of production. Of course private and officers tended to come from different classes and their conditions varied, but the opposition of interests that could form a collective consciousness was largely absent.

It was interesting to see how sailors were more militant than soldiers. The German navy was the driving force in the fall of the Kaiser, and the Russian Baltic Fleet played an important part in the October revolution. Sailors had a less fragmented experience because they worked in large, collectively operated units such as battleships. Many of them were former metalworkers who ran the complex machinery below deck. Like their industrial counterparts, sailors could understand their role as cogs in a great war machine.

The idea that metalworkers had a revolutionary outlook because of their special position in the structure of wartime capitalism is important. It explains why skilled men, rather than semi- or unskilled workers often took the lead in Western Europe. The former had a unique work experience compounded over years of struggle, organisation and participation in the labour movement. This gave craftsmen a strong sense of how they fitted into the production process. This feeling was not shared by the women and young people entering industry for the first time. Indeed for them the war may have brought an apparent advance in social status.

It has been argued that skilled metalworkers turned to militancy and workers' council organisation for conservative reasons — that they wished to preserve their elite status and traditional craft rights.[23] But as the above argument suggests, technically advanced and socially organised factories were the bases of the strongest workers' councils. In Britain, where traditional work practices were most deeply entrenched and energetically defended, the revolutionary drive of the skilled men was relatively weak. In Germany and Italy craft attitudes had never had such deep roots, but a stronger radical tradition existed to make sense of the situation. There the most socially organised workplaces developed the best council movements. To put it another way; skilled men did not turn to the workers' council because of some 'Luddite' fear of rational progress. They were reacting to the irrational contradictions of capitalism, torn by conflict between competitive anarchy abroad and socialised production at home.

Thus the councils were well-adapted to the imperialist age of capitalism. They grew in metalworking — the most technologically advanced and dynamic of European industries. Factories such as the 36,000-strong Putilov works in Petrograd, the DWM in Berlin with 10,000 and Fiat Centro with 15,000 were the birthplaces of the workers' councils. The revolutionary lessons that can be drawn from their experience are therefore more appropriate to conditions today than say the Paris Commune (which was based on small workshops) or Chartism (which had artisan roots).

The wartime crisis of 1914–18 set many forces in motion. It stripped the working class of its traditional defences and forced it to approach self-organisation in a new way. It decided which industry might be the weak link in the social chain, for in munitions the contradictions of capitalism were most acute. It even determined the method of struggle. State capitalism, with its fusion of politics and economics, could be opposed only by a workers' council movement which fought on these fronts — against the economic offensive at work and on the political issue of war. Twentieth century capitalism was to meet a fitting enemy in the revolutionary democracy which grew from the mass production units it had itself created.

But war did not affect only munitions workers. The crisis shook the beliefs of *millions* of workers and undermined the system's greatest ideological weapon — the notion that capitalism, whether good or bad, is fundamentally unchangeable. Total war revolutionised daily life. Out of the years of self-sacrifice in the name of a fictional 'national interest' there grew a feeling that there could be no return to the old way of life, that a radically new world must be born out of such suffering.

It is difficult to grasp the strength of this all-pervading mood, but this conversation, published in a right-wing magazine and overheard 'On the night train to Amiens' conveys an impression of it:

French soldier: We will replace capitalism with a new order . . . call it socialism, communism or what you like, but be sure *m'sieu*, it will not be monarchy, 'democracy' or individualism . . . For the first time in history nations have gone to war *as a whole*. You have seen Germany mobilised to the last man. You have seen the same thing in France and

England . . . Be sure that the young men in the trenches, and the young women in the munitions factories, know now what communism means . . . They receive the same six sous per day . . . They eat the same food. They obey the same commands and live in the same hovels and ditches.

Corporal: Shall we forget these years? Shall we turn the country for which we have bled, *nous autres*, back to the politicians, back to the capitalists, back to your democratic aristocrats who ride through the boulevards in automobiles . . . To whom does France belong? It belongs to us who fought — to the women who labour in munitions factories — the peasants who support the orphans of dead friends. France is ours now *m'sieu*.[24]

If the workers' councils had potential for growth only in the armaments industries, they could never hope to win the allegiance of a majority of workers and hence state power. Although the crisis made it likely that councils would first develop in munitions, it also ensured that the opportunity for a much wider class struggle existed. In this situation engineering could play the role of a *vanguard industry*, that section which could spearhead the offensive of all the exploited. Equally the workers' council had an opportunity to spread until it became the mass organisation of the entire working class, and eventually a workers' state.

Capitalist crisis opened up great possibilities — but they were no more than possibilities. The objective circumstances were favourable to a new form of workers' self-organisation. The pressure of the slaughter in the trenches, long hours in the factories and food shortages led to several explosive upsurges of militancy, often by the least organised sections of the working class. It now depended on revolutionary leadership whether the potential of such spontaneous actions would be consolidated and led to victory. The workers' council was the force which, given the right leadership, could prevent the barbarism into which the capitalist system was dragging all humanity.

While the two great issues of the moment were war and struggle at the point of production, under reformist conditions *it took a conscious effort to link them together*. Any political campaign based purely on state issues was doomed to failure because it could not immediately connect with the material concerns of workers. Any fight that remained limited to sectional economic aims would leave the class divided and invite defeat at the hands of an immensely powerful state apparatus, which included the official leaderships of the trade unions.

The division of politics and economics is a basic characteristic of reformism. In part it reflects the real experience of many workers who, as objects of exploitation in the workplace, can readily understand the need for collective *economic* organisation such as trade unions to fight back against the employers. However, when it comes to the broader political issues, which do not seem so directly relevant to the workers' immediate situation, the need for class organisation and clear class *politics* is not nearly so obvious. However, the division of politics and economics is not a simple reflection of workers' conditions under capitalism. If this were so, this division would be easily and spontaneously overcome when capitalist crisis forced workers to consider problems far wider than their own individual factories, or when the intervention of the state in economic struggles showed the close link between state and industrial issues. In developed capitalist countries organisations — sectional trade unions and parliamentary parties — have grown up which build their very structures upon the separation of politics and economics. Politicians, with a constituency-based organisation, fear losing votes if they are involved in strikes. Union leaders, whose chief focus is in industry, fear attacks by the state if they politically challenge it during disputes.

At the outbreak of the First World War there were many West European leaders of parties and trade unions who had a vested interest in maintaining the separation of politics and economics, even though this ran counter to the needs of workers more obviously than ever. The deliberate maintenance of this division became one of the chief means of protecting reformist organisations. It thereby had the effect of protecting capital from workers' revolution.

If labour was to free itself from the rule of capital, the most advanced workers had to generalise from experience of exploitation at the point of production, to reach an understanding of the need for action *as a class*, both to defeat the bosses and overthrow the capitalist state. Only a fusion of economic and political struggle could make possible a successful revolution on these lines. The workers' council was a form in which this fusion could be accomplished. To build it, and champion its cause against the external enemy of the bourgeois state and the internal enemy of reformism, a new leadership had to be developed.

In Russia the Bolshevik Party was ready to take on this role. No equivalent force existed elsewhere. But there were groups of revolutionaries and of industrial militants who were to have influence far beyond their tiny numbers. In Western Europe they did not, as yet, constitute parties, nor even rank-and-file movements. Nevertheless they showed the promise of a leadership combining the most advanced political ideas (the vanguard of socialists) with rank-and-file activists in the factories (the vanguard of militants). In the crisis of wartime these two elements could set the best organised workers, those in munitions, into motion. They in turn could draw the rest of the class behind them. The Bolshevik Party represented just such a fusion of socialist and militant vanguards and so played the key role in bringing the workers' soviets to power.

The revolutionary movements of Western Europe also attempted to establish effective leadership, but it was difficult to unite the different vanguards into a cohesive force in the midst of war and intense class struggle. Nevertheless, the degree to which such leadership was attained conditioned the strength of the workers' council movements. For workers' councils were not passive institutions with a fixed card-carrying membership. The ability of their leaders to promote unity in action was crucial to growth.

Chapter Three

GLASGOW:
LAYING THE FOUNDATIONS

THE CHARACTER of the British labour movement is best understood if contrasted with that of Russia, which was in some ways its
polar opposite. The latter had a new industrial working class
which, though lacking in permanent trade unions, was politically
the most advanced in the world. Britain had the oldest working
class, some of the highest levels of union organisation, but the most
conservative political attitudes. The fact that for much of the
nineteenth century British capital faced little external competition
meant that employers were able to buy off organised groups of
workers. Full employment and rising living standards from the
1850s onward sapped the political force of movements such as
Chartism. While some sections of the working class maintained
strong economic organisations to extract various concessions, they
felt no need to generalise their struggle or overthrow the system.
Though British labour history was punctuated by short periods of
widespread militancy, such as the 1889 strikes which established
new 'General Unions' and the 'Labour Unrest' of 1910–1914, the
argument that distinctive class politics was unnecessary for workers'
progress was commonly heard right up until the war.

Given this background it might seem that Britain was so
distant from Russia, the home of the soviet, that it would hold few
lessons in the art of revolutionary struggle. Certainly Britain in the
years 1915–1920 was less immediately exciting than Russia or
Germany. But the fact that militants had to start from a very low
point, and solve the most basic problems confronting revolutionary strategy in a reformist situation, in itself makes their experience
valuable to socialists who face difficult conditions today. Glasgow
in particular was the place where the first tentative steps towards
workers' council organisation were taken.

Glasgow before the war

All three of Western Europe's key centres for workers' councils — Glasgow, Berlin and Turin — experienced rapid social and industrial change in the years leading up to the First World War.

Glasgow's population doubled between the 1860s and 1914. Rapid expansion brought new groups such as 20,000 Highlanders and many Irish into the city's mix of cultures.[1] It also meant serious over-crowding, with many people forced to live in cramped 'single end' flats in tenement blocks. As a result Glasgow had among the highest death rates and infant mortality rates of any British city.

Industry mushroomed, with electicity consumption multiplying by 15 times between 1900 and 1913.[2] Factories and shipyards soon extended beyond the confines of municipal Glasgow, running along the Clyde basin from Dalmuir in the West to Shettlestone in the East. The chief industry was metalworking, employing one third of all workers. Its main branch of activity was shipbuilding and marine engineering, though this was complemented by a great expansion of munitions production in wartime. Such turbulent social change profoundly affected workers' attitudes:

> the growth of industry was sufficiently novel for its arrival to be remembered, its growth checked and annotated. To the Clydeside workers industrialism did not appear as the God-given and inevitable environment of mankind, but rather as one phenomenon amongst others, changing and changeable, fit to be moulded by their hands, as it had been by others.[3]

This comment could well have been made of Berlin or Turin.

Even before the war, Glasgow's metalworkers experienced the drive towards social production through modern technology and new management procedures. Arthur McManus, soon to be one of the Clyde workers' council leaders, was a good example. Before the war he worked at pointing needles for the 10,000-strong Singer sewing machine factory:

> Every morning there were millions of these needles on the table. As fast as he reduced the mountain of needles, a fresh load was dumped. Day in, day out, it never grew less. One morning he came in and found the table empty. He couldn't understand it. He began telling everyone excitedly that there were no needles on the table. It suddenly flashed on him how absurdly stupid it was to be spending his life like

this. Without taking his jacket off, he turned on his heels and went out, to go for a ramble over the hills to Balloch.[4]

Not everyone reacted as strongly as McManus, but the alienating effect of modern capitalism with its mindless and repetitious production methods was certainly a factor in labour militancy.

In the war, the workers' council movement took root in a number of modern engineering factories. Weir's of Cathcart was one of the five named by the government as the main plants behind the Clyde Workers' Committee, the embryonic council organisation. Before 1914 Weir's saw a long battle against the aggressive management methods imported from its twin factory in America. Such things as time and motion study led John Maclean, later the leader of the anti-war struggle, to write in the summer of 1914: 'No British firm has been more Americanised than this pump-making monopolist, one that supplies the Navy as well as the Merchant Fleet. It is hustle, hustle, hustle, all the time and every time.'[5]

To combat their 'scientific management', the workers built a strong shopfloor organisation. Harry McShane, a steward at Weir's, shows how socialised production contributed to collective consciousness:

> Weir's was a modern factory with men working in their own bays, at their own benches and not moving around . . . The jobs were so ridiculously simple that anyone could do them . . . The organisation of the factory meant that it was much easier to organise the trade union.[6]

Parkhead Forge was to be another base of the council movement. This mammoth plant was newly built and employed the latest methods, including electric furnaces, cranes and automatic conveyors. By 1914 the factory had a strong shop stewards' committee which negotiated on a day-to-day basis with the owner, Sir William Beardmore. Weir's and Parkhead Forge were almost unique in Britain for enjoying this level of shopfloor organisation.

Indeed the general level of engineering trade unionism on Clydeside was high. Four out of five workers were in their appropriate trade organisation, the strongest being the Amalgamated Society of Engineers. The ASE had authorised the appointment of shop stewards in 1892 and it took little time for a local stewards' network operating independently of the union to emerge. As early as 1896 employers moaned bitterly about the stewards' 'Vigilance Committee'.

This form of rank-and-file unity was hardened by a series of confrontations that made Glasgow the most militant metalworking district. The lockout of 1897–8 was fought by a committee of delegates from the different factories. It went into action again five years later to resist wage cuts, in defiance of orders from union headquarters.[7] By 1914 Glasgow had developed a powerful and independent network of factory militants. They had proved their worth as rank-and-file leaders in the fight for basic improvements in wages and conditions *before* the war arrived. This was to be very important, for this accumulated self-confidence and rudimentary organisation helped the rank-and-file network not only to withstand the floodtide of chauvinism and calls for 'social peace' but to initiate industrial action in direct opposition to the national trend.

However a tradition of revolutionary politics was as important for the growth of a workers' council as a network of shopfloor militants. In Britain as a whole, the socialist movement was very weak. On the eve of war the Labour Party (whose politics were barely left of the Liberals) had just 1.6 million affiliated trade unionists and no constituency organisation. The confused idealistic socialism of the Independent Labour Party (ILP) attracted only 30,000 followers. Marxism had even less support.

The revolutionary movement found it difficult to grow for the reasons outlined above. The ability to extract *economic* advances, such as better wages, without resorting to *political* struggle, meant that the two concepts remained separate entities in many workers' minds. The best organised sections of the working class had acquired the characteristics of a 'labour aristocracy', a group of workers who built a strong trade union movement for extracting economic concessions, but felt no need to generalise their struggle to the whole class. British labour entered the twentieth century with strong sectional organisation but virtually no independent politics.

One striking feature of the British Socialist Party (BSP), the main Marxist current, was the degree to which it had succumbed to the idea that economics and politics are separate. Far from seeking to overcome this aspect of capitalist ideology through class struggle, the party reacted by turning in upon itself to assume the attitudes of a political sect. The BSP was founded in 1911, during the 'Labour Unrest' — a rash of militant strikes which swept the country. Some argued that the new party should be working in this mass industrial movement, but the prevailing opinion was that such agitation would be 'an impertinent interference in a field with which they had nothing to do.'[8] •

The party was supposed to win political power, but it did not intend to soil itself with anything less in its daily work. It divorced socialist politics from industrial struggle, rejecting immediate activity lest this compromise the ultimate goal. As a result it lacked the means to attract the thousands of workers recently radicalised by militant action. The BSP's socialism, expounded from soap boxes Sunday after Sunday, remained irrelevant to the lives of workers. This party was by far the largest 'Marxist' organisation with 10,000 members.

But it was not the only labour organisation which saw an unbridgeable gulf between political and economic agitation. The *syndicalists*, who reached their high point during the Labour Unrest, emphasised the other side of the equation to the BSP. As much as the BSP stressed politics and the ultimate goal of socialism, the syndicalists campaigned for immediate action through militant trade unionism. For them the attainment of socialism would be through the struggle of trade unions. Their aim was 'to amalgamate all workers into one national and international union, to work for the taking over of all industries, by the workmen themselves.'[9] This was the theory; but for syndicalists activity was much more important. And given the limitations of trade union struggle, their activity rarely went beyond the limits of economic action or challenged the system as a whole.

The British left, more than any other, lacked that synthesis of socialist theory and working-class action that is the essence of revolutionary practice. Only the tiny Socialist Labour Party, with a few hundred members, attempted to fill the gap. The SLP considered 'the two phases of working-class activity, political action and industrial action to be "Siamese twins"; each is necessary to the other.'[10] But their position did not amount to a belief in the workers' council. The ideas they inherited from Daniel de Leon, the American socialist, suggested a parallel growth of a workers' political party and alternative revolutionary trade unions of the syndicalist type. Although de Leon's approach proved a sectarian dead-end, the SLP's understanding of the interrelation of political and economic struggle helped put its members at the head of the British workers' council movement.

Despite the general weakness of the British left, Glasgow was a centre of socialist agitation before the war. Its radicalism had been

fed by diverse streams — the highland clearances, the Irish liberation struggle and even contact with revolutionary Russian sailors at
the port. In 1907–8 a sudden recession in engineering and shipbuilding sent local unemployment rocketing from 6 to 28½ per
cent. In the face of such capitalist anarchy, the methods of trade
unionism and parliamentary procedure already seemed woefully
inadequate. Soon afterwards Clydeside was stirred by agitation in
support of the Dublin transport strike, and the Labour Unrest
which preceded the war.

The local ILP claimed 3,000 members and the BSP some 500.[11]
Even the SLP, though minuscule elsewhere, had some 100
adherents.[12] While the British left was generally divided between
syndicalists (who saw economic struggle as the route to workers'
emancipation) and sectarian socialists (who put their faith in party
propaganda for a classless society), to a degree Glasgow's movement overcame the false dichotomy between socialist economic
and political agitation. Many revolutionaries on Clydeside were
involved in both the fields of party activity and shopfloor militancy.
Politics and workshop life met in factory gate discussions, canteen
debating groups and the Trades Council.[13] In addition there were
John Maclean's education classes, attended by hundreds of leading
militants.

Willie Gallacher's political evolution was a good example of
how political and industrial work could interact. He became a
socialist through reading Robert Blatchford's **Clarion** newspaper.
It strongly criticised trade unions as insufficiently socialist. He
then met a Trades Council delegate who was scandalised to discover
he was not even in a union. Convinced of his mistake, Gallacher
joined the Brassfounders' Association, became a leading steward at
Albion Motors and built a group 'which was able to keep up a
continuous stream of revolutionary literature with regular discussion classes at the midday meal hour.'[14] Similar agitation in metal
factories across the Clyde Valley began to break down the walls
separating socialist theory and factory life, making it a fertile
ground for the development of a workers' council.

While Glasgow was not free from the sectarianism which
blighted the left elsewhere, the various groupings worked together
without softening or abandoning their political positions. The
annual May Day celebrations captured the spirit of this collaboration:

There were fourteen or fifteen meetings being held at once and all kinds of socialist banners were flying — 'Socialism the only hope for the workers' — and so on. The Social Democratic Federation [soon renamed the British Socialist Party] would usually have some slogan from Marx. The SLP was there, the ILP and the Clarion Scouts; everybody co-operated very well. The children in the socialist Sunday school came from George Square . . . Even the anarchists led by old Willie McGill made a splash.[15]

The Clyde Workers' Committee

The origins of the Clyde Workers' Committee were to be found in the leadership of an important unofficial strike. While under normal circumstances strike committees are limited in scope and disappear once the particular dispute is over, the continuing crisis of war led to a whole series of rank-and-file grievances. In the process the loose network of militants was called upon to form a solid link between a number of factories, thus acquiring a permanent form. As was the case in the 1905 revolution in Russia, the first appearance of the workers' council is often as a sort of *permanent strike committee*.

Shopfloor agitation peaked between 1915 and 1919 and was led by munitions shop stewards who comprised the bulk of the Clyde Workers' Committee. War and industrial life were inseparable in these years and the committee was a rank-and-file response to the special circumstances of this time. Economic demands by trade unionists were inevitably resisted by the employers on the grounds that everyone must make sacrifices for the war effort. The problems facing those who made even minimal demands were revealed by the first confrontation of munitions workers with their employers in February 1915. When a three-year agreement on wages came to an end, the Glasgow District Committee of the ASE asked for a wage increase of two pence an hour. This demand would normally have had no revolutionary implications, but at that time any threat to arms production was branded as treason.

On 28 January the engineers imposed an overtime ban. They were finally provoked into all-out strike when Weir's of Cathcart brought in American engineers on higher wage rates than their British counterparts. From the start the link between the war and this local wage campaign was apparent. As Gallacher, one of the leading participants, wrote:

. . . because of the 'patriotic' posturings of the national trade union
officials . . . the employers were convinced that there was no possibility of the workers taking action . . . the engineers at Cathcart, by their
prompt action in declaring a strike when faced with such a situation,
maintained in the face of all betrayals . . . the right of the unions to
determine the conditions to be operated in the factories. They demonstrated to the Government and the employers that, war or no war, the
workers were going to see that the trade unions did not go out of
existence.[16]

During the strike the shop stewards' network re-emerged
under the title of a 'Central Labour Withholding Committee'. It
united 10,000 unofficial strikers from 26 firms.[17] Solid organisation and close rank-and-file involvement in decision-making made
the two-week stoppage 'probably the best organised strike' ever
seen on the Clyde.[18] Although government pleading brought a
return to work on 3 March, informal contacts between the leaders
continued.[19] There was now the basis for an organisation covering
engineers right across the valley.

Equally important, within each workplace militants were
encouraged to set up shop stewards' committees. Until then such
bodies had existed in only one or two strongly organised plants.[20]
So this one strike, over a simple economic demand, had immeasur-
ably strengthened workplace organisation — the first stage of the
workers' council process, and paved the way for the second — a
rank-and-file organisation linking metalworkers in a number of
different factories.

The Clyde Workers' Committee, however, was a new departure. It was formed after a direct clash with the state over the
imposition of the Munitions Act. In other words its origins lay in a
political issue.

In August 1915 two shipwrights were sacked for inefficiency
and 26 more fined under the Munitions Act for taking sympathy
action to defend them. When some refused to pay the fines they
were jailed. In response, the unofficial network of militants threatened immediate strike action and the prisoners were released. Days
later the victimisation of a Weir's steward under the Munitions Act
was foiled by similar rank-and-file resistance. It was clear that the
sort of organisation that had led to the 'two pence strike' in February
was needed all the time — so the Clyde Workers' Committee was
born.

The militants who built it had two things in common. They 'were all shop stewards at one or other of the arms firms which had led the February 1915 strike and were to remain the backbone of the Committee through 1915–1916. And they were all socialists.'[21] Willie Gallacher, a steward at the Albion works and BSP member, was chairman. James Messer of the ILP was a steward at Weir's and secretary. The treasurer was Tom Clark of the SLP, who was a worker at Parkhead. The SLP was also represented by Johnny Muir, convenor of Barr and Stroud and formerly editor of the SLP's paper, **The Socialist**, and by Arthur McManus, who succeeded him as editor.[22]

Without this combination of left-wing politics and rank-and-file popularity, Glasgow's embryonic workers' council organisation could never have started, for a very simple reason. The majority of workers accepted the war and the resultant social truce between workers and employers. Only socialists, who believed there was nothing to gain from imperialist war, would fight to save the workers' movement from strangulation in the name of 'King and Country'. But very few workers shared their opinion. These socialist stewards would have had no impact if they had campaigned on their ideas alone. Yet they were able to lead thousands out on strike, because they had a reputation among the rank and file as fighters on bread and butter issues. Having prepared the ground *before* the war, they could argue convincingly that workers should defend their wages and conditions *in spite of* their attitude to war.

These militants were thus able to lead workers in the fight for better wages — an economic issue. But in doing so they soon confronted the Munitions Act — a political issue. So the development of the workers' council movement, from factory organisation to rank-and-file movement, was matched by a shift from the defence of economic gains to resistance to the employing class's political attack.

The Clyde Workers' Committee's first leaflet was written in November 1915, and clearly expressed, for the first time, 'the principle of rank-and-file organisation':

> We will support the officials just so long as they rightly represent the workers, but we will act independently immediately they misrepresent them. Being composed of Delegates from every shop and untrammelled by obsolete rule or law, we claim to represent the true feelings of the workers. We can act immediately according to the merits of the case and the desire of the rank and file.[23]

The militant vanguard was therefore both within the trade union movement but free to act outside it. This was the starting point for effective leadership. Had the stewards been totally integrated into the union machinery, they could have taken no action; had they been divorced from it, their initiatives would have had no following. This discovery was a considerable advance on past practice, which either consisted of a sectarian rejection of union work, or embraced it uncritically.

The leaflet invited attendance from the 'progressives in all Trades', adding that it already had support from miners, joiners, gas workers and so on. Although this broad basis was more a sign of the munitions' stewards hopes than an accomplished fact, their intention was to reach beyond their base in engineering to become a *class* organisation — a workers' council.

But to be able to do this, they had to offer the class something to attract its allegiance. Obviously the appeal had to be wider than the defence of engineering interests. One common threat to all workers was the imperialist war, but the committee would have considerable difficulties in taking on this issue, as we shall see.

The Clyde Workers' Committee was a very simple institution. It assembled some 250 to 300 leading stewards from various factories once a week. There was no full-time bureaucracy, for it drew its strength not from some Head Office divorced from the workplaces, but directly from the rank and file. Its effectiveness could not be measured by the amount of paper work produced, but by its ability to mobilise workers. This ability came from the standing the shop stewards had won in the factories. The munitions stewards were known personally to their workmates, laboured under the same conditions and had fought for the right to lead.

The coming together of such men under the umbrella of the Clyde Workers' Committee thus connected the rank and file in the workshops with a centralised organisation spanning engineers right across the Clyde Valley. The committee was designed for *action*, and so combined authority as a representative body with the freest discussion among the militants, as this interview with one demonstrates:

Question: 'Were you a member of the Clyde Workers' Committee?'
Answer: 'It depends on what you call a member. The Clyde Workers' Committee was a heterogeneous crowd which had practically no constitution. It was more a collection of angry Trade Unionists than

anything else, which had sprung into existence because of the trouble which was going on on the Clyde. [It] was a place of meeting where the different kindred spirits of the different shops met to discuss all our grievances.'

Question: 'Did you think it better to go there than to your own Trade Union officials?'

Answer: 'Oh yes. Our own Trade Union officials were hopelessly tied up . . . under the Munitions Act.'

Question: 'Could you represent yourself alone?'

Answer: '. . . it was not absolutely necessary for your shop to send you; you could represent a minority in the shop just the same as a majority, even though the majority was one.'[24]

The Clyde Workers' Committee had established itself through workplace struggle. But the wider question of war was central at this time, and in this field Glasgow was also to make an original contribution.

At the outbreak of hostilities most of Britain's anti-war socialists, already desperately few in number, were silenced by nationalist hysteria and physical intimidation. Clydeside was the exception. On the first Sunday of war Willie Gallacher shared a platform with John Maclean. Both BSP members, they spoke strongly against imperialism. The majority of workers would undoubtedly have dismissed their arguments outright, but there was just enough popular tolerance of socialist ideas to give the spark of internationalism space to grow into a small but intense flame. Even to achieve this required considerable courage!

When, under the shock of the terrible news and in fear of the widespread, spontaneous patriotism . . . The ILP retreated from the street-corners, stopped their big Sunday night meeting in the Metropole Theatre, and took refuge in their local halls, where they could reach nobody but the converted, John Maclean decided to continue his work among the masses.[25]

Very soon Maclean had rallied the local BSP branches to his position. This was in contrast to the party nationally, which was hopelessly split over the war. The SLP, with a few exceptions, also took an anti-war stance. But Maclean did not confine his work to criticism. His special argument was that 'the only war that is worth waging is the Class War'. Denunciation was not enough, socialists must do everything they could to pit 'the workers against the world exploiters.'[26]

While the Clyde Workers' Committee was an effective defensive response to the problems in the factories, Maclean's internationalist position was the only possible starting point for an offensive challenge to the capitalist system which was creating these problems. On their own, neither Maclean nor the shop stewards had an overall solution to the crisis. The only effective answer was one which used the collective strength of the workplace to confront the general crisis of war. This meant that the committee had, with Maclean, to evolve a strategy that united both the organisational strength of the one and the theoretical clarity of the other.

But there were grave difficulties. Maclean's ideas were not backed up by any solid organisation so had only minimal influence on the rank and file. Apart from three issues of a monthly propagandist newspaper, **The Vanguard**, and a mere handful of direct supporters, Maclean had no mechanism (such as a party rooted in the factories) to fight for internationalism. He therefore depended on the Clyde Workers' Committee to campaign on the issue. But the committee was not a revolutionary party. The leaders might be socialists, but they had been brought together as representatives of the rank and file, and were very conscious of the duties and limitations this implied. Maclean was putting political demands on them which they found it difficult to fulfil, so there were in-built tensions in the relationship between the two sides.

When, in late 1915, Maclean argued that the militant stewards should make the anti-war struggle the central plank of their work, they replied that an open declaration of this policy would destroy their support among the rank and file. Gallacher put it succinctly when he said: 'The Clyde Workers' Committee stands for *Unity*.'[27] Although the co-existence of revolutionary ideas and rank-and-file organisation gave the labour movement in Glasgow a great potential, many obstacles lay in the path of their effective interaction. This was revealed by the issue of dilution.

Dilution — the search for a class strategy

Dilution was the government policy of employing unskilled and semi-skilled workers on engineering jobs formerly reserved for craftsmen. From their strong bargaining position, metalworkers could fight this in two different ways: either as a threat to the privileges of the elite of skilled men, or as the first phase of a war against the hard-won rights of *all* trade unionists. The crucial months of November 1915 to March 1916 saw the militants in Glasgow fighting against the idea of craft elitism and groping towards a strategy that could harness the strength of their workshop organisation to the wider interests of the labour movement.

When the government's proposal for dilution was first discussed, the initial response of the spokesman for the Clyde Workers' Committee was the following statement:

> We have every sympathy with your wish for increased output, but we fear, for reasons which I need not enumerate, the introduction of a class of labour in our industry that will do our work cheaper than we are doing it, and recognise that if employers can obtain the same results for £1 from the new class of labour as they do from us for 30 shillings, nothing except, perhaps, our force . . . can prevent a reduction in our wages.[28]

This 'sympathy' for increased munitions output seems extraordinary from leading shop stewards who, with the exception of Kirkwood and Muir, were opposed to continuing the war. The above statement showed a sharp division between their public pronouncements and their privately held anti-war beliefs.

Such a split between public and private faces was the legacy of pre-war methods. Even in Glasgow, with its vigorous left-wing traditions, socialists such as Gallacher felt they could speak against the war on *political* platforms, but that industrial issues were quite different and could be treated separately. The leading members of the Clyde Workers' Committee were used to wearing two hats — one reserved for their socialist party activities; the other, the shop steward's hat, to be worn as a representative of the rank and file, many of whom were pro-war.

Nevertheless, the wartime crisis was forcing those militants to confront their contradictory ideas. The Clyde Workers' Committee had come into existence only because the trade union officials had succumbed to war fever and abandoned the workers' struggle. Like it or not, the Clyde stewards operated in the space opened up by the clash of wartime state capitalism with a leaderless working class. To make progress in this minefield the stewards needed to preserve the mass unity forged in the two pence strike *and* fight over the major issue of capitalist war.

It is as an attempt to do this that the Clyde Workers' Committee's attitude to dilution in the winter of 1915–16 must be understood. The shop stewards had to take their effective base in the munitions factories as the starting point, but try to lead it away from craft elitism to a general class position. Johnny Muir was given the task of drafting a policy.[29] Its most important paragraph stated that dilution would be tolerated if the government complied with certain demands:

> All industries and national resources must be taken over by the government — not merely controlled — but taken over completely and . . . organised labour should be vested with the right to take part directly and equally with the present managers in the management and administration of every department of industry.[30]

This call for nationalisation and shared control has baffled historians. James Hinton finds it 'surprising — and evidence of the general disorientation'.[31] Even J T Murphy, a leader of the English shop stewards during the war, saw it as 'either window-dressing propaganda, or a complete over-estimation of the power and extent of the influence of the Clyde Workers' Committee.'[32] But it can be understood if looked at in the light of Maclean's proposals in the weeks preceding the issue of Muir's statement.

Maclean's answer to the government's dilution plans appeared in his newspaper, **The Vanguard**:

> Let the Government take over all munitions works, pay the capitalists nothing per cent dividend, double the workers' wages, shorten the hours to eight, and give control of the establishments to the workers themselves. We guarantee that very soon the worker would treble the war output and justify the proposals from a pro-war standpoint. These are only timid immediate proposals, and we are willing to have better ones inserted in the next issue.[33]

These demands were intended to expose the capitalist aims which lay behind the war, for as another article declared:

> If the masters are anxious to win, we challenge them to hand over their land and capital to the people, and to let the workers organise all industries, including those necessary for the conduct of the war, and control the products of labour, and we can assure them that all will go well at the front . . . We know they would rather accept defeat than adopt socialism.[34]

Maclean was challenging the government to admit the class basis of the war, and by so doing, he hoped to lead workers away from their attachment to patriotism.

Within weeks of these articles appearing, the leading members of the Clyde Workers' Committee had taken up their main ideas. On 8 January 1916, Gallacher, writing in the committee's newspaper, **The Worker**, called on the capitalists to

> relinquish their stranglehold on industry. 'It would be a revolution', said Mr [Lloyd] George, in reply to the Clyde Workers' Committee deputation, 'and it cannot be done'. Why not? Simply because the employers would lose the war rather than lose their power over the workers . . . It is for us workers to take that power from them.

A week later Muir's dilution proposals were presented with the full agreement of the committee. His programme, which demanded nationalisation but only a *share* of control, was less ambitious than Maclean's. But both policies were seeking to make the connection between the immediate workshop issue of dilution and the overall question of war. The strategies they put forward attempted to provide a policy which fused political and economic struggle. The organisational base for a workers' council had been constructed; it was now time to give it a sense of direction.

It was perhaps naive to think the state would take this call for nationalisation and workers' control seriously, or that its rejection would bring many workers to see through the imperialist war. Maclean had few followers and a newspaper with a circulation of 3,000. The Clyde Workers' Committee stewards had a rank-and-file base in several factories and a paper which printed 15,000 copies. Clearly neither side was able to give their demands an airing nationally. Nevertheless the dilution proposals were the first attempt since Chartism, seventy years earlier, to escape the separate political and economic compartments of British socialism and lead a mass industrial movement in a revolutionary direction.

Against overwhelming odds neither the strategy of Maclean nor that of the Clyde Workers Committee in opposing dilution had much chance of success, and it was not long before the tensions between the two sides surfaced. An argument developed because Maclean was looking for a short-cut to a broad anti-war campaign, while the committee feared losing the rank-and-file unity it had painstakingly consolidated. Maclean regarded the committee's demand for only a share of control as dangerous, since: 'If the Clyde workers took part-control of the munitions works they would thus accept part responsibility for the War.'[35]

This dispute revealed how each group approached the questions of the day rather differently. The committee's leaders saw its role primarily as a mouthpiece for shopfloor opinion and would go no further than Muir's statement towards making an *overtly political* stand. Maclean, whose immediate tactics did not derive from any single collective unit but from the standpoint of international socialism, found this incomprehensible, and asked: 'How could any man calling himself a socialist come to speak at a meeting at this time and *not* refer to the war that is raging in Europe.'[36] Soon there was an open rift between the two sides.

At the end of 1915, Lloyd George, then Minister of Munitions, declared his determination to impose dilution on the Clyde as soon as possible. He personally confronted local shop stewards at a 3,000-strong meeting on Christmas Day, 1915. The proceedings were punctuated with much singing of the 'Red Flag' and heckling of the platform speakers — Lloyd George and Arthur Henderson, leader of the Labour Party and Cabinet advisor on industrial affairs.[37]

Lloyd George's speech was cunning. By equating nationalisation with socialism he hoped to elicit sympathy from his hostile audience: 'We have started great National factories; state-owned and state-controlled; every timber and nail in them belongs to the state. My friends, these are great socialist factories.' When Henderson declared dilution to be 'the great issue of the present moment', someone called out 'Ay! and profits'. The Labour leader continued — 'You are all aware of the fact that we are engaged in probably the greatest war' — 'at hame' came the reply.[38]

After this rough handling, Lloyd George and his fellow ministers decided to take the unruly munitions workers head on. Secret government memoranda, always with an impeccably polite, but ominous, tone, spoke of certain 'gentlemen' who would be removed from the Clyde 'for an indefinite period'. The targets were workshop leaders like Gallacher, Kirkwood and McManus, as well as prominent revolutionary activists like Maclean. The final offensive followed the general line laid down by William Weir, manager of Cathcart and Ministry of Munitions representative. His approach showed how well the ruling class, unlike the majority of workers, understood the connection between politics and economics.

> An essential preliminary step must be to have the country and community behind you . . .

1. Assuming a strike takes place immediate [dilution is announced],
the policy should be:

a) the immediate issuing of summonses under the [Munitions] Act.

b) the immediate arrest of any Steward who . . . proposes resistance.

c) the immediate declaration by the Central Executive of the ASE or
other unions affected, that under no circumstances can the strike be
supported.

d) a careful watch by detectives on the actions of the members of the
Clyde Workers' Committee and the few others specified.

2. Assuming the strike continues and extends sympathetically to other
shops

a) a proclamation should be issued by the National Advisory Committee [of the Labour Party and unions] clearly dissociating itself . . .
calling on loyal Trade Unionists to return to their work with the full
assurance of Government support against any acts of interference or
intimidation.

b) the repeal of the Trades Disputes Act.

c) arrest of the strike leaders.

d) on no account must any of the shops shut down entirely. Employers
must be instructed to carry on with whatever skilled, unskilled and
female labour they can induce to work. If the shops are closed no
opportunity is given to create the necessary cleavage between the
willing and loyal workers . . . and the rebellious element.

e) military guards should be instituted at every works.

f) at the first attempt of riot or damage to property, martial law should
be proclaimed.[39]

There were many overlapping elements here — government,
judiciary, army, police, prison, 'public opinion', propaganda,
Labour politicians, trade union officials and employers. Weir
planned to use all of these to achieve a subtle articulation of
persuasion and force, state repression and reformist sabotage. His
tactics were copied on a grander scale by the capitalists of Germany
and Italy when confronted by workers' council movements on their
own soil.

The Clyde Workers' Committee hoped for a united stand by
all local factories over the dilution scheme. To force the authorities
to recognise *its* authority, all workshops were to refuse to meet the
Dilution Commissioners individually, but refer them to the committee officials. The Achilles' heel of the whole plan turned out to
be David Kirkwood, convenor at Parkhead Forge. His commitment

to the dilution strategy was weak because, unlike most of the leading stewards, Kirkwood believed in the war effort. Together with John Wheatley of the ILP, he drafted an alternative plan in which dilution could be introduced so long as the employer's overall wages bill was not lowered. While this prevented the boss from using dilution to cash in on cheap labour, it was entirely devoid of political implications.[40]

Kirkwood met the Commissioners, who, anxious to keep dilution an economic issue, readily accepted his proposal. Without solidarity among their own ranks, the Clyde stewards could not hope to generalise the struggle over dilution into 'war against war'. Now there had been an open breach, the left was vulnerable. On 2 February **The Worker**, their newspaper, was banned. Four days later Maclean was arrested, followed by Gallacher and Muir. The key factories answered this provocation with a strike which won the release of their stewards on bail. However, as Weir's plan had shown, this battle was going to be fought to the finish.

An incident at Parkhead Forge served to spring the government trap. On 17 March 1916 Kirkwood's right as convenor to tour his plant was withdrawn and the workers immediately downed tools. Other factories took sympathy action. The authorities then arrested a number of key Parkhead and Weir militants and 'deported' them from the city. This was a clear attempt to smash the Clyde Workers' Committee. Unfortunately the protest stoppage against it involved only half the number of the February 1915 strike. Certainly Kirkwood's maverick behaviour over dilution contributed to this lack of unity, but the chief reason for defeat was the committee's failure to involve workers outside Glasgow's munitions industry in its struggles, which in turn must have contributed to a feeling among the rank and file that resistance to the government was hopeless.

The break-up of the Clyde Workers' Committee that followed was the result of its inability to make its strategy against dilution a serious proposition, either to the mass of munitions workers, those outside the industry, or the government. The weakness of the internationalist current and the separation between public and private beliefs among the stewards made this outcome virtually inevitable. It would take some years before the committee could be re-established. Nonetheless, Glasgow's militant shop stewards had evolved a form of workers' council movement. Tragically they lacked the means with which to carry it beyond the embryonic stage.

The authorities were able to isolate and destroy the committee because, despite its efforts to the contrary, it had not been able to connect its struggle in the engineering industry with a wider campaign against the war. J T Murphy was no doubt correct when he wrote:

> None of the strikes which took place during the course of the war were anti-war strikes. They were frequently led by men like myself who wanted to stop the war, but that was not the real motive. Had the question of stopping the war been put to any strikers' meeting it would have been overwhelmingly defeated.[41]

Nevertheless the unique contribution made by the co-operation of John Maclean and the Clyde Workers' Committee was to try to find tactics which might lead from current concerns to anti-war action, and lead from a rank-and-file organisation in one industry to a class-wide workers' council. There could be no successful workers' council without a tactic which generalised the struggle of the vanguard section.

Although the government gained the upper hand in 1916, the Clyde militants had achieved two important things. By initiating a resurgence of workers' activity despite the clamour for social harmony, they set the workers' council process in motion through an unofficial strike leadership which linked shopfloor organisation in several factories on a permanent basis. This took them from shop stewards' organisation in one plant to a rank-and-file movement across the engineering industry of the area.

Their second discovery, although a tentative one, was a new relationship between socialists and the mass movement. The importance of John Maclean should not be underestimated here. The Clyde Workers' Committee policy on dilution grew from his 'timid proposals'. If they could have been backed by a solid political and industrial campaign, they might have transformed the committee from a defensive sectional organisation into a broad-based workers' council. But Maclean's tiny group lacked the influence which only a revolutionary party could have given, and without a groundswell of anti-war feeling the leading stewards felt trapped in their role of representatives of a patriotic rank and file.

The brief interaction of Glasgow's revolutionary socialists and factory militants was still a step forward. Their common struggle to formulate a forward strategy for the rank-and-file movement at last sought to overcome the distinction between struggle at the factory and struggle against the state. Only from such efforts could there grow a movement that generalised particular struggles and had the potential to achieve socialism through working-class self-activity.

Chapter Four

THE LESSONS OF FAILURE

THE ARREST and deportation of militants from the Clyde in the spring of 1916 suppressed the movement in Scotland for some time, but helped spread it to the rest of Britain. In early November 1916 it was possible to call a national conference of shop stewards. This was duly convened by Arthur McManus, the Clyde deportee. Held in the Hyndman Hall, Manchester, the conference assembled representatives from what remained of the Clyde Workers' Committee as well as stewards from Barrow, Manchester, London and Birkenhead. These people represented propaganda groups composed of militant shop stewards rather than representative organisations of the rank and file.

The national shop stewards' movement which grew from this beginning was slow to grapple with the central question of war, but was primarily concerned with extending shop stewards' control within production. It was clear that the stimulus of Maclean's internationalism did not go much beyond his native city. Nevertheless in May 1917 the national organisation of stewards established just six months earlier was called upon to lead the biggest strike of the entire war.

This began when dilution was taken outside arms production and introduced into private work. The majority of engineers might willingly sacrifice their rights to 'assist the boys in the trenches', but not to benefit individual capitalists. Two hundred thousand workers came out over this issue, and on 5 May 1917 a national stewards' conference met in London to assume direction of the strike. The government stepped in and arrested several of the rank-and-file leaders. The shop stewards' representatives remaining out of jail eventually capitulated under this pressure and by 19 May the strike was over, without Clydeside ever participating.[1] The issue of dilution in private contracts was of interest only to skilled engineers and this meant that despite its considerable size, the May 1917 stoppage was sectional in character.

Although the strike was lost, the national network of shop stewards continued to spread. Another conference was held in Manchester during August 1917 and this time was attended by delegates representing stewards' committees from many places, including Barrow, Bolton, Bristol, Coventry and Leeds as well as those involved in the November 1916 conference. A 'National Administrative Committee' was elected. But as J T Murphy, a leading English steward, later noted, such was the stress put on the *representative* function of stewards as opposed to their role as initiators of action, that the National Administrative Committee 'held theories which prevented it from giving the leadership which the movement needed'.[2]

Nevertheless a measure of the strength of the national stewards' movement was the sale of Murphy's 'Workers' Committee' pamphlet. This sold 150,000 copies in a short time. It contained a detailed blueprint for shop stewards' organisation from the lowest to the highest levels — but made no reference to the war.

In Glasgow a revival was taking place in the labour movement. The release in February 1917 of Macdougall, Maclean's close ally, along with Gallacher and Muir, did something to restore its vigour. By June other deportees had returned to the city. Working-class women, who had proved so important in the famous Glasgow rent strike of 1915, had established a Women's Peace Crusade and its anti-war arguments were complemented by the return of John Maclean in the summer.

International events were also encouraging. The fall of Tsarism in February 1917 put new heart into workers' movements everywhere. Many British workers began to question the continuation of the war. Hope was inspired by the Petrograd Soviet's call for world leaders to meet around the bargaining table to find a negotiated peace settlement. To the extreme left, however, the February revolution symbolised more than a challenge to war; it was a call to overturn the system as a whole.

Supporters of both these pacifist and radical interpretations were present at the Peace Convention which brought a motley collection of representatives together in Leeds on 3 June 1917. Called by the ILP and BSP, the 1,150 delegates endorsed a controversial motion calling for:

Councils of Workers' and Soldiers' Delegates for initiating and co-ordinating working-class activity . . . for a peace made by the peoples of the various countries and for the complete political and economic emancipation of international labour.

Despite the assertion by the proposers that this meant 'the dictator-ship of the proletariat',[3] it was really intended to establish reformist councils which would perform charitable works. The sponsors clearly had no notion of how a Russian 'Council of Workers' and Soldiers' Delegates' actually functioned. The sort of body advo-cated at Leeds was to be just a committee of labour bureaucrats which sought to:

diligently . . . resist every encroachment upon industrial and civil liberty; shall give special attention to the position of women employed in industry and generally support the work of the Trade Unions; shall take active steps with questions affecting pensions of wounded and disabled soldiers, maintenance grants to dependents, provision for treating disabled soldiers and suitable remunerative work on return to civil life.[4]

The Leeds Convention was the first of several abortive attempts in Western Europe to create workers' councils under the control of official labour leaders. Genuine workers' councils could not be built from the top downwards in this way. They were generated by the self-activity of the rank and file coupled with the willingness of militants to lead their struggle in a political direction. Only Gallacher, the Clyde Workers' Committee representative at Leeds, showed any understanding of the Russian example, because he had worked in a movement which had started on the road towards the soviet. He alone suggested the workers' council as an alternative form of state to bourgeois parliament, urging the Convention 'not to resurrect a dead House of Commons, but aided by the Workers' Committee, carry through the revolution by taking over the con-trol and direction of all that goes to make up the life of the nation.'[5]

Bureaucratic councils of the type proposed by the official movement at Leeds did not answer the needs of the rank and file and the idea was soon abandoned, amidst a vicious campaign of press-inspired violence.

But the Convention had shown that after three miserable years of war there was a new optimism in the working class. A sign of renewed energy was the re-establishment of the Clyde Workers'

Committee in late 1917. It was soon confronted by the question of conscription, an issue as potentially explosive as dilution.

Although most workers had been subject to the call-up since 1916, it had not been successfully applied to engineers. There had been one serious attempt made in Sheffield, but this had been rebuffed by lightning strike action. The success of this strike had generated the Sheffield Workers' Committee, the strongest of the English stewards' organisations.

However at the end of 1917 the government decided to take the skilled men on once more and to extend the categories liable for call-up to include engineers. This latest appeal for cannon fodder came at a critical moment internationally. Workers in Germany had staged several mass strikes; socialists meeting at Zimmerwald in Switzerland had issued many calls for peace; most important of all, the new Bolshevik government in Russia was proposing unilateral action to end the war. In the light of this, the chances of a successful anti-war strike in Britain had never been better.

Unfortunately, many engineers echoed the elitist argument of the engineering union officials. This was characterised by the slogan: 'Don't take me. I'm in the ASE'. In other words conscription was acceptable for anyone except skilled metalworkers.

In defiance of this trend Clydeside again seemed to offer the best hope of anti-war action. In the secret reports of the Ministry of Munitions Labour Department, the Glasgow area was judged to be the only one likely to take militant steps to resist further conscription. Local papers spoke of the rank and file refusing to see '*any* man being called up'.[6] The ferment was such that even local union officials felt compelled to threaten strike action.

Again, this militancy did not grow in isolation from economic issues. As well as mobilising against the new Manpower Bill on conscription, the Clyde Workers' Committee was involved in the fight for a 12½ per cent pay rise for pieceworkers, and a strike of moulders and against the victimisation of two women workers at Beardmore's.

To head off the growing opposition, the government sent Sir Auckland Geddes to Glasgow. His meeting on 28 January 1918 with 2,500 local shop stewards was a re-run of the Christmas 1915 event, but this time the political level of the workers was much higher. Where a major concern in 1915 had been defending workshop conditions, now the question of war or peace was paramount. All the questions from the floor of the meeting were to do with international politics in one way or another. Delegates asked Geddes how Britain could ever negotiate an armistice while keeping predatory claims on the lands of its enemies. Arthur McManus made the strongest attack, declaring: 'Not another man for the criminal war for trade and territory! An immediate end to it. This is our challenge to the Government. For this we are fighting and will go on fighting.'[7]

For a time it seemed that the Clyde stewards might form part of a broad stewards' opposition to the war. Just before the Geddes meeting, the *national* shop stewards' movement had taken a decision to strike against further conscription. But the movement had a serious political defect, which was soon exposed.

In the first week of 1918 the National Administrative Council of the shop stewards' movement urged the movement to accept the Bolsheviks' peace proposals and threatened 'national action . . . to enforce these demands.' **Solidarity**, the paper of the English stewards, carried this ultimatum in its February issue. But at the same time it added:

> If we could only be certain that the German workers would follow suit, we would have no hesitation in calling for an immediate policy of 'down tools and damn the consquences'. But we are not in touch with our fellow workers in Germany . . . It may be that the German workers would be willing to do the bidding of their warlords . . . by attempting to invade these islands. In which case, they would get the surprise of their lives.[8]

This argument was *multilateralist*. Worse, it completely lacked the internationalist spirit that had inspired the Russians to strike the first blow against the war, alone if need be. Maclean, like Lenin, had been uncompromising in his hostility to the idea that the war could in any way represent or defend workers' interests, but his influence was far too limited. The tragic results of the shop stewards' hesitation at national level were soon revealed. At the very moment that the **Solidarity** article was penned (and the British engineers waited), half a million German workers were striking for peace. The possibility of workers in both countries linking up in anti-war struggle was not to recur.

The ambiguous position of the national stewards' movement left the Clyde isolated. The anger shown at the Geddes meeting was not acted upon. Soon government-orchestrated propaganda in Glasgow's weaker factories put paid to hopes of an anti-war strike.

In the end it was the British workers who failed their German comrades and not, as **Solidarity** had imagined, the other way round.

In spite of this setback, the Clyde labour movement was powerful enough to stifle local manifestations of jingoism. While in the rest of Britain anti-war socialists felt physically endangered, in Glasgow it was the pro-war meetings that were disrupted. 100,000 people joined the 1918 Labour Day demonstration held in working hours.[9] Havelock Wilson, hysterical patriot and leader of the seamen's union, was given short shrift when he tried to carry his 'fight the war to the finish' campaign to the Clyde. After a street battle lasting several hours and involving 5,000 people, he was driven out of the city. This was not the sort of war he had been expecting![10]

The First World War came to an abrupt end on 11 November 1918 when a workers' revolution overthrew the Kaiser. The action of the German workers' and soldiers' councils was applauded by a demonstration of 30,000 Clydesiders.[11]

Soon afterwards Lloyd George called a general election, hoping to cash in on the war victory. While the Labour vote (in a much larger electorate) stood nationally at five times its 1910 level, it climbed by fifteen times in Glasgow. This showed, in crude statistical terms, how much further workers on Clydeside had developed through self-activity during the war.[12] Revolutionary ideas, which had once seemed the quirky creed of tiny groups, were shown to have a solid base of support when Maclean, running against a pro-war Labour candidate, polled 7,436 votes to his opponents' 14,247.[13]

Those who had believed self-sacrifice in war would bring a better world soon received a rude shock. The alliance between labour and capital, which had been trumpeted so loudly by union leaders and employers alike, was suddenly dissolved once the crisis had passed. The first evidence of a return to the old ways was a reappearance of mass unemployment. As armaments production ran down, the numbers out of work in Glasgow rose alarmingly. By February 1919, with numbers boosted by sacked munitions workers and the first demobbed soldiers, the figure was one in ten. In engineering unemployment rose from its wartime average of 0.5 per cent to reach 11 per cent in February.[14]

The Clyde Workers' Committee insisted that the only solution to the problem was shorter hours. Largely as a result of the campaign it initiated, a meeting of local shop stewards was held in the Shop Assistants' Hall on 5 January 1919. At that time employers were arguing for a standard peacetime week of 47 hours. The reply of the stewards was unequivocal:

> *A 47-hour week means increased productivity, increased productivity means increased unemployment, increased unemployment means lower wages.*
> Lower wages means starvation for the workers and increased profits for the employers . . . a huge standing army of unemployed, and a huge standing army of soldiers to protect the interests of your employers.[15]

Soon official sections of the local labour movement, such as the Joint Direct Committees of the Shipbuiding and Engineering Trades, were taking an interest in the campaign. A Joint Committee 'representing the Official and Unofficial Section of the Industrial Movement' was formed.[16] Emmanuel Shinwell, an ILP councillor and leader of the Glasgow Trades Council, was its chairman. Another conference on shorter hours drew 800 delegates from many areas of Scotland and on 18 January issued a 'Call to Arms' which demanded a 40-hour week and threatened a 'General Strike' for Monday 27 January. 160,000 copies of the call were distributed.

Although the campaign remained regional in character, the Clyde Workers' Committee's newspaper declared:

> We 'British Bolsheviks' have the Russian precedent to guide us, and we believe that in the critical hours of our own revolution, our rallying cry will be: 'All Power to the Workers' Committees'.

Gallacher's tone was even more challenging at this time:

> The decisive hour has come. March forward, strong of heart with the workers of Germany, the workers of Russia . . . Long live the Soviet Republic![17]

But the Forty Hours' Strike was not the decisive hour of revolution. On 27 January most of the Clyde Valley came to a complete halt with 40,000 out. One leading steward wrote later:

> The method of picketing adopted was a new one. Pickets of five to ten thousand workers would march to a particular shop, then line up on either side of the roadway . . . It was a most successful method . . . Another feature of the strike was the use of strikers' wives as pickets.[18]

The climax of the strike came on the fifth day, 1 February. By now there were 100,000 out in Clydeside and 14,000 around Edinburgh. This day was to be called 'Bloody Friday' because the police provoked a violent confrontation with tens of thousands of demonstrators in George Square, Glasgow. What happened next was described in this eye-witness account:

> All Friday night trainloads of troops were brought into the city. When the citizens awoke in the morning from their peaceful slumbers they found themselves surrounded with all the paraphernalia of war. At all points of vantage, guards with fixed bayonets, steel helmets and full war equipment were posted. Machine-guns, tanks, aeroplanes, etc. were brought into the city. Preparations were being made as if a German invasion was imminent.[19]

The government's answer to unemployment vindicated Gallacher's charge of three years before — that the government was as afraid of losing power to the working class as of losing the war.

The joint committee issued a new manifesto calling on workers throughout Britain to resist this 'dastardly attempt to smash trade unionism'. For a time broad action seemed a distinct possibility. Belfast was in the grip of its own struggle for shorter hours and in London a mass meeting of the Electrical Trades Union threatened to switch off the capital's power from 6 February onwards. 'Tell the Clyde men we are coming' was the message they sent north. Despite the military intervention the strike remained solid in Glasgow.

The most serious threat came not from the army but the full-time officials of the national unions. With government support the ASE leaders suspended the Glasgow, Belfast and London district committees of the union. The Electrical Trades Union leaders buckled under government threats that the solidarity action projected for 6 February would be made illegal, and the promised stoppage was delayed. Faced with open sabotage by the national officials, the joint committee recommended an end to the strike — this was accepted at mass meetings on 11 February 1919.

The Clyde Workers' Committee had developed the skill of shopfloor representation to a high degree. But this was not matched by a political analysis of the struggle, or of the way it should be directed (such as would be provided by a revolutionary party). This gap left the official elements in the joint committee free to make the running on national strategy. So it was that after the initial stages of the campaign the Clyde Workers' Committee played no independent role in the 40-hours' movement. It merged its forces with the joint committee, allowing the strike to be conducted more as an industrial dispute than a challenge for power. Whether such a challenge was feasible we will never know, but what is certain is that the tendency of the joint committee to depend on official initiatives to bring support from outside proved a serious mistake.

The Clyde Workers' Committee was not to recover from the strike's defeat, for very soon the engineering militants who formed it were driven out of their factories to join lengthening dole queues. All the bravado of its newspaper, **The Worker**, could not make up for the lack of a national organisation of revolutionary socialists which could have fought attempts by the union officials to defuse the mass militancy of post-war Britain, on the Clyde as elsewhere.

Nevertheless, four years of unprecedented struggle held important lessons for socialists. These were summed up by an SLP manifesto issued just two weeks before the 40-hours' strike. It was significant both as a personal expression of its signatories and as a political statement. Three of its four proposers — Murphy, McManus and Bell — were prominent figures in the shop stewards' movement, a mass industrial organisation. They were also leaders of the Socialist Labour Party, a revolutionary group. They personally connected revolutionary politics with the workers' council movement. In the manifesto every item hinged on this interplay of socialist theory and rank-and-file action.

The first section dealt with a new kind of revolutionary practice:

> It is essential that education and activity should be the concrete expression, one of the other . . . if education and the machinery of action were parts of one organisation, the latter would respond in terms of the former.[20]

This was a break from the old evangelical approach to winning socialism. It suggested an interventionist approach. Socialists working in the Clyde Workers' Committee had led thousands in struggle with the employers, and this mass activity had proved to be the best sort of political education.

Section B of the manifesto dealt with the nature of mass action:

The experience of the war has shown that it is impossible to separate the political and industrial agitation of any grave issue . . . the industrial agitation of today can become the political issue of tomorrow and *vice versa*. Therefore the urgent need of the movement from the standpoint of sound tactics is the immediate creation of a movement which will combine both industrial and political functions.[21]

Here the manifesto broke through the attitudes which had imprisoned orthodox Marxists and syndicalists alike.

The third part dealt with 'Social Administration . . . after the revolution' and presented, for the first time in Britain, a serious alternative to parliamentary politics:

All factories and plants of production should be organised in such a way that each should have its own complete committees of delegates drawn directly from the various departments . . . This organisation extending over a whole District would regulate the local sources and supply.[22]

There were limitations to the ideas in the manifesto. SLP members, like revolutionaries in the BSP, had intervened in struggles not so much as socialists building their party but as industrial militants who happened incidentally to belong to a political organisation. Thus the lessons they drew tended to concentrate on the character of *mass* struggle rather than the way the revolutionary minority attempted to build their political influence. Thus the manifesto made no distinction between the role of the Marxist party, with its conscious political character, and the mass collective movement embodied in the workers' council. An understanding that a revolutionary party was needed to lead mass struggles to successful seizure of power was to be learnt from the Russian example and propagated by the Communist International only in the 1920s.

But the wartime experience had given revolutionaries some insight into the means by which the transition from capitalism to socialism could be achieved. Revolution ceased to be a hollow formula, but was now something which became feasible when the immediate struggles of workers were organised and spread by working-class self-organisation through workers' councils or soviets. The emphasis on the final goal (by 'political' socialists) or on short-term union issues (by syndicalists) was replaced by a synthesis in which the two could be knitted together.

The Clyde Workers' Committee had not simply revamped the

trade union movement, but created something with much greater potential. The collapse of union officialdom during the war had forced militants to look for new reserves of working-class strength. In so doing, they discovered the collective power of the rank and file. The unofficial movement which arose used the most basic level of existing union organisation — the stewards, who alone were closely in touch with shopfloor feeling. If this rank-and-file organisation had been content to rest upon the temporary sectional power of the munitions workers (as the English shop stewards' movement tended to do) it would have lacked the drive towards the workers' council, remaining at the level of 'do-it-yourself' reformism — the sort of purely economic agitation in individual workplaces such as was to be seen in British manufacturing in the 1950s and 1960s.

What gave Glasgow that special edge was a partial recognition of the broad nature of the capitalist crisis. Under pressure from ideas put forward by John Maclean, local militants attempted to fuse economic and political struggle, thus threatening managerial power in the factory *and* the capitalist state. Only such a total challenge to the system could solve the total crisis to the benefit of the working class. Managerial power could not be broken unless the state was overthrown; just as the state could not be smashed unless the working class developed its collective muscle in the factory struggle.

Although the movement could not fully escape the weakness of British socialism, the wartime crisis forced British revolutionary socialists to rethink many basic beliefs. Before the war, socialist politics and workplace activity had been miles apart. But the embryonic workers' council movement on Clydeside pointed the way to a new sort of revolutionary practice whose essence was the linking of the two together. Only this could create a movement which saw its final goal as a state based on the workers' council and working-class self-activity as the means to that goal.

Chapter Five

GERMANY IN WAR

BRITISH workers traced only the first steps towards a workers' council. In the three months between November 1918 and January 1919, Germany was to take the movement to the brink of state power, putting the workers' council to the ultimate test — a full-blown revolution. That period saw a great flowering of workers' councils right across Germany. Although the revolution continued fitfully until 1923, its first phase was characterised by the struggle for power between workers' and soldiers' councils and the old state. There were major battles in the Ruhr, the northern ports of Hamburg and Bremen as well as middle Germany. But the eye of the whirlpool was Berlin.

Imperial Berlin

Berlin resembled Glasgow in many ways, but everything was on a larger scale. In the second half of the nineteenth century the capital of the new German Reich increased its population five times over, reaching four million in 1910. Recent arrivals in Berlin included an important Polish contingent with its own revolutionary tradition. As in Glasgow, this hectic social expansion certainly contributed to the city's radicalism. This was confirmed in the revolution when the majority of workers killed at the barricades were found to have been born outside the city.[1]

Pressure on housing was acute. One survey in the 1900s revealed that 790,000 Berliners lived in 'kitchen/living rooms' containing up to five or six people. Two-thirds of the city's school-children reported sleeping two or more to a bed.[2]

Berlin was not only the administrative capital of the German Empire, but also the heart of its engineering industry. The dynamic growth of this sector was phenomenal. In 1910, for example, employment in the branch of electrical technology grew by 21 per cent.[3] Typically for the imperialist age, the bulk of engineering factories were in the hands of just three giant combines — Walter Rathenau's AEG, Siemens and Schwartzkopff. These modern companies dominated the city and their plants were much bigger than the average.[4] By 1917, Berlin had 37 engineering factories with more than 1,000 workers.[5]

As in Glasgow, the production process was becoming rapidly more social, and this had occurred well before the war. Technical change was spearheaded by the Ludwig Löwe machine-tool company. They advertised products such as the 'Universal Milling Machine' which enabled one man to do the work of six, and the 'Special-Automatic Capstan Lathe' which could replace the labour of nine workers. Not everyone was as independent of spirit as Arthur McManus had been when confronted by new working methods. The following passage graphically illustrates how the machine claimed ascendance over man in one Berlin factory:

> One day the Löwe machine was set up in the workshop. The worker, who for years had been at a different type of machine, began to work at his accustomed pace. The manager, who was standing behind him, leant over and speeded up the belt drive, increasing the cutting rate. Dismayed, the worker said he could not run the machine at this frantic tempo. But the manager brandished a piece of paper which indicated the rate at which such a tool was guaranteed to operate. The worker has now had to adjust to the new rate permanently.[6]

New working practices weakened the control of skilled men over the labour process. A symptom of this was the influx of women. In just seven years the number of female machine tool workers rose by 89 per cent against an increase of 25 per cent in the male labour force. By 1910 one in seven of the workers in this traditionally male preserve were women.[7]

Despite these problems, the engineers were strongly organised. The Deutsche Metallarbeiter Verband (DMV), the German metal-workers' union, was the only labour organisation recruiting engineers. With a pre-war membership of 545,000 the DMV was easily the most powerful of the socialist-affiliated Free Trade Unions. In Berlin it had signed up 85 per cent of turners. Such high levels of unionisation contrasted with most other industries, where bitter opposition from employers prevented major union growth.

Despite its strength, the DMV was less and less capable of

resisting the offensive of new technology. By 1914 the situation in the Berlin engineering industry was critical. A local survey of turners was taken just two months before the outbreak of war. It revealed that in seven years the number of people working as 'craftsmen', yet who had never served an apprenticeship, had doubled. Working conditions had deteriorated since the introduction of new management methods. 'All large Berlin factories and most small ones have been more or less transformed by the Taylor system', reported the union newspaper. 'Management statistical offices are imposing time and motion study, and some have worked this sytem for years.' The once static workforce had now taken to moving from one employer to another, trying in vain to escape the pressure of Taylorism and new piecework methods that were bearing down on them.[8]

The union, however, seemed to be more concerned with expanding its bureaucratic apparatus than defending the membership. Thus between 1900 and 1914 the number of full-time DMV officials grew from 19 to 647 without alleviating any of the difficulties on the shopfloor.[9] The failure of the union to respond to the needs of the members cleared the way for a rank-and-file opposition on similar lines to that which emerged in Glasgow. In Berlin there was an extra spur to such a movement. It took the shape of Adolf Cohen, chief local officer and the epitomy of the new breed of bureaucrat. In 1911, in defiance of the membership, he wrecked a strike by moulders by his refusal to sanction solidarity action. Soon afterwards he broke an unofficial strike of turners in the Wilhelmsruhe district of the city by threatening to withdraw their union cards if they stayed out.

The rank and file soon began to organise local opposition. In the spring of 1912, workers at the Borsig factory began a campaign to replace the worst full-time officials. Their first target was Cohen. A candidate ran against him in the election campaign, but was ruled ineligible on a technicality. Soon the belief that it was possible to simply replace bad officials with 'good' ones had given way to the idea that the basic structure of the union had to be reformed.

The rise of bureaucracy was partly the result of a growth in union size. In the early days, democracy had been safeguarded by meetings of the whole membership in an area. This worked well when numbers were small, but by the turn of the century such assemblies had swollen into mass meetings. The rank and file found it impossible to have any detailed control of the day-to-day running of the union through such a structure.[10]

In July 1912 Siemens shop stewards proposed that the Berlin district committee of the DMV, with its built-in dominance by union officials, should be replaced by an assembly of shopfloor delegates. At the same meeting, Richard Müller, who was a turner by trade and soon to be leader of the revolutionary shop stewards' movement, proposed an equally radical plan. Under this scheme the 'middle level' of the union (in which full-time officials were the largest group) would be entirely replaced by *Obleute* (the German word for shop stewards) chosen from the 40 largest factories in Berlin.[11] Unable to defeat these plans openly, the bureaucracy simply passed them on to the union executive for 'consideration' and nothing more was heard of them.

Shop stewards in Berlin's large plants wanted to solve the problem of union democracy by basing it on workplace representatives. This use of rank-and-file organisation to combat union bureaucracy paralleled later workers' council organisation against the capitalists. That full-time officials and employers should be fought in the same way was not surprising, since the former, by virtue of their high wages, status and social milieu, often acted more as agents of capitalism inside the working class than as fighters for that class. Workers' struggle, even at the purely economic level of the pre-war period, still had to depend on collective self-activity inside the labour movement.

In Berlin as in Glasgow a network of experienced rank-and-file leaders was established *before* the onset of the wartime crisis. It was this group that would later launch the powerful strike waves which led directly to Berlin's workers' council movement.

The political situation in Berlin, however, was a world away from that of Glasgow. It was dominated by the Sozialdemokratischen Partei Deutschlands (SPD) — the German Social Democrats, who claimed a million members nationally and well over 20,000 in Berlin itself. The party was the major force in the Second International, and Karl Kautsky, 'the pope of Marxism' was its chief theoretician. In the 1912 election the SPD took three-quarters of the vote in Berlin, against a national average of 35 per cent.[12] Its local figures included leading revolutionaries such as Rosa Luxemburg and the Reichstag deputy Karl Liebknecht.

Despite the greater strength of German socialism, the SPD, like Britain's BSP, was prone to see a gulf between political and economic strength. Against this background Rosa Luxemburg wrote her outstanding pamphlet **The Mass Strike** which, though it overlooked the question of workers' council organisation, was insistent on the close interrelation between the two phases of workers' action:

> Every great political mass action, after it has attained its political highest point, breaks up into a mass of economic strikes . . . With the spreading, clarifying and involution of the political struggle, the economic struggle not only does not recede but extends, organises and becomes involved in equal measure. Between the two there is the most complete reciprocal action . . .[13]

Anton Pannekoek, a Dutchman active in Bremen, went even further by identifying the precise organisational mechanism of revolutionary change:

> The problem of the social revolution can be put in simple terms: to build the power of the proletariat so high that it is superior to that of the state; and the content of this revolution is the destruction and dissolution of the physical force of the state through the physical force of the proletariat . . . Organisation is the bringing together of atomised individuals to form a powerful instrument . . . In large organised factories, where individual action is subordinated to the collective, the habits are created in the modern proletariat which are the raw materials of such an organisation.
>
> The organisation of the proletariat which we describe as its most powerful physical force . . . is not to be compared with the present forms of [party] organisation or trade unions, which define themselves in relation to the still existing bourgeois order.[14]

But the SPD, with its massive bureaucracy of full-time officials, was impervious to these arguments. Its reply to Luxemburg's view of the interpenetration of industrial and political struggle was summed up by a resolution, adopted at a Second International Congress, which formally separated the two:

> While it falls to the parties of Social Democracy to organise and lead the political struggles of the proletariat, so it is the task of union organisation to co-ordinate and lead the economic struggles of the working class.[15]

Here was the British split between orthodox Marxism and syndicalism in another form.

The SPD was equally hostile to the proposal that it actively work towards the overthrow of capitalism. Nevertheless through its Erfurt programme it clung to the rhetoric of revolution. It needed this because, under the repressive autocracy of the Kaiser, it was 'a cast-out minority' within German society. To abandon revolutionary rhetoric would mean accepting a *status quo* from which it was excluded. Therefore the SPD turned to:

> laboriously using every opportunity to build up its strength through those legal means permitted to it by the state . . . But decades of working through legal aid schemes and insurance schemes, of intervention in the state-run labour exchanges, and above all electoral activities, inevitably had an effect on the party membership: the revolutionary theory of the Erfurt programme came to seem something reserved for May Day and Sunday afternoon oratory, hardly connected with most of what the party actually did.[16]

The Chinese wall that separated the rhetoric of the SPD's leaders from their reformist practices was reflected in Kautsky's teachings. His book **The Road to Power** symbolised a political philosophy which used revolutionary phraseology but refused to turn it into action:

> The Socialist party is a revolutionary party, but not a revolution-making party. We know that our goal can only be attained through a revolution. We also know that it is just as little in our power to create this revolution as it is in the power of our opponents to prevent it. It is not part of our work to instigate a revolution or to prepare a way for it.[17]

This kind of politics, which wavered between reform and revolution in its ideas, came to be called 'centrism'.

The coming of war

On 4 August 1914, the SPD, jewel of the Second International and champion of the anti-war cause, was put to the test, with horrifying results. That day virtually the whole of the party leadership threw in their lot with the Kaiser and his generals. In return for abandoning their principles, the SPD bureaucracy was given a role in the war machine. While the rank and file were now facing the prospect of the trenches, their leaders strolled the corridors of power from which they had so long felt excluded. In 1918/19 this

concession which the ruling class gave its former enemies paid off
admirably. It was then that the SPD saved capitalism from workers'
power.

When the war began, two very different currents grew up to
protest against the betrayal perpetrated by the SPD officials. Both
were handicapped by the traditional separation of political and
industrial agitation: the Spartakists were to become the *political
vanguard* in Berlin, while the revolutionary shop stewards (or
Obleute) represented a *vanguard of shopfloor militants*.

The revolutionary group known as the Spartakist League was
formed only after the outbreak of war. It was led by Rosa Luxemburg, who, though she had recognised the SPD's failings long
before 1914, had done nothing to build an organised opposition.
She had to begin from scratch in August 1914. Her first act was to
despatch 300 telegrams to gauge the feelings of those outside
Berlin. Only Clara Zetkin's reply gave unreserved support to a
campaign against the war. From this meagre beginning came the
Spartakist League. Its core was located in Berlin and consisted of
exiled Polish revolutionaries such as Leo Jogiches, Julian
Marchlewski and of course Luxemburg herself, plus a number of
leading German socialists such as Franz Mehring and Karl
Liebknecht.

Spartakist policies were summed up by Luxemburg's 'Junius'
pamphlet of April 1915:

> For the international proletariat, the struggle against imperialism is at
> the same time the struggle for power, the decisive settling of accounts
> between socialism and capitalism. The final goal of socialism will be
> realised by the international proletariat only if it opposes imperialism
> all along the line, and if it makes the issue 'war against war' the
> guiding line of its practical policy: and on conditions that it deploys all
> its forces and shows itself ready, by its courage to the point of extreme
> sacrifice, to do this.[18]

On 2 December 1914, Liebknecht was the only deputy in the
Reichstag to vote against giving further money to the military
effort. His solitary stand lit a beacon proclaiming that internation-
alism was not dead in Germany. From that point on, he and other
Spartakist leaders were constantly persecuted by the authorities.
Luxemburg, for example, spent nine-tenths of the war in jail.

Liebknecht's work and the publicity given to his famous
slogan — 'The main enemy is in our own country' — made him an

international figurehead for revolutionary opposition to war. But until there was solid working-class organisation to back such efforts, they could remain little more than token gestures. So, despite conditions of illegality, the Spartakists set to work to establish a network of contacts from within the SPD.

They began to organise in December 1914, but the experience of Karl Retzlaw, a young Berlin metalworker, showed how limited were the results. He joined the legal SPD youth movement and discovered that among the 15 members of the local branch there was an inner core of radicals. Through them he became a Spartakist in 1915. The branch of the organisation to which he belonged consisted of a consulting engineer, a former technical engineer now working for the army, a senior foreman, a carpenter and two young workers.[19] These seven individuals were not an isolated outpost of the organisation. This was the entire membership of the Berlin-Moabit section, Karl Liebknecht's own constituency, bounded by the huge industrial complexes of Charlottenburg and Spandau!

Various estimates have put Spartakist membership in 1918 at between one thousand and three thousand members. This was a tiny force with which to try to mould the ideas and actions of a working class of more than ten million people. The Spartakists did not split from the SPD, although they operated as freely as they could within it. Following the organisational pattern of the party, they based their structure on the electoral constituency rather than the factory or industry. This reflected a weakness in Spartakist support in workplaces. It also conditioned the type of activity pursued, which was not designed to lead action on the shopfloor, but to propagate general politics.

Despite a penetrating analysis of the war and capitalist crisis, Luxemburg's followers could not generate mass agitation in the factories. They simply lacked a mechanism by which 'war against war' could be made the practical activity of the rank and file.

A sign of their weakness in the factories was that few Spartakists had positions as shop stewards, so the group tended to be excluded from the leading circle of factory militants — the revolutionary *Obleute*. While many *Obleute* doubtless sympathised with the Spartakists, and were indeed ready to call out their members on strike to support Liebknecht's anti-war stand, there was little formal contact between the two groups. Such was the difference in emphasis which each placed on their activity — the Spartakists concentrating on general propaganda and the *Obleute* on detailed workplace agitation — that in general they operated entirely independently.

The revolutionary Obleute made up for the lack of workplace roots of the Spartakists. But while the latter built a movement around revolutionary politics, the Obleute, for all their individual radical beliefs, lacked the incisive understanding of the crisis which Luxemburg provided. These militant shop stewards developed a large and tightly organised following in Berlin's engineering industry. The core of the group was the turners' branch of the DMV led by Richard Müller. Working in extreme secrecy, numbers were inevitably restricted. Because of difficulties in defining membership, estimates of size have ranged between 50, 80 and 1,000, although the lower figures are most likely.[20]

Like the Clyde stewards, the revolutionary Obleute occupied the ground vacated by the union officials after 1914. While wartime conditions gave workers in Berlin's 300 munitions plants tremendous bargaining power, the DMV full-timers actively resisted the exercise of that power. Evidence of their attitude was given by the boss of the Borsig factory in Berlin:

> I was recently called by the union and was told . . . that it was amazed at the demands made upon the firm by the workers, and we should take every care that the firm make no further concessions to the workers. The wages were already so high and the union could not rescue itself from these demands.[21]

Given this vacuum in leadership and the dramatic rise in inflation, the Obleute were called upon to lead a constant agitation in defence of basic living standards. Throughout the war Berlin had the highest number of strikers of any district in Germany. In 1915 there were 38,000; by 1917 this had grown to 220,000.[22] Largely as a result of such militancy the first two years of war saw real wages in Germany's arms industries fall by only 22 per cent compared to a 42 per cent drop in the rest of the economy.[23]

In Berlin, as in Glasgow, the mass of workers did not immediately reject the war. But they were ready to take action over direct grievances, and again effective leadership for this had to come from militants located on the shopfloor and opposed to the social truce. Müller's description of the revolutionary Obleute portrays them as solid union men who reflected the better industrial traditions of the pre-war labour movement. In his words 'as shop stewards on the lowest rung of the union machine', they 'had virtually the unlimited trust of a great section of workers, particularly in the large factories'.[24]

Stressing their representative function, the Obleute felt little need to develop a distinctive political programme and concentrated on the organisational aspects of grassroots action. So while they were on the left of the SPD, with few exceptions, they stopped short of the radical political stand required by Spartakism. They allied instead with the softer politics of Georg Ledebour and Ernst Däumig. These two SPD functionaries tried to keep alive the anti-establishment traditions of the pre-war party. Though they criticised the new party line they still did not break with the ideas and methods that made the August 1914 betrayal possible. Their position, revolutionary in tone but reformist in content, was centrist.

The Obleute went beyond the stewards of the Clyde Workers' Committee and called political strikes, but their authority still rested on leading at the grassroots in a host of small economic disputes. The big anti-war strikes that were to follow were inconceivable without the straightforward economic agitation that forced the employers, union officials and military to set up a 'War Board for the Greater Berlin Metal Industry' to head off shopfloor discontent.

When they called for illegal stoppages, the Obleute had to be sure they would not be denounced to the authorities. Their radical opinions were not shared by the majority, so survival depended on a general recognition of their worth as fighters for the rank and file. The deep basis of their support was tested after a major stoppage in January 1918. The government offered 3,000 marks for information about its leaders, but though they must have been known to many workers, the Obleute were not betrayed.[25]

However the clandestine methods required to escape arrest led the Obleute to avoid openly challenging the politics of reformism. This was illustrated in March 1916, at a meeting called for the re-election of Adolf Cohen. The 2,000 metalworkers' stewards present were ready to depose this discredited union leader and put Richard Müller in his place. But Müller was unwilling to make a public stand and Cohen was returned by one third of the meeting, with the rest abstaining. The chance to run a rank-and-file candidate who could use this post as a platform for revolutionary ideas was not to recur.[26]

Despite their limitations, the Obleute did manage to connect economic action at work and the politics of war. Compared to the

Clyde stewards the Obleute were more conscious of the task facing
them and operated in conditions more favourable to this form of
struggle. As one historian put it:

> The basic core, whose existence was a great surprise for many in 1918,
> worked in an atmosphere of conspiracy and methodical recruitment
> of reliable stewards in different firms and trades. It was a network
> whose members sought to make use of key positions, exploiting the
> legal cover of the turners' section of the union, working the apparatus
> like a well-organised faction, but maintaining close links with the
> feelings of workers in factories and workshops, able to dominate
> delegate meetings, upholding freedom of speech. It was an organisa-
> tion *sui generis* which was neither union nor party, but a clandestine
> group operating in both . . . thanks to the turners, who were well
> placed in all the enterprises, they formed a compact and disciplined
> unit in the meetings of delegates and were able through a few hundred
> men they influenced, to set tens and then hundreds of thousands of
> Berlin workers into motion.[27]

In terms of mobilising industrially, the Obleute had an
advantage over the Spartakist group because of their direct contact
with the rank and file. This was clear from early on. The Spartakists held two demonstrations in 1915. The first, on 18 March,
attracted 100 people, mainly women; the second, a few months
later, involved 1,500. On May Day 1916 Liebknecht spoke publicly
in the Potsdam Platz, Berlin, and was arrested. Then the Obleute
demonstrated their power — 55,000 workers struck in protest on
the day of his court appearance in June.

The strike revealed an important fact. When the war had
broken out and the SPD voted for it in the Reichstag, many of the
party's leaders blamed a nationalist upsurge among the rank and
file as the reason for their betrayal. The truth was that the
capitulation of the SPD itself created much of this feeling, for it
strengthened the wing of the working class that undoubtedly was
nationalistic and completely disorientated the left wing. It is not
possible to state with certainty that different action by the SPD
leadership could have prevented the war, but it is certain that far
from merely reflecting the mood of the masses in August 1914,
the SPD to an important degree determined that the mood would
be an almost unanimous chauvinism. What the June 1916 strike
showed, in contrast, was that given an organised and principled
leadership a large number of workers, even if still a minority of

the working class, were ready to take a stand against the war.

In Müller's opinion the strike of 55,000 Berlin workers in June 1916 was more effective than what he regarded as the propagandism of the Spartakists. Though he too opposed the war, he saw their revolutionary slogans as dangerously provocative, and argued that direct anti-war propaganda might lead sections of workers into action without proper organisation and so invite defeat. He thought that a political campaign should be worked towards gradually. He commented on the lessons of the June protest as follows:

> The first political mass strike won no apparent gains for the workers, but from a psychological point of view it did more than millions of leaflets and speeches . . . To violently press the German working class for one action after another was damaging in itself and bad for the movement. The Spartakus League failed to recognise this fact.[28]

Müller over-simplified the Spartakist viewpoint, but his statement showed that the sort of tensions which existed between Maclean and the Clyde Workers' Committee also existed in Berlin. The June 1916 stoppage was a great step forward for the anti-war movement. But at the same time it exposed tragic divisions in the workers' camp. The strike was possible only because of the clear-sighted internationalism of Liebknecht, who pointed out the political tasks of labour. Yet action in his defence was not led by his followers, but by the centrist-influenced Obleute, men who were fine industrial militants but politically confused, supporting left officials in the SPD rather than the revolutionary politics of the Spartakists.

The reason for such dangerous divisions was that Rosa Luxemburg and her friends had established no links with rank and file struggles before the war and now found it difficult to develop them under repressive conditions. Indeed the more energetically the Spartakists fought to compensate for the tardiness of their independent current, the more the Obleute saw them as ultra-left and outside the mainstream of the labour movement. It was ironic that Luxemburg, whose pamphlet **The Mass Strike** was the supreme exposition of the mass strike tactic, should be so misunderstood by those who practised it.

Nevertheless, despite their mutual distrust, Spartakist and Obleute currents could not help being complementary on one level. Open anti-war propaganda facilitated rank-and-file action against the advice of union officials who were collaborating with

the employers during the war, just as the confidence and understanding gained through militancy cleared the way for the reception
of revolutionary ideas.

The first councils

The second major strike of Berlin engineers came in April
1917. A disastrous winter brought galloping inflation and food
shortages. But there was no direct relation between worsening
conditions and workers' action. Popular reaction to the 'turnip
winter' was not automatic revulsion to war, but something more
complex. Misery and hunger led to a retreat from the problems of
the world before they brought an angry confrontation with them.
In the words of a Spartakist working at AEG:

> For me this time was doubly difficult. My workmates wished to hear
> nothing more of politics. Indifferent to political writings they all clung
> to the same oft-repeated slogan: 'With decent grub and decent pay,
> we'll pretend the war was yesterday'.[29]

Such feelings conditioned labour militancy. While political action
was rejected, there was a growing sense of dismay at the prevailing
conditions. Questions of food and pay generated a continual build-
up of strike activity which strained the official conciliation
machinery to the utmost.

In April 1917 the dam burst. Despite censorship, two news
items filtered through — the fall of the Tsar in Russia and a series
of demonstrations in Leipzig by women demanding bread. In
Berlin the shop stewards judged the moment ripe to lead a stoppage
against the war. The police pre-empted this by arresting Müller on
13 April. This quelled the agitation. But just three days later Berlin
was paralysed as 200,000 workers came out in a massive show of
strength. They were joined by engineers in many other cities. But
it was no call by the left that drew these workers into action
simultaneously: the government itself had inadvertently given the
signal to strike by imposing a nationwide cut in rations.

Müller's arrest disrupted the Obleute organisation, allowing
union officials to step in. They wished to prevent the strike challenging the state by steering it towards purely economic demands,
such as for better food supplies. Their manoeuvre found no organised opposition until further news from Leipzig suddenly threatened to upset all bureaucratic calculations. What had started there

as a movement for bread had escalated into a political challenge to state authority.

On 16 April the city produced the first German workers' council. A single body representing all the strikers, it was led by a committee of two metalworkers and three left-wing socialists who were members of the newly-formed Independent Social Democratic Party. That day it adopted a resolution which asked not only for food and fuel, but made political demands — for peace without annexations, the abolition of legal restrictions on labour, the end of censorship and the state of siege, freedom for political prisoners and free elections.[30]

Side-stepping the official machinery, the 10,000-strong workforce of the DWM munitions factory in Berlin elected a factory council of three workers and three left socialists. Shortly afterwards, Knorr-Bremse, in the Lichtenburg district of the city, followed suit.[31] Factory councils — powerful rank-and-file leaderships within individual factories — were a step towards the geographical workers' council.

For a moment the revival of an independent shop stewards' initiative threatened to transform the Berlin strike from a protest over food into a broad challenge to the war and the regime which pursued it. But a precondition for revolution is not just workers' mobilisation but weakness in the existing state, and in 1917 the imperial machine was still fairly secure. Hitting back at the militants, the police made numerous arrests and placed striking factories under martial law. Eventually the workers' spirit gave way, and from 17 April they began trickling back to work.

The 1917 strike wave illustrated several important features of emergent workers' councils under bourgeois democracy. Firstly, general strike movements have the potential to move quickly from economic questions to major political ones which challenge the existing order. Secondly, however, such movements do not spontaneously move in this direction. This is determined by the conscious struggle for leadership between reformists and revolutionaries. Thirdly, by the same token, when workers' council organisation is in competition with established reformist institutions such as parties and unions, it cannot easily arise spontaneously out of mass strikes. Spontaneous organisation is not excluded under such conditions, but the likelihood that it becomes a permanent and serious challenge is a lot less than was the case in Russia. A lot more depends on the deliberate initiative of leading militants.

The birth of a centrist alternative

The Independent Social Democratic Party (USPD) was founded just before the April 1917 strikes. Throughout its life it led a tortured existence, trying to combine outright reformists such as Eduard Bernstein with a current of working-class radicalism which eventually found its way into the German Communist Party in 1920.[32] The origins of the USPD were very different from those of the Spartakist group. The Independents' principal leaders, Haase and Ledebour, accepted the declaration of war in 1914. Only when there seemed no end to the fighting did they mount a limited opposition to the SPD-right. Politely questioning the wartime policy of the state, they urged an 'honourable' negotiated end to the war and protested against the more outrageous violations of civil rights.

In a sense, Haase and Ledebour were trying to preserve a viable reformism akin to the traditional stand of the SPD. After 1914 this was menaced by the Spartakists on the left and by the SPD right wing which had abjectly surrendered its independence to the Imperial state. The 'loyal opposition' that grew up did not want to form a break-away party, but was forced into this. The right drove them out of the SPD party fraction in the Reichstag and took away editorial control of **Vorwärts**, the party's daily paper. In January 1917, the right-wing majority in the SPD announced that by its criticisms the opposition 'had separated itself from the party'.[33] The Independent Social Democratic Party was formed in April.

Estimates of the relative strengths of the two workers' parties varied. The SPD retained around 210,000 members, while the Independents took about half that number with them. Berlin swung more heavily to the left, with 14,000 joining the new party and just 12,000 staying with the SPD.[34] The Independents had a very mixed heritage, best classified as centrism. Many of its leaders were reformists who, to head off the challenge of Spartakism, felt compelled to use revolutionary phrases. Internal divisions soon developed however, and the party became an uneasy amalgam of right and left wings. The right, round Haase and Dittman, emphasised the importance of elections and the 'proper channels'. The left, including Ledebour and Däumig, provided an unsteady leadership for the growing number of angry workers in the factories.

The Spartakists joined the USPD although fully conscious of its centrism. It seemed to Liebknecht that the new organisation 'was still about the most productive area for Spartakists, since we could not express ourselves publicly with the required force.' They joined the party 'to push it forward, to keep it at the end of their whip, to find and win its best elements'.[35]

Behind this refusal to form a revolutionary party was the fear that if the Spartakists cut themselves off from a mass political party of social democrats, they would be reduced to a sect on the margins of the working class. It follows that they saw these parties (first the SPD and now the Independents) as the embodiment of the mass movement. But in reality, after the outbreak of war if not before, the active sections of the class had found a different organisational focus than the official party or union apparatus.

The workers' movement was changing. While many activists retained a belief in parliamentary politics, the locus of their day-to-day activity was shifting to factory action and mass strikes. When workers wanted to do something about their grievances, they looked towards their rank-and-file organisations rather than the parliamentary system. This tendency was enhanced by news of deepening revolution transmitted across the front lines from Russia.

Reaction to the final victory of the Bolsheviks and the creation of a soviet state was often on these lines:

> Certainly conditions in Russia were different from those in Germany, but what the Russian peasant could accomplish must surely be within the capabilities of the German industrial worker with his socialist education and organisation. This was the general opinion of many workers in the factories.[36]

With the difficulties encountered in April 1917 still fresh in their minds, the Obleute made careful preparations for a new offensive and sought backing from the Independents' leadership. When reports of a mass strike in Vienna reached Berlin on 27 January 1918, both the Spartakists and shop stewards decided the time was ripe for action. The next day the factories of Berlin lay silent: 400,000 workers were out and the strike was spreading elsewhere.

The workers' council that grew from this struggle was a model of organisation. In the factories, one delegate was elected for every 1,000 workers. The 414 representatives thus assembled elected a central strike committee of 11 rank-and-file leaders who in turn co-opted three Independent and three SPD deputies to assist them. The programme they adopted included many of the economic demands of April 1917, but linked them to an immediate acceptance of the Bolshevik peace proposals then being put forward at Brest-Litovsk.

Here was a movement in which demands and organisation were matched. Economic questions were combined with major political issues, all of which emanated from the workers' council — a body rooted in the industrial foundations of society, but which, as the spearhead of a mass strike, challenged the state. However it was not yet like the 1917 soviets in Russia, for *their* challenge was backed up by armed power.

On 29 January the central strike committee sought in vain to negotiate with the Kaiser's ministers. Next day the first skirmishes between strikers and police took place. The police were overwhelmed by the scale of the action, so the government called in the army.

It was not physical intimidation that proved most damaging to the movement, however, but the wrecking tactics of the SPD. Its representatives entered the central strike committee only in order to deflect the movement. Ebert later admitted that he 'joined the strike leadership with the clear intention of bringing the strike to a speedy end to prevent damage to the country'.[37] When the SPD threw all its weight into ending the strike the tremendous solidarity which had been shown began to weaken.

By early February the first cracks had appeared in the ranks of strikers. The authorities swiftly took advantage of this and used threats of mass conscription, backed up by the military occupation of seven major plants, to intimidate those who stayed out. Soon both the SPD and Independent deputies abandoned the strike committee, leaving the Obleute with the choice of armed insurrection or retreat. Judging the moment premature for revolution, they backed down and on 3 February the strike ended.

The shop stewards had shown their influence, but also their lack of political understanding. Without a clear revolutionary position of their own, they had fallen for pleas of 'unity' of the sort which meant bringing SPD leaders, who were openly hostile to the anti-war movement, on to the central strike committee.[38] The result was division at the crucial moment when they were confronting the state.

Unable to hit at the ringleaders directly, the government wreaked revenge on Berlin engineers by conscripting between 500 and 600 men each day and sending them off to the front.[39] In spite of this the seeds of the workers' council had been firmly planted. It meant a variety of things to different people. In the battle for immediate ends, the mass of disgruntled workers saw the workers' council as the front line in a workers' offensive which the traditional forces of labour were unwilling to lead. The Obleute looked to the workers' council as an engine of revolutionary struggle against the state. But being pragmatic in their attitude, they did not explore the nature of the revolution they were calling up, or the tasks it would have to face. At first the Spartakists were unsure of the significance of the new institution. But by July 1918 they decided that the coming revolution must place 'all power in the hands of the workers' councils, the organised power of the proletarian masses, as in Russia.'[40]

By the end of the year these different views of the workers' councils were to be tested on the streets of every German city.

Chapter Six

THE KAISER FALLS

AFTER the military setbacks of the Marne in late September 1918, Generals Ludendorff and Hindenberg admitted that victory for Germany was impossible. A negotiated settlement would have to be reached with the enemy. In an attempt to defuse the tense domestic situation, a new Chancellor was installed as head of government and two ministries were offered to the SPD. These gestures were not enough to stop the pressure of war weariness, hunger and exploitation breaking the bonds of Germany's imperial state.

Although it was now obvious that Germany would lose the war, the admirals ordered Kiel's sailors out to sea on 2 November. They refused to go, unwilling to die for a hopeless last-ditch gesture of the High Command. Their mutiny set a complex train of developments into motion. To escape the repression that had strangled earlier agitation in the fleet in the summer of 1917, the sailors spread their revolt widely.[1] As fast as the railways would carry them the rebels swept along the northern seaboard. Everywhere they went they were enthusiastically welcomed and workers' and soldiers' councils set up. By 6 November these had been established in the north-western centres of Bremen, Hamburg and Wilhelmshaven. The next day they had spread to Hannover, Brunswick, Hanau and Munich. By 10 November, most of Germany's cities and major towns had workers' council institutions of some sort.

This movement was in direct defiance of the Kaiser's regime and could only survive if it struck down this arch-enemy. With mutinous sailors and soldiers behind it, the workers' council movement had the potential to build a new state, for it possessed the rudiments of armed authority. On the other side disorder reigned. When, on 8 November, General Groener, a major figure in the army, asked 39 senior officers if they thought the Kaiser could be saved, only one answered affirmatively. In an attempt to salvage the crumbling military machine, the Kaiser was asked to leave the country for his own safety.

But cosmetic changes could not stop the march of revolt. Soon the mutiny of sailors had spread to engulf the home army and dissolve its command structure. By 10 November Hindenberg, head of the armed forces, accepted that the soldiers' and sailors' councils were here to stay. To counter the influence of the left within them, he ordered his officers to set up councils under their own control.[2] The next day an armistice was signed and the First World War officially ended.

If the 'November days' had remained a military affair, they would have done little more than speed the end of the war. What carried the movement far beyond this was the entry of the industrial workers. The working class had willingly joined in removing the Kaiser, but its demands did not stop there. The crisis of capitalism drove it to challenge the very roots of its oppression and exploitation in society — and this challenge was articulated through the workers' council.

The title 'workers' and soldiers' council' was given to a multitude of provisional bodies established in the first week of November. Many of these were manifestly nothing to do with workers or soldiers.[3] Only in a handful of large cities with militant traditions, such as Berlin, Bremen, Frankfurt-am-Main, Hamburg and Stuttgart, were there workers' councils which conformed to the pattern of mass democracy established in the strikes of 1917 and 1918.[4] These cities based their councils on elections by workers at the point of production. In Berlin, delegation was on the basis of one per 1,000, as in January 1918; in Bremen one per 180; in Hamburg, one per 600, and so on.

This structure did not spring into existence spontaneously but was learnt from earlier struggles. Only workers who had acquired self-reliance and distrust of bureaucratic leaders, through the test of action, had the organisational strength to initiate such organisations. Elsewhere in Germany a mass of phoney councils were created by backdoor deals. They were frequently composed solely of party and union functionaries who were 'spontaneously' acclaimed as the local workers' council by manipulation of public meetings and demonstrations. In Russia such initial bureaucratic manoeuvres had everywhere been accompanied by an upsurge of

industrially-based elections. In Germany, where unions and reformist leaders did everything to prevent independent initiative,
such shopfloor elections were more rare, tending to be in areas with
a rank-and-file tradition. This did not preclude autonomous self-
organisation in the future, but pointed to the greater importance of
conscious revolutionary shopfloor agitation in the West as an
essential counterbalance to the reformist tradition.

Revolutionary leadership in Berlin

During the months between November 1918 and January 1919,
events in Berlin uncovered the intricate anatomy of a workers'
uprising in which a multitude of struggles, abrupt changes of
consciousness and class forces are compressed into a short period.
In this process the workers' council provided the skeletal structure
of the revolution, and the fusion of economics and politics provided the muscles that propelled it forward.

To describe the driving force of revolution as the interpenetration of economic and political struggle may appear as an abstract
formulation. But it was very real, for it was the cement that bound
the masses of workers embroiled in immediate struggles to the
general needs of a class war. Success in the latter was the only
guarantee of a successful solution to the immediate struggles.

The fusion of politics and economics requires leadership. In an
ideal revolutionary situation, this grows from a strategy which
combines the political aims of conscious revolutionaries with rank-
and-file leadership which can marshall the power of workplaces.
The chain of command which can arise to centralise the diverse
struggles of individual sections is held together only through action.
No paper resolution-mongering can take its place. The chain comes
into being if at each level socialists can answer the *immediate* needs
of the moment but join them indissolubly to the *general* demands of
the class struggle. Such a chain of leadership takes much longer to
prepare than the workers' council itself, which can be formed in
hours.

The Bolshevik party was a good example of how a revolutionary
leadership which was both politically centralised and responsive to
the needs of the base could grow up. The party began in 1903, long
before the soviet appeared. It combined a core of professional
revolutionaries and a number of key workers in the factories. The
1905 revolution and the years of reaction that followed trained and

hardened that fusion of political leadership and factory militants, paving the way for the broad expansion of the party in the 1917 revolution. With an organisation deeply rooted in the key militant industrial towns, the Bolsheviks were well placed, after the fall of Tsarism, to win over first the factory committee movement which represented the most advanced sections of the working class, then the soviets which had the allegiance of millions of workers, soldiers and peasants.

After Russia, Germany had the greatest potential for socialist revolution and Berlin was its most radical city. But the organisational fusion of political and militant vanguards — the Spartakists and the Obleute — had not taken place. This left Luxemburg and her allies powerless to control events. The revolutionary shop stewards were in no better position. They were dominated by the politics of Däumig and Ledebour, centrists who swung erratically from a determination to overthrow the system and replace it with workers' power to a belief that Germany had to be saved from economic ruin even if it was on the existing capitalist basis. This meant the Obleute, who formed the most influential left-wing group in the workers' council movement, were hopelessly confused.

The situation of open class warfare begun in the 'November days' of 1918 imposed on the workers' council tasks of a kind not seen in Glasgow. There the workers' council had been a shop stewards' movement of no more than the most advanced section of the working class. Though a genuine democracy, its leadership was therefore composed of only the most radical workers, and their major problem was how to win over sections outside the skilled engineering vanguard.

In Berlin that difficulty was solved by two things: by the injection of anti-war ideas into the mass strikes of wartime, and by miltary defeat, which deepened the social crisis and forced all sections of the class into action. But this advance brought new responsibilities in its wake. The workers' council no longer represented the vanguard alone, but was a truly *class* institution. As such, its democratic procedures now produced leaders who reflected the ideas prevailing among the *majority* of workers. In 1918, despite the fall of the Kaiser, reformism still held sway over most of the class. In other words, the workers' council came to be led by members of the SPD, people who believed in parliament and rejected the idea that workers' councils might take power. In the 1917 Russian revolution reformist Mensheviks and SRs had won a similar dominant position in the soviets during the early stages. But the rapid changes of consciousness that accompany periods of revolution meant that in Germany, as in Russia the previous year, the hold of reformists was far from secure.

The revolt reaches Berlin

Revolution was slow in coming to the capital. Paradoxically its powerful shopfloor organisation hampered spontaneous initiative. As so often in revolutions, the first move was made by those often labelled 'backward' in class consciousness. Free from experience of the 'usual and right' way of conducting class struggle under normal circumstances, it was the sailors who were to act boldly and nudge the vanguard workers into action. So in November 1918, Berlin, the most militant area in Germany, was one of the *last* to form a workers' council. In this city the masses looked to their acknow-ledged rank-and-file leaders to give the word; but the Obleute were waiting for the right moment.

There could be little delay. Long hours at work might have been bearable if food supplies had been adequate, but since October 1918 rations provided just 50 per cent of the minimum calorie requirement and 16 per cent of necessary fats.[5] Many Berliners were now desperate and needed only one concerted push to set them into motion. At the end of October Liebknecht was released from prison in a last attempt to appease popular discontent. This served only to take the lid off the cauldron. Twenty thousand demonstrators welcomed him home.

Liebknecht immediately set to work with the Obleute to organise an insurrection. In their methodical way, the shop stew-ards had been preparing the ground for some time, and to lead an insurrection they set up an 'Executive Committee of the Workers' and Soldiers' Councils'. The Obleute asked the Independent leaders to back a rising on 3 November, but their request was turned down. Forced to fight alone, the Executive Committee picked 4 November as the new target date, but at the last minute drew back. Liebknecht impatiently declared that it was time to call the masses to action. Still undecided, the Obleute chose to bide their time and perfect the technical details. The second deadline passed and a new one, 11 November, was set.

But an unfortunate incident forced the pace. Ernst Däumig, one of the Executive Committee, was arrested while carrying complete details of the rising in his briefcase. There was now no alternative but to heed the voice of Liebknecht and unleash the insurrection.

On the night of 8 November the executive, comprising Obleute, Spartakists and Independents (who now wanted to be seen playing a part) sent out messages and issued leaflets. The events of the next morning have been described by a Spartakist active at the DWM factory:

> We were in front of the munitions plant for the first shift and distributed our leaflets calling on the workers to come out. We finished that job at 7am and helped other comrades unpack and load revolvers. All went calmly and in order. Finally all the guns were distributed and the demonstration set off.

To topple the state, the workers had to break the last bastion of its power — the army:

> It was our task to join up with the processions from Moabit and Charlottenburg and win the soldiers garrisoned at the Lehrter station to the revolution. The door of the barracks was shut, so the masses called through it: 'Brothers, don't shoot us! Finish with the war! Peace! Down with Kaiser Wilhelm . . .' We, who were armed, expected shooting and were prepared for a gunfight; but our persuasion was enough and to the delight of the workers, the soldiers were prevailed upon to join us in marching to the Maikäfer garrison.[6]

It was at this next destination that the uprising had one of its few martyrs, when officers began shooting on the crowd before they could be overpowered by their own soldiers. In fact, only eighteen people died in the overthrow of a regime which had caused the deaths of millions.

All over Berlin on 9 November the same pattern of moral pressure backed by mass mobilisation was used to great effect. Reaction to miserable conditions and military defeat combined to produce a powerful synthesis of rank-and-file leadership and class action. From the first, shopfloor organisation played its part — linking, directing and growing into a mighty workers' council movement.

The SPD was not silent during the 'November days'. It felt confident of the passive support of a majority of workers. On 4 November **Vorwärts** announced that the party was 'doing all that is necessary through the proper channels'. Four days later, sensing the impending revolt, the SPD leaders called a meeting of their own shop stewards, but this predicted that if the party stood in the way of the insurrection 'it would simply be overrun'.[7] It then attempted to install a hand-picked SPD workers' and soldiers' council in Berlin. This manoeuvre, which worked in towns where the left was weak, could not succeed in a city with a history of independent grassroots organisation.

Throughout 9 November wave upon wave of the population were drawn into the revolution. Jails were stormed and prisoners freed by the hundred.[8] In the early afternoon Berlin's central police station witnessed an incredible scene during which an avowed radical socialist — Emil Eichhorn — was installed as head of a new revolutionary police force.

> Only the terrible fear of retaliation for atrocities committed against the workers of Berlin can explain the frenzy with which police officers and constables tore off their swords and revolvers, casting them into an ever larger mound . . . But the police were not molested by the hordes of people who just streamed through the gates and across the courtyards grabbing every available weapon, right down to the last cartridge belt and holster.[9]

The day after these dramatic events the bourgeois newspaper **Berliner Tageblatt** wrote:

> A week ago there was still a structure of military and civil administration so extensively ramified, inter-twined and deeply rooted that its reign seemed safe from the changing times. The grey motor-cars of the officers raced through the streets of Berlin, policemen stood in the public squares like pillars, a gigantic military organisation seemed to embrace everything, in public offices and ministries an apparently invincible bureaucracy was enthroned. Yesterday morning all this was still there, at least in Berlin. Yesterday afternoon nothing remained.[10]

But the results of 9 November were rather more complex than this report suggested. For the long columns of demonstrators that wound their way from the factories and barracks to the centre of Berlin were soon presented with a fundamental political choice. The collapsing imperial state had turned to the leader of the SPD, Ebert, and made him Chancellor to salvage what he could of the old society.

As inheritor of the 'legitimate' regime, Ebert had no wish personally to confront the masses of armed workers and soldiers who had opened his way to power. However Scheidemann, his second-in-command, felt that the populace needed quieting and shouted to the throng surrounding the Reichstag building: 'Long live the German republic'. His intervention on behalf of the SPD was timely. Nearby, at the imperial palace, a forest of clenched fists was being raised in support of Liebknecht's speech backing a much more radical idea: '. . . a new proletarian state . . . the free German socialist republic.'[11]

Bourgeois republic or proletarian socialist state — these were the choices of a classic 'dual power' situation. Two forces claimed the mantle of power on 9 November — the reformists who traced their rule back to the old state and its parliament; and the revolutionaries, who looked to the workers' council.

The next day saw both sides frantically trying to organise their forces. At the Reichstag, the SPD wrangled with the Independents and the Workers' and Soldiers' Executive over what form a new government should take. An arrangement was reached which provided for a provisional government headed by 'People's Commisssars'. There would be three from the SPD and three from the Independents. The SPD Commissars were Ebert, Scheidemann and Landsberg. The Independents put forward Haase, Dittmann and Emil Barth.

Barth was a member of the Obleute. His seat in the provisional government had been offered to Liebknecht and Richard Müller. Both declined to serve as People's Commissars, Müller saying that 'the way to parliament would have to be across my dead body'. For both believed that the future lay with the workers' councils, not the discredited machinery of parliament.

While the provisional government was one side of the dual power equation, it was by no means the dominant one. The tremendous force of the revolution had shattered the nerve of the ruling class and left the state apparatus prostrate. The situation in the army was summed up by General Groener when he wrote:

> The influence of the home workers' and soldiers' councils prevails among whole sections of the army . . . All authority on the part of officers and junior officers is being undermined by the propaganda of the Independents and Spartakists. The High Command is powerless and no help can be expected from the government. If state authority is not restored, the whole army will crumble . . . If an army on the old basis is impossible because of the internal political situation, an army of volunteers must be created.[12]

Although officer discipline survived for a time on the external fronts, far from the political ferment at home, Groener's assessment was substantially correct.

The People's Commissars were in no happier a position. Scheidemann melodramatically described in his memoirs the sort of conditions under which they worked:

> Noisy processions of many thousands, most armed to the teeth, were continually organised by Liebknecht in front of the Chancery . . . The People's Commissars had hardly any protection. [They] practically did their work as prisoners. The Social Democratic members of the government dared not venture into the streets in daytime as they would have been killed. To Liebknecht's followers we pretended we had a military guard, although we had none.[13]

The Provisional Government and military High Command were weak. But unless they were physically disbanded they still had the power to revive the bourgeois state. As it was, the consciously revolutionary forces were still too small to deny them freedom of manoeuvre, so it was not long before the officer corps had rebuilt an army on the lines indicated by Groener. In place of unreliable conscripts a force of reactionary volunteers was assembled. These new troops, called the *Freikorps*, would be used to confront the power of the working class in the days of revolution. And the political wing of the state, despite the hammer blows dealt on 9 November, was able to recover ground by allying with reformist currents which held sway in the working class.

Standing in opposition to the old state were the workers' and soldiers' councils. The masses had shown their power on 9 November but had still to give it coherent form. The first opportunity to do that came on Sunday 10 November at Berlin's Busch Circus. From the factories and barracks came three thousand rank-and-file delegates, chosen on the basis of one per 1,000 workers and one per battalion. The first decision of the meeting was to claim leadership of the tangled network of councils that had spread across the face of Germany in the previous few days. Then the composition of the committee of People's Commissars was presented for approval and passed. The ease by which this decision was taken showed that few of those present realised that the Commissars, who headed the old state machine, would be the deadly enemies of the workers' council system.

When the meeting came to elect an executive committee for

the Berlin council, Müller nominated a slate which included several revolutionary shop stewards as well as Liebknecht and Luxemburg. The SPD sympathisers in the soldiers' delegation were grouped around the platform and vociferously objected to the list. Only when an executive dominated by reformists was put forward did their disruption cease. This new Council Executive comprised 12 soldiers (mostly SPD members or sympathisers) and 12 workers' delegates chosen in equal numbers from the SPD and Independents. Disgusted by what he saw as the SPD's gerrymandering tactics, Liebknecht refused to stand for the executive, and so the Obleute and their Independent Socialist allies took all six seats open to the left.

The 10 November meeting in Busch Circus was a defeat for those who believed in the councils. Because the delegates lacked a clear idea of the inevitable conflict between the council system and parliament they allowed the old state to regroup around the People's Commissars. The confusion was confirmed by the election of a Council Executive which gave a majority to the SPD — the party which had wrecked all previous attempts to set up workers' mass self-organisation.

The reformists had not retrieved their position merely by clever manoeuvres on the floor of the assembly. The logic of the situation, which had only just begun to educate the masses through struggle, dictated the initial balance of forces in the council. In Berlin the jubilant atmosphere of 9 November temporarily worked to the SPD's advantage. Perhaps the SPD had backed a catastrophic war, done everything in its power to prevent the revolution and jumped on the bandwagon only at the last minute, but to voice such criticisms seemed ungracious and sectarian. Had not ordinary workers from all parties fought side by side to share the same sweet taste of victory? The extreme left had the unenviable task of insisting that the revolution had merely stripped the armour plating off the capitalist system and that the reformist leaders stood in the way of completing its destruction.

But despite the hold of reformist ideas which was demonstrated by the SPD's success at the Busch Circus assembly, reformists found it hard to control Berlin's council movement. The problems they faced there contrasted with the ease with which they manipulated the Provisional Government. This seems surprising, given the SPD's three-to-one majority in the Council Executive compared with their equal votes with the Independents among the People's

Commissars. Both Council Executive and People's Commissars claimed mass backing, but each drew on a different type of support.

The council operated in a context of grassroots struggle which was worlds away from the dusty conservatism of the government. Although outnumbered in the council chamber, the Obleute and their allies often drew ordinary SPD members behind them when it came to practical issues. Thus the Council Executive had to bend its will to the masses *in their activity*. The Peoples's Commissars claimed support from the same masses, but drew *on their passivity*, on the inherited belief that socialism could be granted from above, by voting in reformist leaders. Unlike the council delegates, the People's Commissars felt no direct pressure upon them and remained the willing prisoners of the Kaiser's civil service and generals. The councils could not but express, even if in distorted form, the mobilisation of the proletarian movement. The Provisional Government played upon the confused ideas which lagged behind events, the Council upon the self-activity that changed ideas.[14]

However, although the councils were always under pressure from the base, this meant very little unless this could be given organised expression through revolutionary leadership. To offer such leadership two things were required: a clear understanding of the current situation and a solid base in the mass movement.

This might have come from two sources — the Spartakists or the shop stewards. Circumstances seemed to favour the latter. After all, the revolutionary Obleute had done more than anyone to pioneer the workers' council movement. But its extention to sectors far beyond the metalworkers' vanguard left the Obleute as just one of many currents vying for influence. Though they had proved their worth as militants, they had no equivalent following when it came to general politics. The programme of these rank-and-file leaders took them up to the outbreak of revolution but no further. The Spartakists, on the other hand, did have an idea of where they were going. But they had no solid organisation and were in no position to fill the vacuum of leadership, having only a minimal representation in the councils.

Ranged against the supporters of a workers' state were the SPD and right-wing Independents who deployed an army of officials, tens of newspapers, and party organisations of hundreds of thousands. These reformists had the advantage of years of propaganda plus the habits and beliefs fostered by life under capitalism.

Reformism had not been invented as a plot to deceive workers but was a deeply-rooted ideology which had once *made sense* of the world to the majority. Years during which the system remained stable and capable of offering marginal improvements had led many workers to see gradual change within the legal channels as the way forward. Indeed this seemed preferable to the unknown risks involved in revolution.

By 1918 such an optimistic view of capitalism did not, and could not, explain the chaos brought about by the war or the system's inability to provide even the basic necessities of life. Without abandoning their reformist world view the majority of German workers and soldiers felt compelled to revolt at the end of the war — the crisis forced them to link their struggles together in the workers' and soldiers' councils.

But this did not mean that all workers had immediately and spontaneously drawn revolutionary conclusions from a few weeks of activity. Old ideas do not simply disappear even though they do not fit reality. Unless an alternative was presented which showed a revolutionary way forward the old methods would continue by default. Reformist ideology could be adapted so that even the emergence of the workers' council could be presented as conforming to its ideas. Thus **Vorwärts**, the SPD's daily paper, carried articles arguing that the council might have been necessary to prepare the way for parliamentary government, but once it had fulfilled this role it was redundant.

For the mass of workers to draw revolutionary conclusions, even in a revolution, their direct experience had to be supplemented by the analysis of events and leadership which could only come from an organised body of socialists.

Chapter Seven

THE REVOLUTIONARY CHEMISTRY OF NOVEMBER 1918

IN A DUAL power situation, where the bourgeois state had lost its monopoly of armed force in society, the battle for the minds of the workers and soldiers is all-important. The SPD was clear about what it had to offer in the days after 9 November. **Vorwärts** greeted the new Germany with an article by Ebert calling on all 'citizens' to maintain 'calm and order'.[1] These were the party's watchwords, a non-class jargon which claimed to protect the interests of 'all Germans' by restoring the old 'order'. The paper begged government officials to remain at their posts and urged workers not to settle scores with those who had sent so many to their deaths. 'Do not fight your own brothers' was the paper's headline. With the Kaiser gone, the SPD was confident that in free elections to a National Assembly it would win a handsome majority.

In a situation of deep social crisis the SPD's brand of 'socialism' amounted to the restoration of capitalist stability, at great cost to the working class. There were many reasons why the party adopted this approach. At the most basic level, reformist policies depended for success on the ability of capitalism to grant occasional concessions — so the well-being of capitalism was necessary. Parliamentary deputies and party and union officials retained their relatively privileged status and lifestyle only by acting as negotiators between the working class and the ruling class. If the latter disappered the SPD's very *raison d'être* would disappear too.

On the other hand, one of the chief bulwarks of reformism was the belief that workers' did not have the potential to run society for themselves and that this must be done *for* them. From this belief leaders such as Ebert or Scheidemann derived their influence. If a self-confident, independently organised working class was allowed to develop this would be as much a threat to the SPD as to the capitalist state. That is why the reformist leaders put their efforts

into restoring the health of the system and protecting it from the
challenge of revolution by destroying autonomous workers' organisation. With an alternative to parliament, workers would have no
need of professional politicians to make elegant speeches on their
behalf or negotiate paltry concessions for them.

When General Groener rang Ebert on the evening of 10
November to propose a crusade against 'Bolshevik subversion',
Ebert readily accepted.

The Spartakists were equally clear of *their* aims. Their new
daily paper, printed in the occupied premises of the right-wing
Lokal Anzeiger, was called **Rote Fahne** (**Red Flag**). Out of the
ruins of war, it proclaimed:

> the proletariat must erect a new economy. To do this it must have
> political and economic power. The next step on this road is early
> peace, proletarian economic rule, transformation of the economy
> from phoney war socialism to the real socialism of peace.[2]

The means to achieve this were laid out in the Spartakist
programme:

> 1. *As Immediate Means for Making the Revolution Secure.*
> The disarming of the entire police force, of all officers, as well as of the
> non-proletarian soldiers . . . The arming of the entire adult male
> population as the workers' militia.
> 2. *On the Economic and Social Field* . . .
> Removal of all parliaments and municipal councils, their functions to
> be taken over by the workers' and soldiers' councils . . . Election of
> workers' councils all over Germany by the entire adult population of
> working people of both sexes in cities and rural districts along the line
> of industries . . . The Central Council of the workers' and soldiers'
> councils . . . to elect the Executive Council as the highest organ of
> legislative and executive power . . .
> 3. *Further Economic Demands*
> Election of administrative councils in all enterprises, such councils to
> regulate the internal affairs of the enterprises in agreement with the
> workers' councils, regulate the conditions of labour, control produc-
> tion, and, finally, take over the administration of the enterprises.[3]

The Spartakists put a workers' council state at the centre of
their thinking, but their influence within the actual councils was
negligible. The group had few members and an even smaller
number who had built a recognised following in their workplaces.

While the most prominent leaders such as Luxemburg and Liebknecht appear to have addressed large workers' assemblies, the impact of the Spartakists within the Berlin workers' and soldiers' council seems to have been minimal, an organised caucus only being created in February 1919 — three months after the revolution began. Another sign of the Spartakists' inability to shape the action of the councils was that neither Luxemburg nor Liebknecht was able to attend the First Congress of Soviets in December 1918.

Between the SPD's programme of capitalist restoration and the Spartakist programme of a 'second revolution' to abolish the system entirely, stood the Obleute and their left-Independent allies. Though considering themselves revolutionary socialists, the Obleute lacked the theoretical tools and political organisation to cope with the complexities of dual power. They believed that by the mere creation of workers' and soldiers' councils on 9 November the takeover had been completed, and so did not demand the dismantling of the imperial state. A symptom of this disregard of the old reactionary forces was that Emil Barth, second only to Richard Müller in the Obleute organisation, was allowed to join the People's Commissars.

The Obleute's attitude was summed up by Ernst Däumig's declaration at the Busch Circus that 'Old Germany is no more . . . Political power is now in the hands of the workers and soldiers', and that socialism would be won without further upheaval, merely by 'securing and building' on what had already been achieved. But the Obleute were soon to find the middle ground crumbling beneath them. In the end they were faced with a stark choice — the SPD or Spartakus, a capitalism still bloody from war or socialism through renewed struggle.

The three fronts of class conflict

The chemistry of revolution was not determined by political leaders alone. The masses had been stirred up and demanded immediate solutions to their pressing problems. The war had seen 13 million Germans called up into the armed forces. Of these 1.7 million were dead, 4.2 million wounded and one million missing or taken prisoner.[4] The monumental job of demobilisation could not be ignored. Another legacy of war was economic chaos. By January 1919, 800 Germans a day were dying from hunger.[5]

In Berlin the situation was especially critical. Three babies in every ten died within a few days of birth; food supplies were down to less than half of minimum needs. To add to these problems there came the spectre of unemployment. During the war it had been practically nil in Berlin; by the end of November it had climbed to 19,000 and thereafter rocketed, reaching 230,000 within two months. The city felt the pressure of unemployment acutely because it housed one quarter of the nation's jobless.

In such circumstances, class struggle was not something that could be shrugged off. It forced its way into every shop and street, every factory and office. Battles were staged on three interconnected fronts — the national state, local government and the workplace. On each level a situation of dual power prevailed: the Council Executive disputed with the People's Commissars as to who should rule the nation; local workers' and soldiers' councils tussled with municipal authorities for power in the community; while factory councils challenged management in industry.

By 11 November the masses in Berlin had erected a vast network of councils which constituted a new source of power. When it came to order on the streets, Eichhorn's control of the central police headquarters had been matched by local takeovers. Charlottenburg's revolutionary police chief had been at work within hours of the rising. The Spandau workers' and soldiers' council, in the suburbs, set up a security battalion of 110 radical workers who occupied not only the police station but the arsenal and railway station.

Neukölln played a similar role in Berlin to that of Vyborg in Petrograd as the capital's most radical district. At the heart of the city and housing a quarter of a million people, it frequently acted as a faithful barometer of the wider class struggle. Since 9 November Neukölln had had a revolutionary militia of 500 patrolling its streets.[6] Rather than co-operate with these new powers, the old police force simply melted away.

The situation in local government was less clear cut. Between Saturday 9 November and the following Wednesday, there was a war of words between workers' and soldiers' councils, which claimed that the central Council Executive had given them full powers, and municipal officials who quoted provisional government instructions that they continue as before.[7] In the end a truce, like that reached at the Busch Circus, divided power between the two. Local workers' and soldiers' councils would exercise 'supervision' over the existing municipal bodies and workers' militias would be paid out of local rates. In the prosperous Wilmersdorf district, for example, the most notorious of the Kaiser's men were expelled, but here, as elsewhere, the apparatus of local government was left intact.[8]

However in militant areas, the workers' and soldiers' councils went beyond mere supervision. In Spandau the council decided to abolish the municipal government. Neukölln's workers' and soldiers' council declared its intention to seize control not just of all public offices, but the factories too.[9]

The shaking of the foundations of society could not fail to affect industry. When the central Council Executive called off the revolutionary general strike after three days, factory councils sprang up in virtually every sizeable works.[10] The building of mass democratic organisations, begun in the January 1918 strike, could now be completed.

On the question of control Spandau's workers were the most daring. In the huge Staatswerkstatten, management was driven out and replaced by a radical committee of eleven manual and eight white-collar workers. The factory council ended machine-gun production and planned conversion for peacetime purposes.[11]

Here as in a host of other examples, the masses, despised for ignorance and 'dark passions' by generations of 'cultured' classes, were showing the genius of collective action. Within a few days they had created a marvellously democratic network of councils which could run society for the benefit of the majority. It should be noted that at this point no verbal distinction was made between the different levels of council organisation. The central workers' and soldiers' council was not seen as an institution high above the masses, but simply the summit of a pyramid whose base was found in the combined strength of workers in production. Whether in the factory, community or city, the different types of council were called *'Arbeiterräte'*. Only later were reformists to break this unitary thrust and mentally separate the fight for power in the state, on the streets, or in production, assigning different names to the various sections of council organisation.

Given the weakness of the provisional government and army High Command, it was obvious which class had the greatest potential for power after 9 November. As Chris Harman puts it: 'To the question "Who ruled Germany?" there was only one possible answer: the councils did.'[12] In Berlin it was clear that the working class had the armed capacity to sweep away the old state entirely.

But that was only half the story. The *subjective* element needed for the workers' councils to take power was absent: it was not the conscious aim of most workers. Though 'socialism' was on all lips, even the vanguard workers in the metal trades had no clear conception of what it really meant or how it could be secured.

Reformists and reactionaries were to use this confusion to their advantage. With the carrot and the stick, persuasion and force, they would try to divert the workers' urge to rule their destiny. Their strategy consisted of granting concessions while weakening the councils by restoring the alternative system of parliament and physically eliminating the vanguard sections of the working class.

The provisional government issued its first decree on 12 November. The repressive laws of wartime were withdrawn, the 'state of siege' repealed, censorship abolished and an amnesty granted to political prisoners. So far this was no more than recognition of what had already been achieved by the revolution. In the field of labour legislation, Ebert sought to pre-empt grassroots action by granting a maximum eight-hour day from 1 January 1919. Many workers would not wait that long.[13]

Reforms were accompanied by measures designed to block the advance of revolution. Despite the openly right-wing attitudes of most army officers, the government declared that their orders must henceforth be obeyed. Perhaps the most important decision of the provisional government was to restore parliament. A National Assembly would be elected on the basis of full and equal male and female suffrage. One man/woman, one vote would be an improvement on the old discriminatory 'three class' voting system and, it was hoped, placate many workers.

By counterposing a National Assembly to the political authority of the Council Executive the provisional government was declaring war on the council system as a whole. Ebert's reactionary intentions were soon to be made more explicit. Addressing soldiers' delegates, he called on them to 'smash the Spartakist Red Guard. Up with the Volunteer Corps of soldiers to defend citizens' lives and property. Down with Bolshevism!' The motto of 'don't fight your brother', when the left had been advancing, had given way to one of war on your 'red' brother as soon as the immediate danger had passed.[14]

The central Council Executive lacked the resolve to fight back. It made a half-hearted attempt to form its own militia of 2,000 to

resist the reactionary units being formed by the government — but
the SPD accused it of showing mistrust of the existing army units
and built up such a powerful campaign through its soldier supporters that the idea of a central council militia had to be dropped.[15]

The Executive's problems were compounded by one of its own
recent decisions. It had ordered that 'councils can only exercise
authority within their own enterprises, troop units, etc., and in
relation to their own internal and local problems.'[16] This showed a
total lack of understanding of the dynamics of the workers' council
movement. Workers' and soldiers' councils had been breaking
down sectional attitudes and grasping control of all aspects of social
life, linking factories, local government and militias. Such an
integration of social production and armed power was the key to
unlocking the potential of the working class. The Executive's order
played into the hands of the reformists because it fragmented this
thrust towards unity in struggle.

The muddled situation on the Executive was revealed when
Däumig moved a resolution against the restoration of parliament.
It fell by 12 votes to 10.[17] The Council Executive was willingly
signing away its future to its arch-rival. Nevertheless, in view of the
SPD's in-built majority on the Council Executive, this vote was
surprisingly narrow and showed, not for the last time, how the
higher organs of the council were subject to leftward pressure from
below.

On 12 November Richard Müller wrote to Ebert on behalf of
the Council Executive, reiterating its right, established just three
days earlier, to supervise the work of the People's Commissars.
Disdaining even to reply, the Chancellor made it clear that he and
his colleagues intended to act as the supreme authority in
Germany.

By mid-November, despite their initial advantage, Berlin's
councils were blocked on military and political fronts. Only renewed working-class mobilisation could clear the way. That came
from the factories, and in an unexpected form. Returning to work
after the general strike, employees at the Daimler factory in
Marienfelde made the following demands:

> Equal pay for equal work by women.
> An 8½ hour day with 5 hours on Saturday.
> No overtime.
> Abolition of punitive fines.

All hiring and firing to be undertaken by the workers' council in the factory.

Abolition of piecework.[18]

Such apparently minor claims may seem out of place in the midst of a world revolution, but in their way they were more dangerous than any grand revolutionary speeches. It was far easier for Ebert to give everyone an equal vote in elections to the National Assembly, than to countenance the abolition of piecework, the granting of equal pay, shorter hours and the like. For these demands struck at the heart of the beast — the profitability of a crisis-ridden capitalism.

The example of the Daimler workers was infectious, and was soon followed by a number of other factories. Yet even during revolutions there is great unevenness in the working class. Schwartzkopff was one of the factories that joined the campaign initiated at Daimler, but its workers were less radical. Although they too demanded wide-ranging powers for their factory council, they also supported calling the National Assembly and sacking women with working husbands to make jobs for demobbed soldiers.[19]

The backwardness of Schwartzkopff was confirmed in the so-called 'Spartakus week' of January 1919, when it was the first major factory to break ranks in the mass strike against Ebert. But even in Schwartzkopff, the very fact of a shopfloor debate on the nature of the state was a sign that revolution meant more than a shuffling of political cards at the top. In the battle of ideas which distinguished the advanced factories from the more backward ones it became clear that the struggle at work involved a lot more than mere economics. In dispute were the future of the state, demobilisation and a host of other issues. For the struggle for socialism meant much more than just institutional change, it held out hope for the liberation of all other oppressed sections, whether they be the working-class women of Berlin fighting for the right to work and equal pay or the peasants of East Prussia who had seized the land they tilled.

The capitalists were aware that the trickle of economic demands since 9 November presaged an impending tide. They knew that only trade union officials could possibly provide the flood barriers to contain it. So German businessmen, notorious before 1914 for their rabid opposition to unions, now sang a different tune. As the chairman of the Iron and Steel Employers put it:

Unless we negotiate with the unions we can go no further. Yes, gentlemen, we should be happy that the unions are still prepared to negotiate as they have; for only by negotiations, can we avoid anarchy, bolshevism, Spartakist rule and chaos — call it what you will.[20]

But the officials were far from secure themselves. Having bitterly denounced wartime unofficial strikes, they also had reason to fear the rise of workers' councils.[21] In just the same way as the council threatened the political future of SPD reformism, it challenged the trade union bureaucrats. If the class could organise itself through shopfloor representation, destroying capitalism rather than negotiating with it, there would be no need for bureaucratic wheeling and dealing of any sort.

Unified by a mutual fear of the rank and file, the industrialists and trade union leaders concluded that the dangerous bacillus of workers' *control* could be cured by a mild dose of workers' *participation*. On 15 November they unveiled a grand plan for 'Industrial Co-operation'. Henceforth, they said, the class war would be abolished, and its place taken by a system of arbitration committees in which unions and capital had equal representation.

This attempt to banish the spectre of an independent rank-and-file movement by top-level negotiation did not work, for the officials had already lost influence over important sections of the working class to the councils. It would take bullets to restore it. Nevertheless, encouraged by false hopes, another symbol of bourgeois rule opened its doors on the day the union/employer pact was signed. The Stock Exchange, which had closed on the eve of the uprising, was dealing again.[22]

Friday 15 November was indeed a day of reformist counter-attack, for it also saw an important agreement sealed between the unions and the Council Executive. Under this, responsibility for all factory affairs would be handed back to the union officials. In its final form the accord stated:

> The representation of the economic interests of all employed persons in Greater Berlin is the responsibility of the Free Trade Unions . . . The existing workers' and staff bodies are therefore dissolved. New elections are to take place in all enterprises.[23]

The new role of the union-controlled factory council would be:

> together with the factory management, to decide on all questions of interest to workers and office staff . . . No other matters come into the

terms of reference . . . The factory council must work with the Free Trade Unions in defending the *economic* interests of the workers. It can negotiate independently with the employers, but the union must be informed regularly. If disagreements arise between factory councils and management, the committee must turn for advice to the Free Trade Unions before taking any action . . .
The collectivisation of the enterprise can only be carried out systematically and in an orderly fashion by the socialist government . . . The question of pieceworking cannot be decided at present and must probably be put off until the economic life of the country has been restored.[24]

This deal, signed by Müller himself, threatened to be a disaster for the factory councils. 'Economic matters' were to be hived off to the unions. Official-controlled shopfloor bodies would be expected to act as an extension of the union rather than for the rank and file.

Why did the Council Executive abandon the factory councils? The answer was given by Müller. He felt the Executive was 'not in a position to take care of conflict between employers and workers' because it was so busy trying to consolidate its political position in relation to the national state. What he did not realise was that any claim to political authority was jeopardised if it did not have the force of the factory councils behind it. To expect the central Berlin council to hold state power if it were cut off from its lifeblood — collective organisation at the point of production — was nonsense.

Union officials were quick to take advantage of the Executive's blunder. Cohen, the metal union official, launched his offensive just two days after the deal was signed, declaring:

Industrial life has been disrupted by recent events, but it must be revived. Some businesses have been presented with unbelievable demands. It is obviously stupid to insist that managers be sacked or that wages for an eight-hour day be maintained by the inclusion of payments for overtime that is no longer worked. These things are not in the common interest but only serve to spread chaos.

Cohen, like other bureaucrats, was pursuing a two-pronged strategy. By limiting factory discussion to economic issues he hoped to contain it by negotiation and compromise, at which he was adept:

In my opinion there should be a division of labour between [factory] committee members and workers' council delegates so as to make economic matters the responsibility of the former and political matters the work of the latter.[25]

The intention to break up the *general* class struggle into a host of sectional issues was clearly spelled out here. But Cohen also sought to isolate the most advanced workers by contrasting the 'interests of the community' with those of militants hell-bent on disruption. Talking of community, rather than its constituent parts — employers and workers — he obscured the reality that workers' interests could be secured only at the expense of the ruling class minority.

The Council Executive's deal with the unions showed that even the Obleute were falling under reformist influence. Without a clear political analysis of their own, they bent to whichever force applied the most pressure. Here was an example of the 'vanguard' falling behind those it purported to lead.

Luckily the voice of the rank and file could not be silenced. At the central council assembly on 19 November Müller opened the proceedings with a warning that 'too much militancy' put the economy in danger. Many delegates felt he was parroting the slanders of the SPD, union bureaucracy and bourgeois press. As one of them was to put it:

> It is not the proletariat but the ruling class which through its war has sown the economic chaos. Workers' militancy is directed towards creating a new order that will make such anarchy impossible.[26]

Müller faced many critics at the meeting. One steward explained how in just a few days the factory council had transformed life at his works, introducing the eight-hour day, taking control of hire-and-fire, along with better workshop regulations. But since Müller's deal with the unions, the officials had come in from outside to set up their own puppet committee.[27] Argus motor workers explained that as a result of the Executive/union deal, their employers would only recognise the officials for the purposes of negotiation, while shopfloor opinion was ignored.[28] Railway workshop employees striking against piecework had come in for special abuse from the bureaucracy and bourgeois press. But, as they told the meeting, this nationalised industry had imposed conditions no ordinary worker would tolerate. Enough was enough, and despite Müller's accusations they wanted the Berlin council's support.[29]

Leviathan stirs

Because the leadership of the councils had failed, the rank and file took charge once more. Militant action spread like wildfire.

The Berlin metal industry pioneered the offensive, but now other sections joined it. A conference of white-collar workers demanded collectivisation and recognition of their own councils.[30] Printers insisted on an immediate eight-hour day, and even cigar-makers weighed in, denouncing union officials and bosses alike.[31] On 22 November news arrived of an awakening in Germany's giant coal industry; the Ruhr and Silesia were ablaze with strikes.

Impatient with the slow pace of change, Berlin workers were also on the move. The 3,000 Daimler Marienfelde workers came out for their list of demands, in defiance of management and union officials. The stoppage was supported by office staff and spread to other local factories such as the Deutschen Motorwerke and Siemens.

Boxed into a corner, the employers and unions turned to the Council Executive for help. It alone appeared to have influence in the workshops. But that influence had been squandered in foolish compromises and even the Executive's appeals for a return to work were not heeded. As the press commented: 'The workers believe there is no point waiting for the collectivisation of industry by government.'[32] The Marienfelde strikers soon connected their fight with politics at state level and passed a resolution against the National Assembly and in favour of all power to the workers' councils.

Rosa Luxemburg accurately judged the significance of these events:

> The beginning of this strike movement is proof that the political revolution is shaking the very foundation of society. The revolution stands on its own ground; it cuts through all the phoney changes in which individuals are sacked or swopped around, without the relations between capital and labour being changed in the slightest. Pushing them aside it takes the centre of the stage. In today's revolution, strikes are no 'trade union' event, no trifle concerned with humdrum wage questions. They are the natural response of the masses to the violent shock waves which capital has experienced through the collapse of German imperialism and the short political revolution of the workers and soldiers . . . they announce the commencement of direct and violent class struggles.[33]

Broad sections of the working class sought power over their working lives. There were now great opportunities for socialists. In every well-led campaign on issues such as the abolition of piecework or workshop control, the battle lines of the classes would be clarified and fresh forces recruited to the revolutionary camp. Every time workers acted to secure their immediate interests in this situation of crisis, they would discover the political realities of the time — the old state, management, union officials and reformist party leaders were aligned against them.

The workers' council could offer no magical solutions in this struggle for emancipation. It provided only a framework, a source of authority which allowed arguments to be developed and strategies hammered out, with the knowledge that once a decision was taken, it would possess the support and physical force of the active workers' movement. Certainly the council was something greater than its individual parts. It was not just a collection of factory and battalion delegates, but the recognised front line of a mobil-ised working class. But it could maintain its position only by active leadership, and in its first weeks of life it was not given this.

End of the honeymoon

On 23 November the central Council Executive issued a number of major policy documents. The first summoned a national congress of workers' and soldiers' councils, elections to be held on the basis of one delegate per 200,000 workers and per 100,000 soldiers. The disparate nature of council movement structure nationally was reflected by the fact that the method of election, whether industrial or geographical, was not specified.[34]

The second statement recognised the provisional government as head of the state in place of the Council Executive, but insisted that this Executive still had the right to supervise the government's operation. This apparent compromise masked a defeat. The legal fiction could not conceal that in revolutionary periods the state is reduced to its basic core — the physical force of armed power. The provisional government could defy the Executive with impunity as long as the councils were militarily weak, and the majority of those that were armed were soldiers who, though supporters of the revolution, sympathised with the SPD's distorted version of it. The idea that workers could supervise the state and put reins on it rather than taking power directly comes from the practice of parliamentary democracy, with its division of parliament from the executive arm of government. This idea is inimical to workers' democracy, which needs the direct rule of the majority over the physical force of society.

The real balance of forces a fortnight into dual power was reflected by an incident two days before the Council Executive issued its statements. Scheüch, the provisional Minister of War, had protested when the Council Executive's representative, a certain Oberleutnant Walz, demanded the right to countersign all ministerial documents. The Council Executive insisted Scheüch be sacked; the provisional government wanted Walz withdrawn instead. In the end it was the provisional government that got its way.[35]

The third pronouncement by the Council Executive concerned local workers' and soldiers' councils. Its message was vague: 'Their duty is to build and sustain the achievements of the revolution as well as drive back counter-revolution'. But when it came to specifics, the document flinched from interfering with the old local authorities.

> Recently the workers' and soldiers' have independently taken decisions over food provision and raw material supply etc. As a result the measures of central government have been rendered inoperative . . .
>
> 1. There should be supervision, not overthrow . . . of local authorities.
>
> 2. Arrests should only be made in extreme circumstances and only by the local security force.
>
> 3. All expropriations must receive prior agreement and must be avoided in all cases where provisions are destined for the army or local authorities.
>
> 4. Absolutely no private funds should be seized.[36]

This list of prohibitions gives a clue as to the activities of some local councils — obviously arrests of counter-revolutionaries, expropriations and seizure of the wealth of the rich!

The Neukölln workers' and soldiers' council was a particular target for attack. Its local executive was made up 24 members of the SPD, 24 Independents (many of whom were Spartakists) and 24 soldiers. From the first it kept tight control of local government departments, deciding all major questions of rationing and employment. On 25 November it resolved to abolish the municipal authorities outright, as well as take over the banks and declare all houses communal property.[37]

Before it could put this plan into operation, a contingent of reactionary soldiers, presumably acting for the provisional government, occupied and physically dissolved the Neukölln council. But the right had gone too far and a popular outcry forced it to withdraw, permitting the council to assemble again. The SPD was blamed for these events and its delegates excluded, giving Neukölln a new executive of 48 Independents and 24 soldiers, who took power in the locality once more.[38] With its mini-putsches and counter-putsches this affair was a precursor of struggles that were to involve all of Berlin in the following weeks.

An insight into the atmosphere on the shopfloor of Berlin's factories at this time was offered by the right-wing **Deutsche Tagezeitung** of 25 November:

> The workers arrive on time, then take off their coats, read their newspapers and slowly begin work. This is interrupted by debates and meetings. The employers are as powerless as the managerial staff. All power is in the hands of the workers' committees. On all questions ranging from the reconversion of the factory to peacetime production, the supply of labour, the employment of demobbed soldiers, the implementation of agreements, work methods, and sharing out of work, on all these the workers' committees have the last word.[39]

Real democracy, the employers found, was difficult to live with.

That day, 25 November, representatives of 1,400 Stock workers and 1,600 Zwietusch workers added their names to the growing list of strikers. The Council Executive might wish to abdicate responsibility for economic matters; union officials and bosses might try to side-step the mass movement; but the rank and file, filled with confidence in their own power, would not abandon their fight for justice.

The extended meetings of the central Berlin council at the end of November showed that the intoxication of the first days of revolution was over. In its place was a growing division between those who wanted to take the workers' movement forward and those who wanted to abdicate responsibility to parliament.

Emil Barth, once an Obleute but now a People's Commissar, opened the 27 November session. He began with the familiar warning that the revolution must not be 'degraded' by economic squabbles.[40] Strikes had cut coal output to one fifth of former levels, leaving Berlin with only two weeks' fuel. The provisional government had called for 'Volunteers' to work in strike-bound Upper Silesia, but this attempt at blacklegging was without success.[41] With a mixture of bravado and cunning, Barth pleaded with the meeting to show restraint:

> It is not always possible to keep to an eight-hour day in all industrial sectors as this may harm the interests of the majority . . . The worker who cares only for his own personal interest fights against the socialist republic. He who sees the revolution as a wage movement does not understand socialism . . . *But any sabotage on the part of the employers will be answered by immediate expropriation without compensation.*[42]

Thankfully, many council delegates were quick to see through Barth's threat of expropriation as no more than a sham. The workers at the meeting did not accept his version of socialism but argued for their majority interests, realising that any call for working-class self-sacrifice could benefit only the Krupps and Rathenaus of Germany.

One delegate laid the blame for the economic chaos on a blood-stained capitalism. The only solution, he said, was to build the councils into a properly organised class force to take over from the bosses. A speaker from Daimler showed how this could be begun in practice:

> We have abolished piecework. The workers now do all hiring and firing. Recently the Daimler Company paid out 130,000 marks to shareholders. From now on we want these dividends for ourselves and measures such as the abolition of piecework will bring them in our direction.[43]

Other delegates lambasted the Council Executive for delivering the class into the clutches of discredited officials such as Adolf Cohen. His latest ploy was a general engineering contract, something of which he felt proud. Such a contract had been the aim of the union for many years. But events had outstripped Cohen. What might have been welcomed as an advance before 1914 was now seen as woefully inadequate. Although under Cohen's deal metalworkers' hours would be reduced, this was a concession many had already won by direct action. The sting in the tail was that, in Cohen's deal, in return for better hours wages would be cut by one-sixth. When Cohen rose to defend himself at the council meeting he was silenced by a hail of abuse.

At the heart of the late November debates was the question 'Who should the councils serve?' It was obvious from the first few weeks of their life that while their democratic electoral system put them in far closer touch with the grassroots than any parliament, they could be destroyed from within if their leadership remained indefinitely in the hands of reformists or centrists who either did not understand their nature or consciously opposed them. The disastrous concession made to the union bureaucracy symbolised a dangerous tendency which many rank-and-file activists would not tolerate. Repeated criticisms from the floor of the central council meetings compelled the Executive to set up a commission to reconsider the whole vexed question of union/council relations. Alas, while it met the striking factories were left to fend for themselves on an individual basis.

There was a central contradiction here. On a *general* level workers accepted reformist ideas, but when it came to specific issues raised by the crisis, many instinctively took revolutionary direct action. Yet with the council in reformist hands and the revolutionary groups incapable of providing any organised alternative strategy, the struggle reduced itself to resistance on an individual factory level.

November had shown that the leading stewards and their left Independent allies had no way out of the confusion. Indeed they contributed to it by standing half-way between the two real choices of reaction or revolution. Understandably Däumig and Müller kept a low profile in the stormy meetings of late November. They were responsible for the discontent because their centrism had led the rank and file into one reformist trap after another.

The Spartakists had no such hesitation. For them the fundamental choice outlined by Luxemburg back in 1915 remained the same — a barbarous reign of capitalism or advance to socialism. But the influence of this group, which seemed considerable in street demonstrations, was pitifully small inside the council movement. Their rapidly-growing following had little experience of work in the organised labour movement — a fact which was to cost them dear when they set up the Communist Party one month later.

In the factories the struggle had reached stalemate. Despite the antics of the Council Executive, workers had reasserted the rights of their factory councils and forcibly dragged the movement back from capitulation to the union officials. Yet the situation was still unsatisfactory, for there was no response to the growing military and organisational strength of the employers and provisional government. By the end of the month the first strike wave had lost its impetus and was breaking up.

The grand hopes of 9 November had not been fulfilled in the first wave of struggle. Yet the social forces unleashed were no less active than before. December was to carry them to new levels of conflict.

Chapter Eight

REACTION VERSUS REVOLUTION

THE STRUGGLES of December 1918 soon revealed a new mood in the working class. The dizzying optimism of the November days had evaporated like the morning dew, and in the cold glare of daylight, workers could see that the war of the classes still had to be fought and won. In battles at the end of 1918 the ruling class abandoned the tactic of chipping away at the workers' recent gains. For Ebert and his generals only a decisive confrontation, through bitter but localised class war, could disarm the leading section of the working class and banish the spectre of socialism.

Berlin's engineering workers sensed this change of atmosphere and showed a tenacious determination to resist violent counter-revolution. Conscious of the poor performance of the Council Executive, the most advanced workers made their struggle more deliberately political and rank and file in character. Two mass meetings summed up this new temperament. The first, held at the Oberspree Munitions Works, passed a resolution which said:

> The call for a National Assembly is not the end, but only the very beginning of the revolution whose fruits are yet to be tasted by the working class. This meeting believes it vitally important that the proletarian revolution is carried forward, achieves more than the current miserable results and is unswerving in the battles against the steadily encroaching intrigues of counter-revolutionaries.[1]

The second meeting, at the 10,000-strong DWM munitions factory, brought together that explosive combination of factory and state issues which had proved so powerful in the final weeks of the war. But now, in December 1918, it was on a far higher plane than before. The proceedings began with a speech by Liebknecht, which was followed by a motion that said threats to close the factory should be countered by prompt collectivisation. This was passed unanimously. Only seven people voted against another resolution calling for Ebert's government to resign.

Growing combativity was symbolised by events at the Piechatzek Liftgear Company. The manager went into work one day to find his 700 workers standing idle. He was briefly informed that the plant had been expropriated and that he should hand over the keys of the safe and details of all accounts to complete the transfer. Distraught, the manager tried to telephone for help, but alas, the local switchboard was also under workers' control. However the manager was eventually saved by an unexpected ally. Richard Müller intervened to scold the workers for acting 'prematurely'. In the face of such prestigious advice from the leader of the Obleute, the Piechatzek workforce agreed to bide its time.[2] Müller had to work hard to forestall similar takeovers in the Schutz, AMBI and AEG Hennigsdorf factories.[3]

These were not the only storm signals in early December. The home army had been disintegrating by the hour so Ebert and company put their final hopes in units returning from abroad. On 1 December any belief that these would form a reliable counter-revolutionary force was shattered. A congress of 326 front-line units which met at Ems turned against its officers. It decided to reinforce the soldiers' councils, send delegates to the Berlin council and abolish badges of rank such as epaulettes and separate mess-halls.[4]

Shaken by these setbacks, the government began a new offensive. Given the strength of the opposition, it kept up its soothing reformist facade, all the while testing its forces for the coming civil war. The first step was a conciliatory response to calls for workers' control. A 'Socialisation Commission' was set up with the following daring mission(!):

> The aim of collectivisation is not to hurt the property owners, but to benefit the propertyless . . . The task of the Socialisation Commission is henceforth to exercise a calming influence in such a way that nothing unreasonable is to be expected and no-one suffers the slightest damage.[5]

It is easier to walk on water than collectivise without expropriating the capitalist, a fact proved by the hefty volume of Commission proceedings to be found in the dustbin of history.

The mailed fist beneath the velvet glove did not take long to appear however. Deliberately stirring up middle-class hysteria, the

Berliner Tageblatt led its 4 December issue with dire predictions
of the Bolshevik apocalypse and the pure lie that the Council
Executive had wasted 800 million marks in just a fortnight. The
next day armed detachments under SPD leadership paraded against
'red terrorism'. Then on 6 December they invaded the Council
Executive building and arrested its members, while elsewhere
other units sought to proclaim Ebert president of Germany.[6] A
Spartakist procession was fired on without warning and 16 people
gunned down.

This coup was altogether too small to break the confidence of
the workers. The following day an armed demonstration bearing
Spartakist placards and headed by workers from Argus, Siemens
and the Aron factories, all recently in dispute with their bosses,
filled the streets.[7] Soon thousands from the DWM, AEG and Löwe
works downed tools and a further demonstration of 150,000 sent
the putschists running for shelter.[8]

These were not the only demonstrations in early December.
On the 12th **Rote Fahne** reported a march of Siemens workers who
had walked out over a management ultimatum — accept our offer
on pay and piecework, or be locked out. This report from their
factory council uncovers the complex and volatile chemistry of
class forces involved in workplace struggle at that time:

> Our dispute began with the absolute rejection of a union/management
> agreement. Siering, the DMV official, claimed sole negotiating rights
> on behalf of the rank and file, but we did not accept that. Instead our
> shop stewards set up a delegation composed of members of the factory
> council for the most part. Neither the delegation nor the council were
> recognised by Siemens. So we brought in Scholze from the central
> Council Executive. He supported our assertion that the boss must
> negotiate with the shopfloor commission we'd set up.
> In the meantime the stewards met in the works office to discuss the
> intransigence of Siemens, our boss. He had been spouting off about
> how the sooner the whole bag of tricks (by which he meant the
> Republic) fell to bits, the better it would be . . . Well, Herr von
> Siemens had better watch out that he and his cronies are not arrested
> for counter-revolutionary machinations and treason . . .[9]

This was no idle threat on the part of the Siemens workers.
On 7 December the directors of the giant Thyssen coal and steel
group were seized by their employees in the Ruhr and shipped off
to the Berlin Council Executive to face revolutionary justice, though

Ebert successfully had them released without charge.[10] Things had
not gone that far at Siemens yet. Instead the workers imposed a
work to rule and eventually called a mass strike meeting.

> It was an extraordinary event . . . Barth and Cohen came along and
> abruptly took control of the proceedings. Barth begged us 'from his
> heart and on his knees' to go back to work. Accusing anyone who
> disagreed with being a Spartakist saboteur, he effectively split and
> confused those present. This Barth was the same man who had always
> prattled on about the unity of the class. When Cohen tried to say his
> piece he was shouted down. However, these two eventually had their
> way and won a vote to stay at work, largely because of the support of
> the office staff and white-collar workers.[11]

The Siemens dispute was eventually settled by compromise
and, despite the wrecking tactics of Barth and Cohen, the factory
council was recognised and higher pay with shorter hours granted.[12]
This dispute demonstrated the dramatic ups and downs of the
movement, the confidence of the rank and file, and the continuing
influence of reformist leaders who, in the absence of a coherent
revolutionary alternative, often had their way.

In the Siemens case the Council Executive was forced by
grassroots pressure to mediate *for* the workers and *against* the
unholy alliance of unions and management. This also happened in
two other major disputes. In early December Berlin moulders
struck for the abolition of piecework. Again the employers would
not recognise the existence of those they had happily exploited over
the years, and refused to negotiate. The Council Executive intervened to break the deadlock. At the AEG Hennigsdorf, 10,000
employees backed an egalitarian wage rise which gave the lowest
paid a 20 per cent increase against the top grade's 5 per cent. In this
case Council Executive pressure could not soften management
opposition and though the workers conceded temporary defeat,
they warned that 'the behaviour of the Managing Directors, in our
young Republic's greatest hour of need, will not be forgotten.'[13]

A pattern of militancy had become established. Every issue of
the bourgeois **Berliner Tageblatt** was filled with complaints about
'strikes and overpayment':

> What we have seen is a series of demands, and each time these are
> conceded the workers become more radical and demand more. The
> semi-skilled get wage rises taking them up to the level of the old

qualified workers, these in turn demand increases, soon the white-collar workers will join in this leapfrogging . . . Unofficial strikes are placing the viability and profitability of whole businesses in jeopardy.[14]

On 16 December 1918 all eyes turned to the first National Congress of Workers' and Soldiers' Councils. Its composition reflected the various methods by which delegates were chosen. In Berlin, election was by industrial sections — metalworkers, state employees, professionals — all held meetings in their workplaces. Even the unemployed met to choose their representatives. The larger units elected one person per thousand; the smaller ones were grouped together into units of a thousand. Berlin's poll topped one million and gave the SPD 49 per cent of the votes, the Independents 40 per cent (this included the Spartakists who did not stand under their own colours) and the bourgeois Democrats just 11 per cent.[15] Both Luxemburg and Liebknecht were excluded as non-workers.

In Dresden, on the other hand, balloting was by constituency, open to anyone earning below a certain level and on the basis of voting for party slates. Many of those who attended the National Council Congress were chosen by such means, which barely differed from parliamentary methods. As **Rote Fahne** pointed out:

> The election in Dresden falsified the composition of the workers' council . . . In elections to councils, unlike those to bourgeois parliaments, delegates are elected in the factories and obtain their mandate directly from the shopfloor. They are chosen for their class position as proletarians and are given a mandate with no precise time limits. The representative can be removed as soon as he loses the confidence of his electors. Obviously an election by party slate on the basis of geographical area makes this impossible . . . there can be no accountability.[16]

Of the 405 workers' council delegates to the Congress, the 179 workers were outnumbered by a bloc of 71 intellectuals and 164 full-time party and union officials. Phoney elections and the weakness of the left outside radical centres such as Berlin combined to produce a Congress dominated by the SPD, which had 288 delegates to the Independents' 90 (of whom only ten were Spartakists).[17]

It was no surprise therefore that one of the first decisions of the Congress was to support National Assembly elections to be held in January 1919. On hearing this, Däumig scornfully characterised the Congress as a 'suicide club', for it was signing the death warrant of the council movement. Only on the question of army reform, where the rank and file of all parties shared a fear of the old officer corps, was a radical motion carried. But such was the control by reformist bureaucrats at the Congress that the seven 'Hamburg points', as the motion was known, were simply handed on to Ebert, who ignored them. After the Congress closed, the leader of the small Spartakist delegation wrote with irony: 'What then were the points of vital and decisive significance upon which the Congress had to decide? Above all those that were rejected.'[18]

While reformists had tight control inside the Congress chamber, protest marches filled the streets outside. On Monday 16 December, 250,000 joined a procession led by Liebknecht to demand all power to the workers' and soldiers' councils. The core of this demonstration was formed by metalworkers' contingents. All the workers of Borsig, Daimler Mariendorfe, the DWM, Schwartzkopff, Knorr-Bremse and Löwe stopped work for the day. They were joined by at least 10,000 Siemens' workers.

This march was not a purely Spartakist show of strength, for they alone could not have pulled out the big engineering factories. One leaflet backing the demonstration was issued by a 'revolutionary committee' which also warned against 'Spartakist putschism'.[19] There is little doubt that this committee consisted of the revolutionary Obleute who, disillusioned by failure in the Council Executive, felt they had to operate as an independent force once again. This was an important development and marked a shift in Obleute thinking.

Now, after one month of social upheaval, the leading militant workers recognised that once the workers' council movement spread beyond the vanguard engineering plants to embrace the whole class, they faced new tasks. If socialists were to push the movement forward they could not sacrifice their independence to the workers' council itself, because this would make them no more than a mouthpiece for the mass of still non-revolutionary workers. The Obleute had learnt that to lead the class they must work *within* the mass movement of the councils, but as an *independent* current. To be wholly outside would mean sacrificing influence over organised labour, to be wholly inside without an autonomous position deprived one of the power of initiative.

The new orientation, shown in the 16 December demonstration, cleared the way for the Obleute to act once again as a vanguard, but did not imply that they had shaken off their confusion entirely.

This could be seen when Richard Müller introduced his new line at
a tempestuous five-hour meeting of the full Berlin council on 23
December:

> collectivisation was the most important task ahead; he insisted that it
> was the key question if one wanted to take political power. Mr Müller
> maintained that wage struggle should be considered as the initial
> phase of the second revolution, which could only occur if and when
> collectivisation had been directly implemented.[20]

This was a reversal of the relationship between politics and
economics in Müller's thinking. Until then he had seen the primary
task as wresting state power from the provisional government and
securing it for the workers' councils; economics had been secondary
to this. His lack of concern over the workplace struggle had in fact
led him to hand jurisdiction over factory councils to the union
officials on 15 November. Now he turned the equation upside
down — collectivisation at the point of production would have to
precede the seizure of political power. Unable to understand that in
the interplay of politics and economics, each struggle complements
the other. Müller swung from too much emphasis on one factor to
an equal but opposite exaggeration of the other.

Nevertheless Müller's recognition of the need for a second
revolution, taken in conjunction with the demonstration outside
the Council Congress, suggested a left turn by the Obleute and a
new alignment of revolutionary forces. On 16 December's demonstration, as in the days leading up to 9 November, Spartakists and
Obleute co-operated. Banners with slogans such as '8 hours' work,
8 hours' play, 8 hours' rest' were coupled with 'All power to the
workers' and soldiers' councils' — reproducing a fusion of economic
and political demands. It seemed then that the political and militant
vanguards needed for the first links of a chain of revolutionary
leadership were coming together. Unfortunately, the temporary
co-operation of the two was not at all the same as fusion within a
disciplined revolutionary party. Both sides mistrusted each other,
and their final marriage, in January 1919, was to come under
extreme pressure and too late to bear fruit.

While the National Council Congress had proved a disappoint-
ment to the left, in Berlin many workers turned their attention to
local battles. Yet again Neukölln saw skirmishing. On 16 December
an armed squad of provisional government supporters invaded the
Neukölln workers' and soldiers' council for the second time. They

had more success than before. The council was forced to postpone its plans for wholesale expropriations and allow the SPD to take up its seats on the local executive once more. The reactionary troops were withdrawn only when the Neukölln council permitted the municipal authorities to resume work.

In the factories the situation was equally unstable. One instance of this was the Cassirer Cable Company, whose workforce had been notably conservative during the war.[21] So with managerial blessing some right-wing white-collar workers tried to whip up a campaign of mass meetings to denounce the revolution. But the plan badly misfired. It was dangerous to bring any group of workers together in the atmosphere of 'red Berlin', for far from joining the reactionary witch-hunt, as had been expected, the mass meeting was in favour of collectivising the factory. To retrieve the situation the boss had to promise double wages for the day and payment for time lost attending the funeral of victims of the 6 December shootings.[22] For the moment the workers were placated.

As the tide of conflict lapped at the foundations of capitalism, new forces were drawn in. Printers, gasworkers, navvies, salesmen, shop assistants, even barmen were discovering the power to mould their working lives through their own activity.[23] The class struggle had gone beyond its usual limits, a civil war was approaching and the slightest spark could set it off. A typical incident during December was described by one young militiaman who was instructed to collect arms for the Neukölln workers' and soldiers' council:

> In the Spandau munitions works our leftist comrades were influential. They had taken over supplies of arms and ammunition to offer to soldiers' councils in the various districts. We set off to Spandau in two empty trucks . . . Our vehicles stayed together for we had heard that 'citizens' guards were operating in the western part of Berlin. Little bands of reactionary troops had formed in Charlottenburg, Wilmersdorf and Steglitz and there had been shooting incidents between them and weak, unarmed groups of workers . . . In Ruhleben . . . a dozen guards with rifles and grenades blocked our path. They were all youngsters. A lieutenant ordered us to hand over our arms, but soon our second truck came abreast. Sensing what was up our comrades arrived with primed grenades in their fists. This gave us the advantage. We disarmed the little uniformed sons of the bourgeoisie and sent them packing while we carried off their arms and helmets as booty.[24]

It was just such a struggle for control of armed power that set off a new right-wing offensive around Christmas time. Berlin was the home of a detachment of radical sailors led by Heinrich Dorrenbach and known as the People's Marine Division. On 21 December the government tried to reduce the division's strength from 3,000 to 600 men. To the sailors this did not just mean joining a rapidly growing dole queue, but was a challenge to the whole working-class movement.[25] The most serious combat took place around the military complex in Berlin's Marstall:

> . . . groups of civilians had joined in the fighting, members of the Spartakist League and other organisations — as well as sections of Eichhorn's Security Force and the Republican Soldiers' Corps who also backed up the sailors. Above all, working-class women, ignoring danger, had infiltrated the ranks of the Guards and made clear to them the outrage that was taking place. That broke the cohesion of the besiegers. The Guards threw their guns down and arrested their officers. By midday the sailors had won an all-out victory.[26]

As this was consolidated popular anger against the SPD erupted. This party had instigated what was nothing less than an attempt to destroy the military strength of the revolution. There was a spontaneous occupation of the building where its paper — **Vorwärts** — was printed.

The fighting had electrified the situation in Berlin. So blackened was the reputation of the Provisional Government that even the three Independent members felt compelled to resign from the Council of People's Commissars. Abandoning all semblance of radicalism, the SPD continued to stoke up the fires of reaction and called its supporters to an anti-Bolshevik demonstration. The 40,000 who turned out were no longer the workers who had supported the party in the years before 1914, but were overwhelmingly middle-class, for these now recognised the SPD as their political ally.[27] At the outskirts of Berlin the Freikorps prepared for another, larger offensive.

On the left too, the events of late December galvanised people into action. After years of hesitation, the Spartakist leaders decided to go beyond the limits of a primarily propaganda group operating within social democracy and form an independent organisation of revolutionaries — the German Communist Party (KPD). **Rote Fahne** explained the importance of this event:

> The revolutionary vanguard of the German proletariat has decided to form an independent revolutionary political party . . . It is the natural product of the development of the revolution, and with its foundation the second phase of the revolution begins . . . The illusions of 9 November are dashed . . . Now the contradictions have been clarified, the struggle sharpened and the maturity and self-determination of the revolution prepared . . . In place of the spontaneous we must set the systematic.[28]

But the course of the party's founding congress did not bode well for the creation of 'systematic' leadership. On 30 December 1918, its first day, the Spartakist leaders proposed that, despite their opposition to bourgeois forms of democracy, the new party should use the forthcoming National Assembly elections to publicise its views. Wrongly believing such elections to be irrelevant, the floor of the conference voted 62 to 33 against participation.[29] In another debate Paul Frölich argued for a slogan of 'Out of the Unions'. Though his position was neither endorsed nor defeated, the Communist Party did not regard consistent union work as important.

History was to prove these opinions terribly wrong. Just three weeks after the founding of the party, elections to the 'irrelevant' National Assembly saw 1,131,927 out of a possible 1,385,527 inhabitants of 'red' Berlin at the polls.[30] The Free Trade Unions which Frölich declared moribund grew from 1.5 to 8 million members between the end of the war and 1920.

Why did the floor of the conference not listen to Luxemburg and her experienced colleagues? When supporters flocked to Spartakism in the heady weeks following the 'November days', the organisation filled with enthusiastic young revolutionaries. Many of these had never confronted the difficulties of winning workers to their ideas, or tried to lead them in the daily class struggle. Such lessons could not be learnt overnight. They could only be developed over a long period of party building. The German Communist Party began 1919 with a membership all too easily tossed and turned by the swirling current of the moment, a membership which could not shape events but was instead shaped by them. The old Spartakists around Luxemburg were at the helm of the new party, but they could not control the rudder.

These problems were compounded by the Obleute's obstinate refusal to join in the new party. Politically both sides claimed full agreement. The apparent reason for failure of the unity talks was that the Obleute would not have adequate representation in the leading bodies of the party. But this excuse concealed deeper divisions, as Müller showed during the unity negotiations:

> On basic questions we and the Spartakist League are one . . . Like Liebknecht we do not favour abstention from parliament. But why then the obsession with street action? . . . Of course, we ourselves have argued that street action will become necessary, but in my opinion . . . **Rote Fahne** consistently inflames the masses to all manner of adventures. They are so aroused by this that they can easily fall prey to provocation . . .
> The masses outside are not as experienced as we are and cannot make as balanced judgement of the situation as ourselves. We must use a little foresight. I spoke against putschist tactics yesterday . . . and I oppose combination with the Communists.[31]

The sort of articles which Müller was referring to in **Rote Fahne** included passages like this one:

> Destruction and liquidation by the anarchy of capitalism, or re-birth through social revolution. The hour of decision has struck. If you believe in socialism, now is the time to show it through action.[32]

In the delicately poised situation of dual power such calls, unless they are going to be backed up by solid planning and organisation, can easily play into the hands of the enemy. While Luxemburg used reasoned arguments concerning the need to convince people how the bourgeois parliament was a dead-end, her paper treated the subject thus:

> The clenched fist of the revolutionary proletariat will rise from the National Assembly and banners will fly inscribed with the fiery letters — 'All power to the workers' and soldiers' councils' — that is our reply to the National Assembly.[33]

Whatever the theoretical maturity of the Spartakists, their daily paper did not reflect it. Lenin had approached the Russian crisis of dual power most carefully. With the situation balanced on a knife edge, the great danger was that a minority section would leap into action before the working class was ready. **Pravda**'s policy had been to 'patiently explain' the need for workers' power. Only when this had been done and a majority of workers won to the idea was the call for an all-out offensive conceivable.

In Germany the problems facing revolutionaries when they attempted to found a revolutionary party fully two months into a revolution were now revealed. If the fusion of the political and militant vanguards had been made some years before, it would have quickly shown that the methods of both, the one tending towards propaganda, the other to factory agitation, were complementary. If the Communist Party had grown on this basis, it could only have benefitted from the enthusiasm which its youthful recruits now brought with them. As it was, the party that was created at the end of 1918 was poorly equipped for what was to come.

In spite of these troubles, the extraordinary atmosphere at the New Year brought thousands towards the Communist Party. On 2 January 1919 Spandau's Independent Socialists voted by 400 to 5 to join the Communists. The next day Charlottenburg's Independents came over *en bloc*. In Neukölln the local Independent branch dissociated itself from Barth after he debated with Liebknecht over the future of the revolution.[34] But this rally to revolutionary ideas was still not general enough to be decisive.

Workers' struggle in January 1919

Victory over reaction at Christmas inspired militant workers with a feeling of confidence unknown since early November. This was illustrated by an amazing meeting of the engineers' union on 29 December. A full-time official named Tirpitz announced that he had negotiated substantial pay increases for grinders, drillers, millers and several other grades of metal craftsmen. The assembled workers were impressed by the unprecedented progress made, but to Tirpitz's astonishment the deal was thrown out unanimously! The general feeling was that

> there should be no more bargaining with employers. Henceforth branch representatives should consider themselves servants of the established power of the workers, and in a socialist state there is no longer any room for negotiations with private capitalists.[35]

For once the tables were turned — the workers were refusing to recognise the employers!

Even the central Council Executive was revitalised. It reclaimed the absolute political authority it had enjoyed in its heyday, and announced that workers' councils were once again to be treated as the supreme power in the land.[36] Its claims were reinforced by demands at workshop level. Delegates from Berlin's factory councils announced that from now on:

> The workers' [factory] council *will* use its revolutionary authority and no-one dare stand in its way . . .
>
> 1. In the large factories the workers' council has executive powers over production, wages and working conditions. During the transition to socialism it will take care of the maintenance of production, attentively and energetically organising for the imminent collectivisation of the large industrial concerns.
>
> 2. The workers' council of every large enterprise will act as the management. It will supervise and intervene in all technical and financial matters.[37]

The local workers' councils met and presented their own ultimatum concerning municipal government:

> All political power is to be in the hands of the workers' and soldiers' councils as executive organs of the revolutionary proletariat. These councils are called upon to direct the authorities in the community towards the aims of revolutionary socialism . . . Therefore the communal workers' and soldiers' councils must not only have rights of supervision but possess absolute executive power.[38]

The three threads of struggle, at the level of the central state, local community and factories were now woven together.

However there were limitations to the upsurge of militancy. The workers' council movement was registering a growing determination to build on the foundations of the revolution, but the general attitude to the coming struggle was still fairly defensive. Franz Beiersdorf, an ex-sailor who now worked at Siemens, described the tenor of workshop discussions at the beginning of 1919:

> All comrades were of the opinion that emphasis must be put on the factory; each factory must be made a fortress in which collectivisation could be carried through. It was suggested that I take charge of organising military supplies to the factories so that when the time came, as it must, they could be defended.
>
> I thought the slogan 'make every factory a fortress' was correct. A whole number of my colleagues wanted arms for they took the call for a National Assembly to be open treason to the achievements of the revolution. They demanded, as before: 'All power to the workers' and

soldiers' councils' until our major demand is won — collectivisation of the big factories.[39]

The truth was that the majority of the rank and file wished to use their collective strength to *protect* the achievements of 9 November rather than take a decisive military step forward. Beiersdorf's assessment was to prove thoroughly accurate in January 1919.

This period saw a complex situation. The councils had passed resolutions which challenged the authority of the old state, management and municipal government; but they were not part of a consciously planned revolutionary advance, and the clearest revolutionaries (a minority even within the ranks of the new Communist Party) were hardly in a position to approach the new crisis with the necessary organisation and leadership. The more impatient revolutionaries judged the time ripe for the armed overthrow of Ebert's government. They knew that the most advanced section of workers in Berlin had survived two reactionary coups in as many weeks and now had an education in class warfare without parallel in the rest of Germany. But what they did not seem to appreciate was that this very uniqueness could cause problems. Only certain groups in the capital would support an immediate insurrection. Even if the new revolution were successful in Berlin, there was little guarantee that the rest of the country would follow. A solitary 'red Berlin' was doomed.

Once again the question of vanguard leadership was all-important. If the revolutionary socialists, together with the best militants, could pull the mass of Berliners behind them and if their action met a sympathetic response in the rest of Germany — then the sort of combination that made the October 1917 insurrection in Russia a success would have come into being. As it was there were serious obstacles in the way of such a combination — obstacles that could have been spotted by simply referring to the workers' council. For revolutionaries quite simply lacked a majority in the workers' council movement in Berlin and elsewhere in Germany. No amount of heroism could change that fact, or substitute for widespread support.

In a revolutionary struggle, when social conflict is at its highest, the forces of entire classes are pitted against each other. Socialists are often accustomed to working in smaller-scale sectional struggles. But even on this level the question of leadership — that vital connection between a vanguard and its base of support — is tremendously important. When the fate of a whole class is involved, the close relationship between the two is still more essential. The connection between the vanguard and its base cannot be measured passively, by secret ballots and the like. In class war the opponent will allow no time for such legal niceties. There must instead be a sober assessment of the likelihood whether masses of workers will be willing to *act* on forward initiatives, for these need the central-ised authority of mass workers' organisation behind them to be effective. In the case of Germany, the workers' councils still had the support of a vast number of the most revolutionary workers and could not be ignored.

Even if the left had understood this, the upsurge of feeling generated by the attack on the People's Marine Division during Christmas had to be channelled in some direction. In Russia the Bolsheviks faced a similar situation of localised action in Petrograd during July 1917. They knew that insurrection was premature on a national scale and so, while marching with the mass demonstra-tions of the 'July days', they convinced Petrograd's workers that they must wait for the rest of Russia to catch them up politically. Only a mass party with roots deep in the working class could have shaped and controlled this local explosion of feeling.

In Berlin the situation was reversed. Despite the wish of many Communists and Obleute, both groups were dragged into all-out combat by the forward momentum of the most revolutionary, if not the most politically perceptive workers. In doing so they fell into a government trap.

On 4 January 1919 the provisional government sacked Emil Eichhorn, Berlin's Independent Socialist police chief. This move was more than a personal attack, it was an act of open defiance to the left. Both the Obleute and Communists were divided about what to do. A section of the Obleute around Richard Müller hesitated before unleashing a civil war for which they were not prepared. The Communist Party's Central Committee also coun-selled caution in dealing with Eichhorn's dismissal and resolved that:

> all slogans which would necessarily imply the removal of the govern-ment at that stage, must be avoided. Our slogans had therefore to be precise and were as follows: annul the sacking of Eichhorn, disarm the counter-revolutionary troops . . . arm the proletariat. None of these slogans implied the overthrow of the government.[40]

But Ledebour, a founder of the Independents, and Liebknecht, who flouted the line of the Communist Party's Central Committee, decided to make an attempt at an insurrection. Bowled over by the confused but angry mood prevailing among many workers, the various organisations of the left were drawn behind these two undisciplined leaders. On 5 January a statement which *did* imply the removal of the Ebert government and bearing the signatures of prominent Communists, Independents and Obleute was circulated. Its key passage stated:

> By this blow directed against the Berlin police headquarters, the entire German proletariat, the entire German revolution is to be struck. Workers! Party Comrades! *This you cannot and must not permit!* . . . Down with the despotism of Ebert, Sheidemann, Hirsch and Ernst![41]

The response to this call was one of the largest demonstrations Berlin had ever witnessed:

> From the Roland as far as the Victoria stood the proletarians, shoulder to shoulder . . . An army of 100,000 men such as Ludendorff never saw.
>
> Then a miracle happened. The crowd stood solidly in the cold and fog from nine in the morning. Somewhere their leaders were sitting in council. The fog descended and the masses still stood. But the leaders were deliberating. The masses were all agog with excitement; they wanted something to do, only a word to quiet their feelings, hardly anyone knew what, for the leaders were deliberating. The fog came down once more, and with it the dusk. The crowds went sadly home; they had intended great things, and had done nothing. For the leaders were deliberating.[42]

Those who had conjured the mass protest into existence were in a difficult position. To retreat now would be seen as cowardly. To go forward would mean all-out insurrection. Furious debates again confirmed how deeply opinion was divided. In separate discussions Luxemburg, Müller and Däumig maintained that the moment was premature. They were again beaten by the alliance of Ledebour for the left Independents, Scholze of the Obleute and Liebknecht.

The lessons learnt by the Obleute concerning the need to operate freely but *within* the organised workers' and soldiers' council movements, the insistence of the Spartakists (now the

Communist Party) that the majority of workers must agree with their programme before they would take power — all these were swept aside. That this should happen was almost inevitable because neither the Obleute nor Communists were capable of directing the movement in such a way that it could tread the narrow path that divided the mass protest from open insurrection. Instead the effective choice was to join the onward rush of the revolutionary minority, or abandon it completely. There was no more time to lament preparations left undone. Despite their doubts the Berlin left threw in their lot with a 52-strong 'revolutionary committee'.

The decision to form a 'revolutionary committee' to take on the government was not made by the workers' councils, but by people acting outside them. Indeed, despite their recent resurgence, the councils would no doubt have opposed immediate insurrection against Ebert. To attack without the support of the councils proved a dangerous gamble. The revolutionary committee called for a general strike, and once again demonstrators streamed in to occupy the **Vorwärts** building. By 7 January the strike was gathering pace, accompanied by sporadic fighting on the streets.

A full-scale military confrontation with the armed forces of the government was now inevitable. They were well prepared: a small but strongly organised force of Freikorps quickly descended on the city. Against these ruthless and disciplined troops there were, despite the hundreds of thousands of strikers, fewer than 10,000 men resolved to fight for power.[43] Even the People's Marine Division, whose support for the insurrection Dorrenbach had rashly promised without consulting its members, doggedly refused to be involved.

Furthermore, Eichhorn's position as police chief, which had an obvious significance for Berliners, did not immediately command interest outside the capital. Leftists in other areas only added their active support in the last stages of the fight, when it was too late and too limited to affect the outcome.

When the German working class had been united against the Kaiser, or stood against armed attacks during December, its power had been immense. But when the vanguard took a step which separated it from the masses, *both* were paralysed.

Between 9 and 12 January, right-wing troops — the Maikäfer, the Reichstag regiments, Rheinhard volunteers and Potsdam battalions — took control of the capital in fierce house-to-house fighting. The massive strike movement remained at the level of factory defence. Schwartzkopff, always one of the less radical workplaces, was the first factory to crack. As the bloodletting reached a climax, the workers there, together with those at AEG, called for an end to civil war. With 40,000 people behind it, this appeal did not stop the fighting, but sowed confusion amongst those in the midst of battle.

There had always been some on the revolutionary committee who were half-hearted in their commitment to the insurrection, and this call for peace from Schwartzkopff gave the waverers their chance to quit. The Communists, committed against their will by Liebknecht, were left to take the brunt of the attack. On 13 January the Obleute appealed for a return to work, leaving those in the **Vorwärts** building to a hopeless defence. Pulverised by artillery barrages it soon had to be surrendered.

In Spandau too there had been bitter fighting during which workers' forces occupied the town hall and strategic points. The Freikorps retaliated to reimpose the hegemony of capitalism. This took a brutally simple form — 60 machine guns were deployed around the munitions complex and the workers were literally driven back to their benches at gun-point.[44]

The rising was smashed and the Freikorps, under Noske — Social Democrat and self-confessed 'bloodhound' of revolution — exacted a deadly revenge. About 200 people were killed in January, nine-tenths of them coming from the ranks of the revolutionaries. This compared with 18 on 9 November, the same number of 6 December and around 70 during the suppression of the attack on the People's Marine Division.[45] The most famous victims of January 1919 were Luxemburg and Liebknecht, whose murders were a terrible blow to the young Communist Party.

The January confrontation began and ended outside the workers' council movement. With incredulity **Rote Fahne** asked in the thick of the fighting: 'Where are the workers' councils, the organs called to lead the revolutionary masses? They do not exist; they are not even meeting.'[46] **Rote Fahne**'s question was put wrongly — if the workers' councils were absent from the fighting, it meant the masses were not ready to be led in a revolutionary direction at that moment, for despite their mistakes, the councils were still the only organisation which had the allegiance of the rank and file. Neither the small and inexperienced Communist Party, which was a political head without a body, nor the Obleute, militants acting without the support of their shopfloor base, could substitute for the vital elements of a mass revolutionary party or class unity through the workers' council.

But though the workers' movement was bowed, it was not broken by the Freikorps in January 1919. In fact the mass of Berlin workers were driven leftwards, for the action of Ebert and Noske was a powerful lesson in political reality.

The aftermath

The revolutionaries had misjudged the situation. Even in the capital there had been insufficient preparation, not only militarily, but above all in politically winning the majority for action. The fatal flaw in timing was illustrated by a series of elections that followed soon afterwards. While even geographical ballots showed a general leftward shift in voting,[47] the swing away from the reformist SPD inside the workers' and soldiers' council was even more striking:

Percentage of votes for workers' parties in Berlin council elections[48]

	Nov '18	Dec '18	Jan '19	Feb '19	Mar '19
SPD	61	55	51	43	36
Independents	39	45	49	47	64
Communists	—	—	—	9	—

So just one month after the murder of Luxemburg and Liebknecht the SPD had lost its lead in Berlin, and the leftward trend was to continue.

History has given the events of January 1919 the title of 'the Spartakist rising'. The left did indeed fall for Ebert's provocation, but the fighting was as much caused by a counter-revolutionary attempt of the right Social Democrats and reactionaries as by an offensive of the left.[49] The following account shows both the defensive attitude of most workers in the January fighting, and the government's intention to exploit the pretext of insurrection not only to eliminate 'the reds', but to strike at the very roots of working-class confidence on the shopfloor:

> In the arms and munitions factory of Charlottenburg-Martinickenfelde the workers arranged a voluntary rota on 6 January to defend the factory and its stocks. The workers wanted to secure their workplace

for everyone, irrespective of party affiliation. They refused to deliver machine guns to the Military High Command. With great care the guard made sure that the factory would not be damaged. But on Friday night government troops shot at those on duty. When Sunday morning arrived and the military advanced, the factory was surrendered rather than provoke bloodshed.

Unaware of this earlier decision, the relief watch arrived at midday to begin their tour of duty, only to find the army in occupation. There was one lieutenant and 40 soldiers. They seized each of the nine members on the watch and searched them for weapons. Three were bearing arms and all were taken prisoner. The officer threatened to blow them apart with grenades if they so much as moved!

The men were eventually released, but when the return to work came:

> the manager behaved like a petty dictator. Secure in his authority once more, he slandered the workers as a bunch of thieves and a rabble . . . Believing he was king of the castle he announced that the factory was to shut on 31 January . . . and that the workers' council would have no more say on the matter.[50]

All those pleas by managers and reformist politicians to save the economy, all the dire warnings of economic decline, were a sham. The real concern was not the maintenance of production, but the full bellies of the capitalists. For, once the workers' resistance was broken, those who had bleated about the 'common interest' had no qualms in shutting factory after factory. The repression was of benefit to union officials too. Tirpitz, the man who had been told to refuse recognition to the employers, now won a demoralised acceptance of his wage deal.[51] The most militant engineering plant in Berlin, the DWM, had been on the point of collectivisation, but now the bosses sacked thousands and cut back on output. When the factory council protested to the government, the 'socialist' Minister told them that their only hope was to appeal to the 'moral generosity of the capitalists', an answer greeted with bitter laughter by the workforce.[52]

Conclusion

The period discussed was by no means the whole history of the German revolution. Even as the last pockets of workers' resistance

were wiped out in Berlin, an insurrectionary coal strike was
developing in the Ruhr and in Bremen and Hamburg workers'
councils were moving to seize full local power. And as early as
March 1919 Berlin was again embroiled in a massive strike.

Yet the months of November 1918 to January 1919 were
enough to reveal the fundamental dynamics of a revolutionary
process — how the complex articulation of politics and economics,
organisation and action, contributed to the development of history.
Within this the workers' council did not have a clearly mapped-out
course. It played only a part in determining events and was stretched
and moulded by the wider struggle of workers. In revolution no
single element could be treated in isolation. The process involved
integration of struggle at the point of production, the local community and the state. Any strategy for workers' power had to take
account of these intersecting social relations as well as trying to
master the kaleidoscopic transformations of class consciousness
that occur in such periods.

Although the first Berlin workers' and soldiers' council of
January 1918 had been disbanded after the general strike, it had
established a tradition, an authority acknowledged by millions. So
on 9 November 1918 the clandestine Council Executive acted as an
umbrella under which the Spartakists and Obleute were able to
bring the whole Berlin working class on to the street. Shopfloor
organisation and confidence prevented any attempt by the SPD to
foist Berlin with a council dominated by party and union bureaucrats as it had done in so many other places. Outside the capital
many workers' and soldiers' councils were no more than committees of union officials and Social Democratic functionaries, but the
structure of workers' power in 'red Berlin' was firmly based on the
rank and file. By extending their control into production, the
community and the state, the councils revealed their potential to
liberate the whole of society and abolish the sham of parliament.

However once the workers' council ceased to be the property
of the engineering vanguard but was established as a class organisation, its democratic nature put it into the hands of its enemies —
the SPD. Still, the situation was far from static. The Council
Executive was caught in a contradictory position. As a mass forum
the council reflected a clash between the general reformist ideas of
the majority, and the immediate impact of the social crisis which
was driving this majority to the left. Thus it was the Obleute who,
though in a minority position on the Executive, were often its

effective mouthpiece, because they faithfully reflected these tensions in their centrist positions.

Every time the council leadership lost the route of the revolutionary process — the integration of economic and political struggle — rank-and-file initiatives acted to correct its course. This was the clearest in the case of the Executive/union accord. Wave upon wave of economic strikes dragged the central council back from capitulation to the unholy alliance of full-time officials and management. Dependence on action from below was also illustrated in the battles of December 1918. Both times the central council itself did nothing, for its reactions were not nearly as swift as the situation required. It took a determined initiative by the most advanced sections to use mass activity at the base to free the Council Executive from imprisonment and at Christmas, protect the revolution from physical emasculation.

The council had an indispensable part to play in the revolution: first as a barometer of working-class feeling and second as the legitimator of action. If the revolution was to be carried forward it was essential that the left should work as an independent vanguard within the council movement. This necessity was tragically overlooked in January 1919 when Liebknecht mistook an enthusiastic but essentially defensive reaction to the Christmas events as the green light for insurrection. The workers' council was still controlled by the SPD. Until revolutionaries had displaced it as the dominant force in the workers' movement, not only of Berlin but of other key working-class centres, an overthrow of the SPD-led government was premature.

The extreme care taken by Lenin and the Bolsheviks to integrate their party's action with the development of the soviets was in striking contrast to the situation in Germany. While the Bolshevik Party fought for its own political positions through its press and daily agitation, Lenin took a party majority in the workers' mass organisations — the soviets of Petrograd and Moscow — as the essential prerequisite for a successful insurrection. Once this was achieved, the vanguard party led the most advanced soviet in Petrograd to seize power. It presented this power to the national Congress of Soviets, thus establishing a workers' state on an all-Russian scale. This meant the second Russian revolution became the act of the masses themselves, led by the most far-sighted section of the working class.

The Spartakists, for all their belief in the workers' councils, were unable to play a role equivalent to the Bolsheviks. The latter had a mass organisation with deep roots in the working class. Therefore the party was able to judge the mood of the workers far more accurately than the Spartakists. The Bolsheviks had a long experience of campaigning for mass support and were in sufficient numbers to ensure their arguments were voiced in every part of the class. The rank-and-file Spartakists lacked knowledge of how to win people to their ideas and did not have enough supporters to make themselves heard clearly by any but a limited number of workers.

The German working class was larger and potentially just as effective as that of Russia. It began the revolution in November 1918 with a system of workers' and soldiers' councils which held real power in society. Though council debates were not recorded for posterity, it is clear from contemporary newspaper accounts that they were unequalled as a forum for debate, in which rank-and-file leaders could thrash out arguments and begin to organise society democratically from the bottom upwards. The councils were the creation of a truly revolutionary situation, and contributed to deepening its effect both by destroying the old society and attempting to establish a new one.

The revolution in Berlin was not something that happened outside the daily life of the masses. The future could not be determined by the grand phrases of professional politicians. Much as Ebert would have loved political activity to remain at the level of a National Assembly elected geographically every few years, the workers pulled politics down from its pedestal. On the streets the working class assumed local power directly through militias of workers and sympathetic soldiers. In the factories control was wrested from the employers. There was a continual interplay of politics and economics at the most basic level.

The effect of this process was clear. The political upheaval of 9 November 1918 gave workers the confidence to fight at the point of production. While the majority began the revolution with reformist ideas, the experience of direct struggle pushed them towards more radical political positions. If in the revolutionary whirlwind the workers' councils took false steps, stumbled and eventually fell, they were the steps of the working class itself, groping forward towards its liberation.

The working class had established the machinery of a socialist state, but what was lacking was the subjective will to set it in

motion. The tragedy was that through lack of guidance, a movement with immense promise had been halted. This was not just a
disaster for Germany, but also for the beleaguered soviet power in
Russia, whose survival depended on international revolution.

1919 began with the defeat of the 'Spartakist rising'. But the
months that followed showed that the flame of revolution had been
kindled in country upon country. A new opportunity presented
itself in Italy, now entering upon its 'two red years'.

Chapter Nine

ITALY: COUNCILS AND BEYOND

THE CIRCUMSTANCES in which the Italian workers' council movement took shape mark it out from previous examples. It grew up towards the end of 1919 — later than its counterparts. So whereas socialists in Petrograd, Glasgow and Berlin worked in difficult wartime conditions and had to improvise at almost every step, in Turin, Italy's most militant industrial centre, revolutionaries had these earlier experiences to draw on. This later beginning gave the Italian movement a theoretical overview of the workers' council that was missing in the rest of Western Europe. Also, because the war was already over, there was not such an obvious focus for the political activity of revolutionaries.

Under the leadership of Antonio Gramsci workers in Turin attempted to build a workers' council movement to which all other workers' organisations — such as the Socialist Party and the trade unions — were subordinated. This exclusive emphasis on an attempt to build a workers' council state made Turin the site of an experiment in 'pure' council socialism which allowed some very clear conclusions to be drawn. Although ultimately unsuccessful, this experiment took Gramsci, the most capable of Turin's revolutionaries, through the workers' council movement and beyond — to glimpse a *total* process of revolutionary change which was especially relevant to socialists working in the reformist conditions of the West.

Turin, capital of the Piedmont region of Italy, exhibited many of the characteristics typical of Glasgow and Berlin, but in a more extreme form. It was a supremely modern engineering city. Population grew from 200,000 to 430,000 in the latter half of the nineteenth century, but the greatest expansion occurred in the early twentieth century. In the first two decades the numbers living in the industrial districts of Barriera di Milano and San Paolo rocketed from 4,400 to 90,200! In the war years alone the number of factory workers in the city doubled, to reach 150,000.[1] The resultant overcrowding in housing was terrible, with almost half Turin's families crammed into one and two-roomed dwellings.[2]

In 1920 Gramsci wrote: 'Today Turin is the industrial city, the proletarian city, *par excellence*. The Turin working class is solid, disciplined and *distinct* as in few other cities in the world.'[3] But to reach this position the workers had to go through important struggles before and during the First World War.

In the nineteenth century nothing pointed to a special destiny for the capital of Piedmont. It was the arrival of car manufacture with firms such as Fiat in 1899 that set Turin on the road to revolutionary change. The car companies had such a dynamic growth that they soon emptied the local reservoir of skilled men in the old foundries and small workshops. Employers had to find new sources of labour and they were not choosy. As the first leader of Turin's employers' organisation put it: 'There was a formidable scramble for all sorts of workers from the most diverse trades. Carpenters, masons, simple labourers were trained and in a few months were baptised as mechanics.'[4] This was a very different workforce to the engineers of Britain, where the ASE imposed a minimum of five years' training before a man could be considered properly skilled.

Many workers came to Turin from the backward agricultural regions of Sardinia and the South, and working in a car factory catapulted them from semi-feudalism into ultra-modern industrial capitalism. In Italy large-scale capitalist enterprise was limited to one area — the 'industrial triangle' formed by Turin, Milan and Genoa. This pioneering bloc of capitalism had a dramatic impact on the labour force and produced both a spontaneous and unorganised anarchist reaction and a more orderly, if innately conservative, socialist movement.

The contrast between Italy's labour movement and the older established movements in Britain and Germany could hardly have been greater. Workers in Glasgow's engineering factories, for example, had evolved from a situation in which the skilled man had a definite status (even if management was doing its best to undermine it). Here is a description of one Clyde metalworker:

> He used to resent being watched at his work. When the manager brought guests through the shop he used to switch off the power and

walk away from his machine — 'bad enough to have to work in a
factory anyhow without being put on exhibition doing it.'[5]

Turinese workers had no established position to defend. They
were often unused to factory life and saw themselves as peasants in
overalls rather than conscious members of a working class. Their
style of protest was conditioned by this. As one Fiat worker put it:

> Before the First World War, we workers were humble, despised,
> exploited, scorned; we counted for nothing. We had everyone against
> us, the boss, white-collar staff, shopkeepers, local government offi-
> cials, everyone, yes, everyone was against us. Understandably, even
> without organisation there were spontaneous walk-outs. Naturally we
> came out for serious reasons, but what happened then? First of all we
> chucked stones at the street lamps smashing the glass, then we
> overturned the first tram that came along, ripping out the seats and
> anything that could be destroyed. Why? Because the street lamps
> stood for the local government which was our enemy, the tram was
> owned by local government, the boss was associated with this local
> power. They were all part of an establishment that despised and
> scorned us, and if any of it could be smashed up, that was okay by us.[6]

In Turin the clash between workers and employers concentrated on control of the production process rather than wages. The
high investment costs of modern factories made bosses keen to
maintain a continuous flow of production and they demanded a
pliable and disciplined workforce to go with it. The struggle,
therefore, was not so much about the price of labour in the market
place, but the fact that employers felt they should have an army of
obedient wage-slaves once their money had been handed over.
This was to make the battle for workers' control a central concern
of the workers' council movement.

Italy's labour movement included a strong rank-and-file
current. In Turin particularly, workers first entered production at
a time when it was organised on mass production lines with a
thorough division of labour. The main British engineering unions
had, in the mid-nineteenth century, grown on the basis of more
backward production methods in which the craftsman had a virtual
monopoly of technical know-how. This basis did not exist in
twentieth century Italy and the Italian Federation of Metalworkers,
FIOM, was pitifully weak. Formed only in 1901 it had just 11,471
members in 1914, despite being the strongest union in the country.[7]

Such trade unions as did exist faced serious competition from independent shopfloor organisation based on the large collective units. This first appeared at the turn of the century as a spontaneously elected strike committee or *internal commission*, involving trade union members and non-members alike.

> The idea of retaining permanently a body intended to lead a particular strike, and entrusting it with the job of making agreements and defending rights was natural enough. By this means a form of workers' representation covering a whole factory was created. It was superior to a trade union as it was linked to the way work was organised in modern factories.[8]

Despite the undercurrent of rank-and-file revolt, independent shopfloor organisation was not easy to sustain over long periods, and these germs of the workers' council withered in the unfavourable conditions before the war. When they were not buoyed up by a generalised militancy they tended to fall into the hands of a few committed activists — usually the trade unionist minority.

Thus in the period before the First World War the embryonic rank-and-file organisations were co-opted by the unions and came to be a method of control by union officials. Whereas the original spirit behind the internal commissions had been mass rebellion against management, the union bureaucracy wanted them to enforce negotiated agreements.

In spite of these constraints, a tradition of shopfloor organisation did survive in a distorted and bureaucratised form, until militancy after the war liberated it from the shackles of the union full-timers. The internal commissions became the fundamental building blocks of the Italian workers' council movement during the *Biennio Rosso*, the 'two red years' of 1919 to 1921. They alone could harness the potential of the working class.

The problems facing other forms of mass organisation were highlighted in two contrasting strikes just before the war. The background to these strikes was a boom in car demand which in one year led to a 23 per cent increase in productivity at Fiat.[9] To sustain this expansion and avoid stoppages, the employers wanted a new contract with the metalworkers' union, FIOM. The officials tried to balance their members' wishes against these management demands and the 1912 contract reflected these pressures. Although only a small minority of car workers were members, the union was made the sole negotiator. Workers were to receive an 8 per cent rise plus a cut in hours. The carrot of higher wages was designed to make the stick of managerial discipline more acceptable. For under the new deal the employers had the right to instant dismissal and the strict enforcement of regulations, while shopfloor representation was abolished and unofficial strikes banned.[10]

FIOM's contract was bitterly opposed by Turin's anarcho-syndicalists. Since Bakunin's anarchist ideas had taken root in Italy in 1872 this movement had been a potent force. The acknowledged leader of Italian anarchism was for over 50 years Errico Malatesta. His work centred on propaganda for a 'society without authority, agitation by anarchists in the workers' movement and trade unions, direct and revolutionary action.'[11] Action, rather than any rigorous theory, was the hallmark of the anarchists. They easily adapted to the influence of French syndicalism at the turn of the century with its emphasis on a general strike to bring down the system.

In union affairs the anarcho-syndicalists rejected centralised organisation because they believed authority of any sort weakened the free initiative of the masses. Their union method consisted in presenting demands to the employers and refusing to compromise in any way. One example of their approach was the strike they led in Turin. A gut reaction against managerial dicatatorship as embodied in FIOM's deal, which sacrificed rights at work for higher pay, led to a prolonged and desperate anarcho-syndicalist-inspired strike directed as much against the engineering union as the employers. After two months of struggle, maintained with virtually no organisation or funds, the workers had to accept defeat and the loss of those few concessions offered in the original agreement.

In their journal FIOM officials wrote of the strikers as a disorderly rabble. Yet within the year the same workers received unqualified praise from FIOM's officials when, under *their* leadership (and in the best disciplined union manner) they undertook a 75-day official stoppage which effectively recovered the ground lost in the earlier anarcho-syndicalist strike.[12]

These two strikes symbolised the divided soul of the Turin labour movement — veering from unformed rebellion to organised but officially constrained action. Despite its defeat, the anarcho-syndicalist strike had touched a chord with those who hated to compromise with capitalism. It had tapped their revolutionary enthusiasm. The FIOM-led stoppage showed there were also those who, though perhaps more used to the system, also better understood how it had to be fought through combination in disciplined ranks. But neither pure spontaneism nor bureaucratic unionism could bring these vital elements of revolt and organisation together in one movement.

The major political force among Turin workers was the Italian Socialist Party (PSI). It was much smaller than the German SPD on the national scale, with just over 58,000 members in 1914 on the eve of war. Locally the party in Turin had doubled in the previous ten years to reach a membership of 2,412, four-fifths of whom were manual workers.[13] Even before the war the Turin Socialist branch was dominated by radicals. They were soon complemented by the growing intellectual power of Antonio Gramsci and Angelo Tasca, leaders of the local youth and student movement.

Nowhere did the First World War have such a profound economic and social impact as Turin. But the road to the trenches was not smoothed by the open betrayal of labour leaders, as it had been elsewhere. This was partly because Italy joined the alliance against Germany only in 1915, which gave time for the true horrors of modern warfare to be revealed. A few days before Italy's declaration of hostilities against Austria and Germany a spontaneous general strike swept the city as workers fought on the streets against pro-war campaigners. While many ranks of the Second International had been crushed by the steamroller of imperialism, Turin's socialists threw themselves onto the barricades and battled to resist the violent repression that followed.

In the process 'the local Socialist Party succeeded, for the first time, in going beyond the restricted confines of the internal life of the party.'[14] This extension of activity began the process by which the political vanguard joined with the vanguard of militant workers to grapple with the common problem of war. Political ideas were inevitably sharpened by the difficult issues which developed as military involvement came closer:

> There was an acute struggle between reformists and revolutionaries in the unions and party. This was not a struggle outside the factory, but bonded together all the forces of the left, creating an intense and direct relationship between politics and industry, for the daily problems of the workplace, bursting forth on all sides, were carried into all the workers' organisations.[15]

Wartime struggles

To their credit, the leaders of the PSI rejected imperialism throughout the war, but while socialists in Turin manned the barricades, the party's national directorate passed resolutions. They criticised those socialist parliamentary deputies who urged collaboration with the military effort, but behind the PSI's internationalist rhetoric there lay a dangerous passivity. The party's attitude to its wartime tasks was expressed in its daily paper, **Avanti!**:

> Study, yes, for today we can collect the materials necessary for action tomorrow.
> But action, today, on concrete and immediate questions? No, no, no!
> . . . The party acts . . . through the press and meetings to arouse mass pressure — this is parliamentary work. But today even such action has been blocked . . . by censorship, the banning of meetings and restrictions on parliament.

Far from fighting such limitations on its work, and despite its denunciation of nationalism, the party directorate lacked any notion of political action outside parliament, concluding:

> Even supposing action were possible . . . What might it be? . . . Winning demands that cost the state money (social legislation), no, because no money is available on account of the war. Winning demands that undermine the defensive or offensive powers of the state (penal legislation), no, because the state demands all its strength on account of the war. Winning demands that diminish capitalist profits (relations between capital and labour), no, because capital will not give up without struggle and for the time being class struggle is forbidden on account of the war.[16]

The party maintained a position of intransigence in principle, but did so while remaining totally passive in practice. Its left-wing rhetoric did however have an influence on many leading revolutionaries. Thus it was not until the end of 1920 that Gramsci felt the absolute need to finish politically with the Socialist Party. He made the organisational break *after* the revolution had passed its peak.

The reason for this was that the PSI appeared to have somewhat different politics to the more conventional parties of the Second International such as the BSP in Britain or Germany's SPD. The outbreak of war exposed the majority of BSP and SPD leaders to be unashamed reformists. But the reformist wing of the PSI, around Turati, was a minority among the party leadership. Although Turati had the support of the PSI's parliamentary deputies the party's directorate, which represented the majority of members, took a position of 'intransigence'. Prominent national figures in the party such as Giacomo Serrati proclaimed themselves to be revolutionary Marxists and unwilling to compromise their opposition to the war. He like others spent some time in jail for sticking to these principles.

However, in terms of practical leadership in the class struggle, a mere refusal to compromise revolutionary principle is woefully inadequate if answers to the day-to-day problems of workers are not offered as well. In reality the PSI's intransigent wing left the field free for wheeling and dealing by reformist elements in the parliamentary group and the trade union leaderships.

Turin's socialists, however, were more energetic in their opposition to war than the directorate, and the party's branch here remained one of the most radical in the country. From the start its paper, **Il Grido del Popolo (The Cry of the People)** condemned any compromise with the warmongers. It attacked right-wing socialists in parliament and criticised union participation in the Mobilisation Committees as a 'veiled form of collaboration with the war'.[17] In November 1916 left influence was confirmed by elections to the local branch executive. The successful slate included revolutionary metalworkers such as Giovanni Boero and its manifesto stated: 'We, the intransigent faction, say that only the class struggle can bring victory for the workers . . . Responsibility for the war must remain squarely with the government — no collaboration can be permitted.'[18]

Radical feeling was encouraged by news from Russia. Even before the October 1917 revolution, Turinese workers showed an affinity with the Bolsheviks, who were still barely known in most of Europe. A delegation of Mensheviks and Social Revolutionaries who visited Turin on 5 August 1917 were astounded to be met by 40,000 people shouting 'Viva Lenin!'[19]

Two weeks later riots gripped Turin. As in the case of Glasgow's rent strike of 1915 and the Leipzig general strike of April 1917, working-class women were the initiators. They faced intolerable pressures in Italy. In near famine conditions they were expected not only to queue for hours to collect what meagre rations were available but to work up to 12 hours a day in the factories. What

began as a hunger riot soon reached insurrectionary proportions
when the women made that crucial link with workers' industrial
power. This took the form of a walk-out at the Projectile Arsenal,
which had a predominantly female workforce, and at Diatto-Frejus.

German workers needed years of struggle to connect their
economic demands fully to the political campaign against the war.
In Britain the two were never joined. But reformist thinking was
barely implanted in Turin and the transition from one form of
action to another could be made in minutes, as this account from
the Diatto-Frejus strike shows:

> We stopped work and gathered outside the factory gate, shouting at
> the tops of our voices:
> 'We haven't eaten. We can't work. We want bread!'
> The boss of my firm, Pietro Diatto, was very worried and addressed
> the workers with words of milk and honey:
> 'You're quite right. How can anyone work without eating? I'll tele-
> phone military supplies straight away and order you a lorryful of
> bread. But for your own good and the good of your families, please go
> back to work in the meantime.'
> The workers fell quiet for a moment. For an instant they looked each
> other in the eyes, as though silently gauging each person's opinion and
> then all together, they cried:
> 'We couldn't care a damn about the bread! We want peace! Down
> with the profiteers! Down with the war!'[20]

On 24 August the movement reached its peak when angry
crowds converged on the centre of Turin, only to be driven back by
machine-guns and tanks. Four days of rioting followed, at the end
of which 50 demonstrators were dead and 800 jailed. For all its
intensity, the August 1917 riot had only begun to tap the collective
power of the organised workers. A wind of revolt had blown swiftly
through Turin's streets, but when it subsided the only evidence of
its passing were the corpses. Without organisation, no amount of
self-sacrifice and courage could overcome the centralised military
power of the state.

Physical confrontation having failed, action in the factories
was to acquire a new importance. Italian union leaders had been
paying lip-service to anti-imperialism, but covertly participating in
recruiting the working class for the war. Like the PSI their attitude
was 'neither support nor sabotage', which in practice left the
workers to fend for themselves. The rank and file soon revived the

system of shopfloor delegations, which now had to act without official blessing.

The trend to factory organisation was continually reinforced by the dramatic changes locally since the outbreak of hostilities. Vehicle production had been raised from the pre-war level of 9,200 to 20,000 a year and Turin was now the chief munitions producer for the Italian army.[21] Although new labour flooded into the factories, the continuing scarcity put the Turinese workforce in a powerful bargaining position. Even so, workers soon had to cope with a tremendous rise in prices. By 1918 real wages had dropped to 65 per cent of their pre-war value.[22] Shopfloor commissions alone stood in the way of a complete collapse in living standards, for they championed economic struggle in a whole series of industries.

During the war the Turinese labour movement again exhibited its characteristics of discipline and revolt, organisation and spontaneism; but now they were all transmuted by the demand for munitions. The internal commissions became a battleground: the union bureaucrats wanted to use them to impose negotiated compromises on the workers; rank-and-file militants wanted to see factory organisation leading the battle against longer hours, lower wages and deteriorating conditions. By early 1916 it seemed that the rank and file were winning and that the internal commissions would regain their original spirit of grassroots rebellion and shopfloor democracy. Battista Santhia, a young Fiat engineer, wrote of how workplace organisation developed:

> In the course of their agitation the workers would nominate a commission to put demands to management. At the end of the negotiations the commission reported back and workers would examine the part each representative had played . . . Thus there grew a process of creating a recognised workplace leadership.[23]

Although a minority of metalworkers were unionised, everyone in the factory shared bad pay and conditions, so it was not surprising that such commissions were chosen by '*all workers on the job on the day of election*'. Thus the Farina commission claimed that unlike the officials, it spoke for the mass of workers rather than the unionised minority 'because we were elected by every worker, not by the union'.[24]

Understandably, full-time officials feared such independent procedures. Unions were founded on card-carrying members and if workers felt their interests were better served by directly elected representatives, there would be little point in their continuing to pay dues. An official counter-attack soon followed. The non-union majority were banned from elections and the independent militants expelled from the commissions.

Such conflicts between rank-and-file activists and union officials continued throughout the war. In 1917 the officials temporarily gained the upper hand. They were helped by the bloody defeat of the August 1917 insurrection and a wave of patriotism following Italy's military disaster at Caporetto in October 1917. With an Austrian invasion a strong possibility, the Orlando government stamped on workers' agitation of any kind. Recalling this difficult period, Tasca wrote of the internal commissions:

> . . . Half had disappeared. Everything had to be rebuilt from scratch . . . Those internal commissions that survived not only failed to grow, but were reduced to meekly performing the tasks set for them by the bosses. The war dominated everything. In government-controlled factories the army, though frequently incompetent, was put in charge . . . any sign of dissent might lead to conscription and despatch to the front. Workers lost any influence over their wages, hours and conditions . . .
>
> No-one can understand Italy's post-war militancy . . . without taking account of this massive repression and daily humiliation which preceded it.[25]

The internal commission, like any other form of shopfloor organisation, was dependent on workers' self-confidence. When this was high, the commission could be a transmission belt for channelling demands *upwards*, but at other times it could serve the interests of the officials, transmitting their orders *downwards*.

In April 1918 internal commissions were recognised and incorporated into an agreement reached between FIOM and Turin's employers. Bonuses were raised and unemployment insurance introduced.[26] When this was put to the local union branch it was accepted. But Maurizio Garino, an anarcho-syndicalist active in FIOM, predicted dire consequences in a speech which echoed the rejection of Tirpitz's deal in Germany:

> Garino conceded that the union had negotiated well. He even admitted that the contract was a notable achievement. But for reasons of principle he was compelled to speak against it. It was bound to

diminish the combativity of the working class, because it would make the union unwieldy, prone to bureaucratic compromise and domination.[27]

Garino's speech was the first conscious expression of a new current in Turin. We have already remarked on the importance of militants such as Willie Gallacher and Richard Müller whose involvement in workshop militancy *and* left-wing policies created the possibility of fusion between the political and militant vanguards. In the engineering factories of Turin this role was played by a 'provisional committee' of FIOM activists. It consisted of 'intransigent' socialists such as Boero and Parodi, and anarchosyndicalists such as Garino and Ferrero.

The provisional committee was not hampered by reformist illusions. From the start its leaders combined a revolutionary rejection of the war with a programme for workshop activity. Garino argued:

> it is time to finish with the bourgeoisie, with the industrialists. The time is right to act in a revolutionary direction. Government and rulers are busy fighting the war and could be taken by surprise by an insurrection, in which case we would be bound to win.[28]

In the union the committee proposed a four-point programme:

> 1. Workers' unity should be built on the basis of factory organisation.
> 2. There must be action to achieve the immediate introduction of an eight-hour day.
> 3. All workers (including conscripts) must have the right to strike and act freely in disputes with industrialists.
> 4. There can be no co-operation with the Mobilisation Committees.[29]

This programme was defeated in a referendum of all Turin's FIOM members, for only the active minority in the union agreed with such radical measures. Nevertheless, the provisional committee included all the key militants who were to animate the mass workers' council movement after the war.

It was significant that militants from such deeply contrasting traditions as Marxism and anarchism should share a common platform. By joining together in the provisional committee they showed an understanding that whatever their ultimate aims — workers' dictatorship or libertarianism — revolutionaries must link the solution of day-to-day problems with the political struggle against capitalism if the working class is to make real progress.

The direction in which their thoughts were moving was shown in a second FIOM manifesto. This was an important advance on the first, which made demands only in relation to the existing union apparatus. The new manifesto proposed:

> *Reform of branch affairs* — greater participation of the masses in the conduct of the branch. Continuous consultation with the dues collectors. Review of the internal commission's role. Election of a training and propaganda committee to study the problems of society as they affect the union and the proletarian movement.[30]

The idea of extending union democracy by involving the dues collectors and internal commissions paralleled the methods of Glasgow's unofficial movement and the Obleute's campaign in the DMV. The final suggestion that there should be a study committee to investigate possible links between industrial action and the broader movement as a whole, showed how the authors thought in broader terms than sectional struggles in the workplaces alone.

By the end of 1918 even Modigliani, a prominent right-wing socialist, recognised and feared the potential of factory organisation:

> Today the short-sighted regard the internal commissions as a collaborationist instrument, useful for the defence of wages within the workshop. But those who set them up and organise them see the commissions as the nuclei of the technical body that will carry through, in the first place, administration, and later expropriation by the workers.[31]

He had accurately judged the trend of the militants' thinking. The internal commission was shortly to be transformed into the factory council — the highest level of workers' organisation achieved in post-war Italy.

Italian socialism at the end of the war

Victory on the battlefront did not bring peace at home. When the war ended in 1918, the spoils of conquest could not allay the disintegration of Italy's fragile economic and political structure. One government supporter described with alarm how returning soldiers were singing revolutionary songs, a popular favourite being 'Let's follow Russia', while at home agitators were inciting insurrection — and all this had occurred 'after the victory! And if we had lost?'[32]

Social crisis tore Italian society apart in the so-called *biennio rosso*, the 'two red years' that followed the war. Within a few months of the armistice the *lira* had lost half its value against the dollar. In the frantic reorganisation of industry for peacetime conditions production fell by almost 40 per cent in the same period.[33] The turmoil had many sources. Nationalists and imperialists were dissatisfied with the spoils they were granted at the peace conferences and spoke of a 'mutilated victory'. The middle class complained about the effects of inflation and nervously watched the disorder they felt to be growing up around them. But it was above all the working class that mobilised, and on an unprecedented scale.

Each of the two red years one million workers came out on strike — six times as many as during the war. In 1919 alone 18 million working days were consumed in strikes, engineering accounting for 11 million of them. But militancy touched every section of the class. Agricultural labourers, for example, fought great struggles to unionise and improve their pay and conditions. They seized some 27,000 hectares of uncultivated land, the occupations often being led by ex-soldiers. The industrial unions multiplied their membership five times over during 1919. Even these rates of growth were dwarfed by the PSI that year. The party ended the war with 24,000 members but boasted 200,000 just 12 months later. The structure of the Italian labour movement was not designed to cope with such a multitude of struggles which, though for better pay, conditions, hours and the like, were fought with an unparalleled aggressiveness and unwillingness to compromise. Everywhere the official organisations creaked under the stress.

In the PSI opinion was divided as to the next step. The right wing, led by Filippo Turati, were still pursuing the well-worn if discredited ideas of the past: 'An attempt at violent revolution . . . can have only two possible results: either *the bloody suppression of the revolt*, or in the most favourable case — *a purely formal and superficial transformation of the political structure* . . . Reforms are the only great and sure path.'[34]

The majority of PSI members were represented by the directorate. On 14 December 1918 this issued an iconoclastic 'Programme for immediate action'. This bold document demanded no less than:

1. Collectivisation of the means of production with direct management by peasants and workers . . .
2. Distribution of commodities through collective organisation, cooperatives and communes.[35]

This would all have been very impressive if the directorate had had
any intention of implementing it. But this programme, like everything else the directorate produced, was just another example of
centrist confusion — noisy posturing devoid of real meaning. For
while the directorate hurled defiance at Italian society, it was in fact
prisoner of the reformist trade union leaders and right-wing socialist deputies.

Apart from propaganda, the PSI had no independent activity of
its own. Its centrist position was epitomised by Giacomo Serrati,
the party secretary. He saw his job as maintaining party unity,
which he did by throwing his weight alternately behind its revolutionary and reformist wings whenever one side threatened to gain
the upper hand. Serrati coined the immortal phrase: 'We Marxists
interpret history, we do not make it', which about summed up his
role in the Italian revolution.[36]

Serrati and the directorate underlined their determination not
to make history during the extraordinary rash of food riots that
rocked Italy in the summer of 1919. The scale of protest was such
that, unlike August 1917, the state was quite unable to isolate one
region from another and suppress individual revolts. There were
many examples of fraternisation between troops and the masses
intent on holding down food prices. Shops were forcibly opened
and their contents distributed by market-place 'soviets'. For a time
the state was powerless and the revolutionary rhetoric of the
directorate was put to the test.

The PSI leaders failed completely. For although they were
unwilling to collaborate with the capitalist authorities in finding a
compromise solution, neither did they wish to lead a rising. As
always, they left the running to the right wing in the party. After a
week of rioting, the movement went into rapid decline as union
officials and local reformist leaders patched up temporary price
freezes. The shallow nature of the directorate's revolutionary
pronouncements was exposed when this potential for a revolution
of national proportions was squandered. But no-one dared say the
PSI had abandoned its principles, for as the rebellion evaporated in
the hot summer air, **Avanti!**, the party's daily paper, declared: 'As

events hasten towards their conclusion, all comrades will remain on duty, alert and at the ready.'[37]

Centrist ineptitude did have its critics in the PSI, however. The extreme left of Italian socialism was championed by Amadeo Bordiga in Naples. He wanted nothing less than 'the proletariat organised as a party against the bourgeoisie, for the revolutionary conquest of political power, and collectivisation of the means of production by a socialist government.' Bordiga, almost alone among European socialists at this time, stressed the centrality of the revolutionary party. But he was a sectarian who thought socialists 'must not strive for any measure which might render the bourgeois regime more tolerable and so longer lasting.'[38] Bordiga was the most intransigent of intransigents, but by dismissing any short-term struggle for immediate reform he reduced socialism to the mouthing of ultimate slogans.

Bordiga's main campaign was for PSI members to abstain from elections, arguing that 'participation can only distract from the struggle for socialism and waste energy. Revolutionary seizure of power is the direct antithesis of parliamentary activity.'[39] Revolution is indeed the antithesis of parliamentary procedure. But if the concrete steps needed to win the masses to it are not taken it will never come to pass. The purely passive method of abstention is not one of those steps, because it does not begin to address the problem of changing workers' ideas through mass self-activity. Bordiga's polemic was directed into the PSI and never looked outside the confines of the party. However, his tiny, hardened faction was the only nationally organised revolutinary current and it had supporters in Turin, of whom Boero was one.

Bordiga's sectarianism was soon eclipsed by a revolutionary strategy of a very different kind centred around the figure of Antonio Gramsci. Gramsci based his approach on the militant activity of Turin's engineers, who were about to embark on an experiment in workers' councils.

Italy, unlike Germany or Britain, had a political vanguard which was deeply divided ideologically and politically: between Bordiga with his national but sectarian vision of the revolutionary party, and Gramsci's small grouping based exclusively in Turin which sought to build a workers' council state. The one position saw Marxism as a doctrine imposed from outside, the other saw it growing from the class struggle. Experience was to prove these twin polarities to be less antagonistic than both sides supposed.

WS-L

The internal commissions reborn

Wartime struggles had produced a layer of militant engineers organised in FIOM's provisional committee. This body had identified rank-and-file democracy and the internal commission as the key to further development in union democracy. The work of Gramsci and his journal the **Ordine Nuovo** (**New Order**) was to lift the movement beyond the narrow horizon of trade unionism and pose the question of workers' council power.

The Piedmont region and its capital Turin were particularly affected by the social turbulence of the two red years. Workers' confidence was helped by the fact that the end of the war brought no serious drop in demand for automobiles (as opposed to more specifically military items). So while much of the rest of Italy suffered, the local economy remained buoyant.[40] The FIOM branch increased its membership from 13,000 to 20,000 in 1919,[41] though this still represented no more than a quarter of the metalworkers in the region.[42]

When the draconian wartime laws were lifted, Turin's metalworks fell into 'an unusual state of agitation'. As the local edition of the socialist daily, **Avanti!**, reported:

> The key forces of the metal industry — workers, white-collar staff and technicians — are now moving simultaneously. It is true that the struggle is not yet uniform in character; the programmes and demands are still distinct. But tomorrow perhaps they will merge to become a single demand: the factory for those who produce the wealth.[43]

In contrast to Glasgow, where militants wrestled with problems of craftism and war, or Berlin, where workers were preoccupied with the struggle for power at all levels of society, Turin's movement concentrated on the question of control of production, almost to the exclusion of everything else. The roots of this concern were to be found in recurring battles over discipline in the workshops. Time and again the Turin edition of **Avanti!** reported disputes arising from the conduct of foremen, the 'arbitrary behaviour of management' or just general discontent with workshop regulations.[44]

A clear indication of the strength of this feeling came in the campaign for the eight-hour day. Agitation for this demand swept Europe after the war, but nowhere was it as fiercely championed as Turin. Once again the comparative novelty of large-scale industrial capitalism lay behind it. Higher wages could compensate workers for selling their labour power, but did not determine *how* it was used once sold. In contrast, the fight for a reduction of hours was an assertion of the rights of workers as human beings to put a limitation on their exploitation, whatever the current price of labour. Turin always led the way for the rest of Italy and the eight-hours' campaign was no exception. The engineering factories won their demand in mid-February 1919 and the Turin example was used to extend a similar agreement to all Italian metalworkers soon afterwards. In March workers in paper, printing and chemicals followed suit. Then came railway and tram employees, but they had less immediate success.[45]

Despite the widespread militancy and the fact that many workers looked to Turin's engineers as the best-organised and most aggressive wing of the class, no direct links were made between rank-and-file workers in the various industries. Organisations remained *sectional*. The PSI certainly had no intention of creating rank-and-file links since, despite its rhetoric of intransigence in general political questions, it had no intention of interfering with what it considered to be trade union matters. The trade union leaders, for their part, feared losing influence to the rank and file and anyway thought of conducting all struggles union by union rather than on a united class basis. So in spite of all the agitation in post-war Italy, struggles still remained fairly isolated from each other, both geographically and one industry from another.

As a result, even the concessions won in Turin's engineering industry were limited in their scope. The eight-hour working day was bought at a high cost. Granted that the new contract cut the working week of between 60 and 70 hours to 48 with no loss of pay, and that piece-rates were raised to match increases in hourly rates, but the other clauses in the contract introduced a three-shift system along with a charter for complete managerial dictatorship. Article 20 stated, for example:

Management has the right to fine or suspend workers who
a) leave their posts without justification
b) work badly or excessively slowly
c) damage workshop machinery or materials through carelessness
d) smoke, bring drink into the workshop without permission
e) arrive drunk for work
f) take collections or subscriptions inside the factory

g) delay completion of work, stop work or anticipate its cessation
h) break the agreement . . .
Further, management will instantly dismiss without pay in the case of
a) insubordination to superiors
b) damage to the factory
c) brawls in the plant[46]

The new agreement also dealt with the internal commissions which, though recognised, were now severely restricted. They had to meet outside working hours and the commissars (as the shop stewards were called) had no right to circulate freely among their members. Management fixed when and where they would meet the internal commissions for negotiations. Failure to observe the regulations in the contract would mean a loss of one week's pay.[47] Fiat workers were again saddled with a disputes procedure which meant grievances had to work their way right up to national level before any strike could legitimately be called.

There was a continuing market for Turin's wares, so the bosses were keen to guarantee unbroken production; but hopes that the new contract would buy peace in the car plants were soon disappointed. Although a cut in hours had broad appeal, the employers had focussed attention on the sensitive area of workshop discipline by their repeated efforts to secure absolute power. **Avanti!** received a letter on 15 March 1919 in the name of 'ordinary workers' who rebuked the union officials for accepting the socially disruptive three-shift system, the ponderous disputes machinery, and compulsory overtime (which nullified the reduction in hours). These workers also opposed the continuation of piece-work, with its taint of sweated labour and divisive multiplicity of wage rates.

The reply of the union officials two days later was vitriolic. Accusing the letter-writers of actually being anti-union anarchists masquerading as 'ordinary' engineers, the FIOM Central Committee added:

> They protest because we want the development of industry, and therefore of the industrialists! No! Whether the industrialists get fat or thin has no importance. In Turin, where industry is fairly well developed, the workers are better off than in Rome, where there is no industry. In New York the working class is better off than Turin, because industry is more highly developed.[48]

Turin's metalworkers were indeed the best paid in Italy, receiving some 34 per cent more than those in Rome and 18 per cent more than the next highest paid, the Genoese.[49] If it had been simply a question of wages the officials' case might have been accepted. But at no price would the workers willingly endure industrial slavery. FIOM's reply did not pacify the malcontents, but it did expose the full-timers as people more concerned to develop capitalist industry than fight those who ran it.

On 18 March the new contract took effect. It was soon clear that despite the hopes of the employers and officials, the influence of the internal commissions could not easily be contained. Only they had close enough ties with the rank and file to be able to sort out the teething problems associated with revised workshop rules and piece-rates, because they alone were on the spot.[50] By the summer, discontent was simmering beneath the surface and the commissions were ever more active.[51] As they grew in confidence the power of the official machinery diminished in proportion. Union leaders were now genuinely worried, for even negotiated improvements in rates later in the year failed to restore their waning influence over the mass of engineers.[52]

March 1919 also saw a long strike by white-collar staff in Turin's metal factories over regrading. Although many manual workers were laid off as a result, they demonstrated their solidarity with the strikers throughout. Soon the idea of a permanent blue and white-collar alliance had become popular. It was supported both by the extreme left and reformist union officials, but each for their own special reasons. The left hoped to unite all workers against capitalism, and saw the cooperation of technicians as important in the takeover of production during the revolution. They could have cited the example of Russia, where such 'specialists' proved indispensable for the industrial revival of the young soviet republic. However union officials saw such an alliance as a step towards harmonious relations between capital and labour to solve production problems under the present system.

Many people were unclear about the difference between the two approaches. A number of workers, eager to control their shopfloor situation, were enticed by a vision of technical co-operation in industry even if it came *before* the revolution. The trend was illustrated by workers at Aeronautics Ansaldo, the factory which built the successful SVA fighter plane. Peace meant the plane was no longer required and the industrialists planned to shut the factory down:

> So our first peacetime demand . . . was the safeguarding of workers' jobs . . . by insisting the company design a civil aeroplane capable of seating several passengers. As a result, Aeronautics Ansaldo was the first to develop a four-seater aircraft for civil and tourist transport.[53]

This type of agitation was ambiguous. The drive for workers' control could lead either to workers' power or to their becoming involved in solving the employers' problems.

The tendency to see the productive process in isolation from its class context (in other words, from who owned and profited by it) grew at this time out of the special conditions in Turin. Many metalworkers took a pride in the advanced nature of their industry, surrounded as it was by a sea of primitive manufacturing and peasant agriculture. Some carworkers received high pay and possessed real technical skills. The social character of their work gave them a choice. They could act as the vanguard of the entire working class, or see themselves as a separate group who, like the officials, were concerned with 'the development of their industry' without regard to 'whether industrialists got fat or thin'.[54] Though the basis for craft sectionalism was weaker in Turin than in Glasgow, nevertheless the choices facing skilled workers — to form a privileged labour aristocracy or act as vanguard of broad class struggle — were present in both cities.

In Turin as elsewhere revolutionary socialists, though few in number, were to have a decisive influence on the choice that was made. Militancy had carried the workers a long way towards independent rank-and-file organisation, but as yet this was only aimed at improving wages and conditions within the factories of Turin. A bi-weekly journal titled **Ordine Nuovo (New Order)** now entered the scene. It wished to give the workers' struggle a more universal significance and lead it towards class emancipation. The **Ordine Nuovo** was started by a group of young Turinese socialist intellectuals — Antonio Gramsci, Angelo Tasca, Umberto Terracini and Palmero Togliatti. Its first issue set out the aims of its editors: 'The main problem to be solved is not how to create or initiate the revolution, but how to guarantee its success.'[55] The second talked of constructing a new type of workers' state on industrial lines.[56]

In an article entitled 'Workers' Democracy' published on 21 June, Gramsci and Togliatti developed this theme further:

> How are the immense social forces unleashed by the war to be harnessed? How are they to be disciplined and given a political form which has the potential to develop normally and continuously into the skeleton of the socialist state in which the dictatorship will be embodied? How can the present be welded to the future, so that while satisfying the urgent necessities of one, we may work effectively to create and 'anticipate' the other?[57]

There were problems with this argument. It treated the actual process of revolution as a simple technical problem which would find an easy solution. But the experience of the Russian revolution shows that this was not so, and that socialist revolution is not just the creation of 'a form which has the potential to develop normally and continuously.' The 1917 crisis of dual power had to be resolved by a decisive push from the left. The power of the soviets was fashioned in abrupt collisions with the capitalist regime, and eventually it required the cataclysmic destruction of the bourgeois state to establish its own rule.

Nevertheless, despite some faults in the 'Workers' Democracy' article, by seriously posing the question of how to 'weld' the present to the future, Gramsci had gone further than Bordiga's ultimatist pronouncements. This was an essential step towards finding a solution, which the same article suggested was as follows:

> The socialist state already exists potentially in the institutions of social life characteristic of the exploited working class . . . the workshop with its internal commissions, the social clubs, the peasant communities . . . Today the internal commissions limit the power of the capitalist in the factory . . . Tomorrow, developed and enriched, they must be the organs of proletarian power . . .
> The workers should proceed at once to the elections of vast assemblies of delegates, chosen from their best and most conscious comrades, under the slogan: 'All power in the workshop to the workshop committees' together with its complement: 'All State power to the Workers' and Peasants' Councils.'

This article became the theoretical foundation of Turin's workers' council movement. Its ideas were not plucked out of thin air. They were a synthesis of information about Russian soviets (of which limited information filtered through the civil war lines) the

Hungarian and German experiences and British example (Gramsci
was in contact with Sylvia Pankhurst, the British revolutionary, at
this time) *plus* local working-class achievements. Contrary to the
beliefs of today's Eurocommunists, Gramsci's strength was not his
'mammoth' brain or an obscurity in his writings which provides
rich ground for academic interpretations and reinterpretations. It
lay in his ability to listen to and learn from the class struggle. As
Togliatti put it:

> To speak with workers individually, simply, without self-importance
> or condescension, but like a comrade or a pupil . . . not only to test
> our aims and influence, but to collaborate with the worker in discover-
> ing the paths open to his class, to investigate the accuracy of a policy,
> orientation or slogan — very few of us, perhaps only Gramsci, knows
> how to do this.[58]

Gramsci's own explanation of his method is worth quoting:

> No initiative was taken unless it was tested in reality, unless
> workers' opinion had already been sounded out through a multitude
> of channels. Therefore our initiatives almost always met with
> immediate and broad success, appearing as an interpretation of a
> widespread and felt need, never like the cold application of an
> intellectual schema.[59]

Such an approach could not have been further from the
sermonising of Pope Kautsky with its prediction of the inevitable
march of history which no-one, least of all the workers, could
change. But it was a double-edged weapon. Gramsci could use the
experience of Turin as a springboard for a leap forward — as a
guide to *political leadership* for all workers in Italy; or he could treat
the local workers' movement as self-sufficient, thus abdicating the
question of leading it further. The latter approach could be called
workerism — making a virtue of the particular struggles of one
group at the expense of generalising and drawing overall lessons.
The history of the *ordinovisti* (as supporters of **Ordine Nuovo** were
called) until mid-1920 showed a continual tension between the two
alternatives of workerism, in which they tailed the Turin workers,
and revolutionary leadership, in which they tried to take them
towards socialist revolution. At first these choices were masked by
some phenomenal successes.

Factory councils

In August 1919, inspired by the 'Workers' Democracy' article, a factory council movement sprang into life. Gramsci's identification of workshop organisation with the ultimate aims of socialism was an explosive concept. For years Turin's militants had operated on two separate levels. Politically they preserved themselves from the corrupting compromises of reformism by intransigence or anarchism — the refusal to collaborate politically in any partial struggles. But they were also shopfloor activists and had developed the idea of rank-and-file democracy through the internal commission. As yet the connection between their two roles was unclear. The **Ordine Nuovo** theoretically linked both political and economic strands, connecting the fight for shopfloor control with the struggle for workers' power.

If the internal commissions could be genuine mass organs *and* function as the basic cells of a future socialist state, then ultimate aims could be linked with immediate action without any sacrifice of principle. The *ordinovisti* gave the inherent tendencies of the movement a theoretical stamp of approval, incorporating them into the grand sweep of socialist strategy. The militants who had been in the wartime provisional committee enthusiastically swung behind this new line, although the libertarians retained their mistrust of centralised organisation[60] and the Bordigists continued to stress abstention from parliament as an important issue.

One serious problem still had to be solved. The internal commissions that survived the war were chosen by a minority — the union members. To become real rank-and-file bodies they had to be restructured. Throughout August, the pages of **Ordine Nuovo** were turned over to a debate on this question. A breakthrough came when two innovations were suggested. First, the commissars should be elected in individual workshops, rather than at factory mass meetings as in the past. This would greatly strengthen direct rank-and-file control. The second was that *all* workers should be allowed to vote (although only union members, being more organisationally experienced, would be eligible as candidates). As a result the new democracy would be based on the mass of workers in the factory. These proposals revived the spirit of the early internal commission, but the factory councils, as these new bodies were called, would be more ambitious in their aims.

The first indication that the **Ordine Nuovo** scheme might catch on came at Fiat Centro. Here workers took up the idea of workshop elections, but gave only union members the vote. But the next factory, the 2,000-strong Fiat Brevetti, followed the plan to the letter. On 31 August the following resolution was passed;

> 1. The current needs of the class struggle compel workers to build factory organisations exterior to, but alongside craft organisations (unions) . . .
>
> 3. This need generated the growth of internal commissions in Italian factories. The present problem is this: how can they be more flexible and articulate, how can they provide a channel of communication by which the commissars can explain their work and ensure that their organisational structure parallels the industrial production process?
>
> 4. To solve this commissars must be elected in each individual workshop . . . ensuring that they are the most active and capable workers, personally known to the electors and in possession of their full confidence and authority when it comes to presenting demands.
>
> 5. The workshop commissars will solve workshop disputes. They will assemble to nominate an Executive Committee that will be the central workers' institution of the factory.[61]

This scheme corresponded to the formal criteria set by the **Ordine Nuovo** but it was a long way yet from making the factory council the basic cell of a socialist state. As it stood, Fiat Brevetti workers had installed a shopfloor organisation that was far more responsive to the workers than trade unions. But that was all. Gramsci could either recognise the merits and limitations of this move, and now call for workshop bodies to be used as a step towards class-wide workers' councils, or accept it as sufficient in itself. He chose the latter path.

In the pioneering article of summer 1919 on 'Workers' Democracy', he and Togliatti had outlined the different components of a workers' state. They had differentiated between workshop organisation to win control in the factories, and 'Workers' and Peasant Councils' which would operate at the higher level of state power. Gramsci's writings of late 1919 blurred the important distinction between these two forms. Now he portrayed factory councils as an existing socialist state when previously he had seen them as merely a prerequisite for much broader soviets. Gramsci now saw the force that would build this alternative state power, not as the armed strength of the working class, the solid 'bodies of armed men' that

Lenin spoke of, but as the 'illuminating light' of workers' control. He saw the revolution, at this time, not as the physical seizure of power, but as an effort to raise consciousness on the part of the workers, as though this would be enough on its own. The establishment of an alternative state power, according to his current ideas, depended not so much on the armed strength of the working class but the experience of controlling events in the workshop.

> The working class is now aware of the possibility of *doing things itself* and doing them well. Indeed from one day to the next it is acquiring an ever clearer certainty that it alone can save the entire world from ruin and desolation. Hence every action that [the workshop commissars] undertake, every battle that is waged under [their] leadership, will be illuminated by the light of that ultimate goal which is in all of your minds and intentions.[62]

Important as workers' control was, it had of necessity to be supplemented by the physical dismantling of the capitalist state.

Another adaptation of the original 'Workers' Democracy' argument was the role now given to the party in the process of change. In June Gramsci had seen the factory councils as a terrain for party propaganda, the PSI retaining a decisive role as 'the furnace of faith, the depository of doctrine, the supreme power harmonising the organised and disciplined forces of the working class and peasantry and leading them towards the ultimate goal.'[63] By September this stress on the party's central importance had disappeared, with the factory council assigned the role of mass democracy *and* vanguard leadership.

Factory councils were indeed a tremendous advance. They alone provided a framework to channel the energy of Turin's labour movement in an organised way. But the advanced militants, and Gramsci with them, were prey to the illusions of achieving workers' control in isolation. They saw that the mass hatred of managerial authority could create a following for socialist ideas. But to see shopfloor organisation as sufficient in itself, irrespective of who *owned* the factories and how that ownership was maintained, was a dangerous deception and led to curious arguments, as this passage by Gramsci shows:

> The working masses must take adequate measures to acquire complete self-government, and the first step along this road consists in disciplining themselves inside the workshop . . . Nor can it be denied

that the discipline which will be established along with the new system will lead to an improvement in production . . . So to those who object that by this method we are collaborating with our opponents, with the owners of the factories, we reply that on the contrary this is the only means of letting them know in concrete terms that the end of their domination is at hand. [64]

How the power of the employers would be destroyed by increased output is far from obvious.

During the war, partial struggles had been forcibly generalised. Peace won through industrial action, for example, would have had an obvious relevance for all Italians. Production and politics could be fused. But as war conditions ended, the threads automatically linking these elements snapped. The state no longer intervened directly in industry and its overall importance appeared to diminish. The historic weakness of the Italian state machine lent credence to the idea that power was a function of economic strength alone.

The hazy ideology surrounding the question of workers' control fed on these influences. Working-class self-government was stressed in isolation from basic social facts: firstly, the means of production were owned by capitalists; secondly, high pay in Turin was an incidental spin-off from a system designed to maximise profits, not some inherent function of advanced technology on its own; and thirdly, the production process was ultimately secured for capitalism by the armed force of the state.

The revolutionary workers' council, as opposed to the kind of shopfloor organisation that can exist at other times, has to be a fusion of politics and economics. The power of workers in industry must be directed at overthrowing the bourgeois state. Although in this respect the Turin factory councils never reached the level of the workers' councils of Russia or Germany, their foundations were sound in terms of rank-and-file support. By linking the organised militants with the mass of the unorganised and uniting them all around a common rejection of capitalist management, the councils were able to tap the energy of thousands of workers. They went much further than the Clydesiders in creating a mass rather than skilled workers' organisation. In a short time a vast and cohesive movement was created. Between September and December 1919 factory councils swept through Turin like wildfire. On 17 October, for example, no fewer than three major factories — Spa, Dubosc and Ansaldo S Giorgio — introduced the new system.

However the sort of negotiations in which the councils were involved showed their limitations. When Fiat's bosses demanded that output be raised to compete with American levels, union officials told their members that 'socialists cannot oppose speed-ups, only refuse to let workers suffer as a result.'[65] This was a chance to test the factory councils in action, for the rank and file angrily rejected these arguments. A series of mass meetings denounced the new working practices, only to be calmed by the intervention of two leaders of the factory council movement — Boero and Garino. Fudging the issue with the idea that workers' power would ultimately grow from the productive capacity of the working class, they prevented strikes breaking out before talks with management were completed.[66] The confusion spread among even the best militants by ideas of workers' control *under capitalism* was never better demonstrated than in this episode.

Gramsci, wanting to avoid early confrontation, had denied that the factory councils were opposed to the union apparatus, seeing the official and unofficial structures as complementary. He repeated this in September 1919 when he said that one of the main tasks of the workshop commissars was ensuring that workers follow procedures negotiated by the unions.[67] However the officials hated the councils on account of both their novel features: they looked to the shopfloor rather than to the union bureaucracy for leadership, and the commissars took their mandate from a workforce three-quarters of which was non-union.

Many workers had a better understanding of the question of council/union relations than Gramsci and on 22 October they decided to storm the citadel of union bureaucracy. Delegates from 17 different factories put forward a slate of workshop commissars for the local FIOM branch executive 'with the aim of infusing the trade union with the new communist spirit'.[68] Their slate was successful and put the union branch into the control of the factory council movement.

This breakthrough heralded advance on all fronts. The local PSI branch had been won to the idea of councils back in June,[69] but in October the movement really took off. Sales of the **Ordine Nuovo** climbed from 3,500 to 5,000 in one month. Factory councils took root throughout Turin's industry, from metals to textiles and rubber,[70] and were even proposed in Milan's offices and Rome's gasworks.[71] Still the movement rolled on.

The last bastion of official labour organisation in Turin was the prestigious *Camera del Lavoro* (Chamber of Labour), the equivalent of a trades council. In mid-October it received a bloody nose from rank-and-file workers opposed to its decision to ban anti-nationalist demonstrations for fear of disorder. At the end of the year its officials mounted a last-ditch defence against the councils. Despite assistance from the national leaders of the PSI and unions, a general meeting of union representatives at the *Camera* passed a resolution backing the council movement by 38,000 to 26,000.

It seemed that in Turin nothing could resist the councils and their leadership — the alliance of *ordinovisti*, PSI intransigents and anarcho-syndicalists. Enthusiasm brimmed over in the workshop commissars' **Programme** of 8 November 1919. Its general aim was clear. The **Programme**, it said,

> is meant to be an exposition of the concepts which underpinned the rise of a new form of proletarian power . . . Its purpose . . . is to set in train in Italy a practical experiment in the achievement of communist society.[72]

The Declaration of Principles went on to state:

> The factory delegates are the sole and authentic social (economic and political) representatives of the proletarian class, by virtue of their being elected by all workers at their workplace on the basis of universal suffrage. At the various levels of their constitution, the delegates embody the union of all workers as realised in organs of production (work-crew, workshop, factory, union of the factories in a given industry, union of the productive enterprises in a city, union of the organs of production in the mechanical and agricultural industry of a district, a province, a region, the nation, the world) whose authority and social leadership are invested in the councils and council system.[73]

But the practical regulations embodied in the **Programme** were much more limited. They laid down election of commissars by section, once every six months (though subject to instant recall by a majority of the section). Voting was to be by secret ballot in working hours, the council meeting two days after elections, and so on. Commissars were to elect the local executive committees of the trade unions. All agreements negotiated by local unions would have to be submitted to the relevant delegate assemblies. In each factory commissars would represent all workers' interests on the shopfloor and organise 'workers' schools' for self-education. In addition these rank-and-file delegates were to elect an Executive Commissariat (replacing the old system of internal commissions). According to the **Programme** the Commissariat was to meet every evening to 'assess the situation in the factory' and would claim equal rights with management to post notices. It would produce a fortnightly factory bulletin and organise weekly meetings of the full council of workshop commissars.

Gwyn Williams has explained the contradiction at the heart of the **Programme**:

> The first point to note about this remarkable manifesto is its earnest and resolutely *communist* tone and language. On the other hand, when one turns from 'spirit' to 'content', particularly in the 'constitutional' detail of the proposals, what is no less striking is how much of the **Programme** is simply an exhortation to good, democratic, trade union practice: an exemplary biography of the Ideal Shop Steward.[74]

The gap between the professed aims of the **Programme** and its practical suggestions was a reflection of a real problem on the ground. The tremendous enthusiasm for council organisation could not be doubted. In Turin the resistance of political and trade union opponents was overcome because the commissars were able to win for the rank and file a tangible sense of control over aspects of workshop life. Although the precise activities of commissars in the workshops were not recorded in any detail, it is clear that in the rapidly changing conditions of Turin's advanced engineering plants, they were involved every day in raising workers' grievances, challenging arbitrary management decisions, interpreting negotiated agreements and so on.

But this was not yet a threat to the state. It would be several months before the forces of 'law and order' saw in the factory council movement enough of a challenge to attack it physically. Similarly the factory owners took no concerted action against the new institution at this time, being more interested in maintaining full production than provoking confrontation. This was soon to change, but at the end of 1919 it was the officials of FIOM and the PSI who took the threat most seriously. In the last months of 1919 their verbal artillery was employed to great effect. Warning workers outside Turin against the 'facile illusions' being peddled by the commissars, FIOM officials answered their critics as follows:

> Of course trade union leaders must be close to the mass of members . . .
> We want the mass to be involved in the life of the organisation. But that
> is no reason why blacklegs [the non-unionist majority who voted for the
> commissars] should have the right to dictate union policy.[75]

Serrati, on behalf of the Socialist Party, joined the fray at the same time. He too disapproved of giving a say to those who would not even join the 'organised labour movement'.[76] An elaborate diversion was now put into operation. **Il Comunismo**, a centrist alternative to the **Ordine Nuovo**, was issued under Serrati's editorship. It was bursting with models of 'soviet' constitutions. Gennari, a leading party member, unveiled a plan for 'Communal Soviets' (hardly more than local government bodies larded with some popular consultation) while the fiery Bombacci, another member of the PSI directorate, proposed a 'National Soviet' of even more ambitious proportions. Even the unions wanted to get in on the act with their own system of factory bodies.[77]

Some of these blueprints sounded very radical, but they all had one basic fault. They were to be built from the top down, by the separate labour organisations. Thus the division of politics and economics would be strictly maintained. PSI 'soviets' would worry about the seizure of power and similar 'political' questions, while the unions would accept factory-based organisations that stuck to economic matters.[78] This was a repeat of the reformist tactics used in Berlin.

At the Bologna Congress of the PSI in October 1919 the party leadership wrote 'the dictatorship of the proletariat' into its programme.[79] To those unfamiliar with centrism its opposition to the Turin experiment, which alone could make that dictatorship a reality, might seem surprising. Despite the 'sound and fury' of the Bologna Congress, the PSI was caught between the opposing poles of reform and revolution. Serrati's position would have been hilarious if its effects had not been so tragic. Here is the full quotation:

> We deny voluntarism; in both its anarchist [revolutionary] and its
> reformist versions . . . The first assigns to man the task of remaking
> the world by means of violence . . . the second equally endows the
> individual with the possibility of social transformation . . . These are
> two utopias . . . We Marxists interpret history, we do not make it.[80]

The practical implications of such a position were revealed in November 1919 when the party entered the general election with a zest certainly not shown during the hunger riots of the summer.

The Palermo paper **Proletarian Dictatorship** (**Dittadura Proletaria**) captured the centrist fantasies of the campaign. One pre-election issue was headed: 'Elections under universal suffrage are an experiment in revolutionary will.'[81] Although the PSI won 156 seats to become the largest single party in parliament this was not enough to defeat the ruling coalition and put the party into government. Yet the paper trumpeted the election result as 'a triumph of the revolution!'[82] Despite the comic opera atmosphere surrounding much of the official labour movement in 1919 the PSI and trade union counter-attack did succeed in halting the extension of council organisation beyond its heartland in Turin.

However the situation was far from static outside the city. In February 1920 anarcho-syndicalist metalworkers in Liguria occupied their workplaces and declared the factories under workers' management. It took the army to eject them after four days. Soon their example was followed by workers of Mazzoni's cotton mills. They continued production on their own account, but eventually acceded to a negotiated withdrawal from occupation that was arranged by textile union officials. The **Ordine Nuovo**'s report on the latter showed the journal's curious attitude to workers' control:

> The work-in, in which the workers achieved a high level of production without the bosses, leads one to conclude that the experiment in self-management succeeded insofar as it achieved a speed-up of disciplined work and maximised output.[83]

Despite these signs of militancy and the general struggles for better wages and conditions raging in the Italy of the two red years, the Turin movement was soon to be put on the defensive. The isolation of its factory council movement, despite these symptoms of broader support for revolutionary ideas outside of the city, continued into 1920. But that time the question of workers' control was overshadowed by a threat to the very existence of independent shopfloor organisation. In the spring of the new year the Turin factory councils found themselves battling for their very survival.

Chapter Ten

RE-ASSESSMENT AND CONFRONTATION

AT THE end of December 1919 the workshop commissars in Turin wrote that unless revolutionary consciousness inspired the council movement 'you will not have created a new institution, a really proletarian institution, but merely a fruitless change of programme, individuals and procedures.'[1] The danger they pinpointed was real. Since the summer the *ordinovisti*, the only group capable of giving a revolutionary leadership, had abdicated their role, believing that the advance of the council institution was of itself enough to ensure victory for the workers.

Gramsci said that 'the factory council is the model of the proletarian state.'[2] The test of his assertion had to be the factory council's practice. No-one could doubt the support it enjoyed because of its ability to organise workers' resistance. That support was shown by the readiness of masses of workers to act immediately upon its directive. The *ordinovisti* claimed, with justification, that

> it was possible within five minutes to get 16,000 workers scattered throughout 42 departments at FIAT to down tools. On 3 December 1919 the Factory Councils provided tangible evidence of their capacity to lead mass movements on a grand scale . . . Without any preparation whatsoever, the factory councils were able to mobilise 120,000 workers, called out factory by factory, in the course of just one hour.[3]

The strike referred to here was a one-day protest over physical assaults by nationalists on socialist members of the Italian parliament in Rome. These assaults were one of the first signs of a reactionary backlash against the working class which in four years' time would culminate in fascist rule. At this stage, however, the government was in the hands of a bourgeois liberal, Francesco Nitti. His policy of offering social reforms (compulsory insurance against unemployment, sickness and old-age, universal suffrage, promotion of the eight-hour day) and using police rather than the army as the usual method of control, was still seen as the safest policy by the ruling class.

Unlike in Russia, the Italian state had not collapsed under the pressure of war, and seemed able to withstand the social strife that followed. One crucial difference was that the Italian army had been victorious in the war. Nevertheless the stability of the state could not be guaranteed. The upper ranks of the army showed it could not be relied upon when an extreme right-wing group of officers showed thinly-veiled sympathy for the poet d'Annunzio and his macabre nationalist invasion of Fiume, a territory disputed with Yugoslavia. The rank and file, on the other hand, proved somewhat untrustworthy in dealing with the food riots of summer 1919 although they never came to the point of electing soldiers' councils as happened in Russia and Germany.

There was another potential danger too. This came from the hundreds of thousands of men being demobilised and now facing unemployment in the cities or inadequate farms in the countryside. If these ex-soldiers had been offered a workable solution to their problems by the left, a potent force could have been created in alliance with the workers' movement. The PSI offered them nothing.[4]

However the army was not the decisive factor in determining the outcome of the 'two red years', for it was never put to the test on any scale. More important was the failure of the Italian working class, despite its widespread militancy, to articulate a decisive challenge for power. The chief obstacles to such a challenge were the leaderships of the PSI and the CGL union federation. Though they differed in their approach, both enjoyed substantial influence, and both were unwilling to lead the Italian revolution.

Although the struggles of industrial workers and agricultural labourers were amorphous and lacked a clear direction, they still constituted a real threat to the stability of Italian capitalism, even if this was not yet a threat to its state power. During 1919 and 1920, however, the jackboot methods of government later used by Mussolini were not a viable alternative for the ruling class. The working class had first to be weakened. This was eventually to be brought about by a number of defeats which resulted from reformist leadership. But that is running ahead of our story.

In 1919 the newly-formed factory council movement seemed blissfully unaware of the national situation, with both the opportunities and dangers it contained. The 3 December strike in Turin, though a significant protest, was one of the few occasions in which the councils reacted to an issue external to local factories. For much of the period preceding the Piedmontese general strike of April 1920 and the military occupation of Turin which followed, the commissars were entirely preoccupied with settling new pay scales with the engineering employers.[5] While negotiations continued, several politically important national public service strikes took place. There were stoppages in telegraphs, telephones and the railways during mid-January 1920 but these simply passed the councils by. In Turin solidarity action was initiated, not by the factory councils, but by the *Camera del Lavoro*, which was still heavily dominated by officials.

However the position seemed much better when it came to factory issues. Between October 1919 and March 1920 Fiat's commissars alone dealt with 800 separate disputes at a rate of three per day.[6] These concerned every detail of workshop life. Only the councils had the structure and authority among the rank and file to organise workers' demands on such a multitude of questions. The precise nature of this small-scale agitation was rarely recorded in detail, although the **Programme of the Workshop Commissars** indicated the range of areas in which the factory council took an interest:

> The most important and delicate of the delegate's duties is inside the factory. He must at all times be the faithful interpreter of the feelings of his comrades before representatives of the employers' authority and within the council . . . The role of the delegate during working hours may be summed up in the word control. He must exercise control:
>
> a) to ensure that existing work agreements are faithfully adhered to, and to resolve any disputes that might arise between the work-force in the shop and representatives of management;
>
> b) to defend the interests and personal feelings of the workers in the event of foremen abusing their power, by mis-assessing work unjustly or through incapacity, in the event of changes in the work process or in the event of a crisis of production on the market;
>
> c) to maintain order on the job, in the face of either management provocation or bad conduct on the part of dissenters from the wishes of the majority;
>
> d) to obtain precise intelligence on: (i) the value of capital employed in his own shop; (ii) the output of his shop in relation to all known

costs; (iii) the possible increase in output that could be achieved;
e) to prevent the capitalists from removing any of the fixed capital invested in the plant.[7]

It is impossible to quantify the precise degree to which the factory council movement made inroads into management power, or to judge how directly the position of Turin's workers was improved. However, one sign of its growing impact was that the trade union officials were no longer alone in seeing the movement as a serious menace. In March 1920 *Confindustria*, Italy's confederation of industrialists, conducted a major reorganisation to equip itself for imminent war on the workers' movement. It was significant that its first target, chosen among the many centres of militancy dotted across Italy, was the factory council stronghold of Turin.

Not only did *Confindustria* realise the futility of individual employers attempting to defeat their workers single-handed, it recognised something that was still not understood by the commissars — that the bosses needed an army, the physical force of the state, to solve problems which conventional industrial relations methods could not cope with. *Confindustria*'s collective state of mind after a year of battering at the hands of an aggressive workforce was revealed by a statement made at its March conference:

> The active bourgeoisie must commit itself to the conviction that it serves a useful function and through organisation find means to energetically combat deviations and disillusion in its ranks.[8]

At this time the internal concerns of the factory councils filled the pages of the **Ordine Nuovo**. Here is an extract from an article of 3 January entitled 'The Factory Council in Operation'. It indicates both the activity of the factory councils and the attitude of the **Ordine Nuovo** which chose to highlight this particular case:

> One workshop of 100 employees suffered from low morale and production well below capacity. As a result the workers got low wages. Inevitably the employers blamed the labour force for this low productivity, singling out the eight-hour day and new wage rates for criticism. The internal commission intervened to explain the root cause of the trouble. 'For weeks,' it said, 'you have been preparing to transfer to line production, but progress on this has been very slow. What is worse, you have taken no account of the expertise of those who

actually do the work . . . Finally, the worst feature of this case is that the managers think only of their promotion and personal intrigues. All this damages workers' morale. Now we don't want to stand in the way of technical progress, but workers don't come here for eight hours a day to do nothing and play about . . . they come here to produce, because they realise that their social power depends on their productive capacity. It is not our fault output is low' . . . The result of this altercation was an immediate improvement in production.

The factory councils were supreme instruments of rank-and-file democracy, but the question must be asked — to what end were they working? The **Ordine Nuovo**'s answer was at one level perfectly correct. 'Class struggle can have no other aim than the conquest of State power . . .' However the journal saw the transition to workers' power in the following terms:

> . . . the whole of the working masses must co-operate; they must adopt a conscious structure in accordance with the position they occupy in the process of production and exchange. Thus within the context of the council, every worker and peasant is summoned to collaborate in the effort of regeneration, to build the apparatus of industrial government and the dictatorship. The present form of the class struggle for power is embodied in the councils.[9]

The idea of industrial regeneration *before* the revolution had some extraordinary repercussions. When one long-standing supporter of the **Ordine Nuovo** was asked why the council was better than parliament he replied:

> Elections take place in every workshop, and in each workshop according to work crew, a procedure which means there is no need to halt production. This proves the superiority of the council system over the bourgeois electoral system, allowing a saving of energy for the full benefit of production.[10]

Such attitudes were encouraged by the peculiar conditions of Turin, where a few giant companies such as Fiat seemed to be independent empires. Here is the **Ordine Nuovo**'s vision of the city in early 1920:

> The Fiat-Centro factory with its 42 sections brings together a mass of around 15,000 workers. The 15,000 workers of the Fiat Centro are the daily breadwinners for a working population of around 60,000 human

beings. There is a gigantic industrial apparatus which corresponds to a *little capitalist state.*[11]

The implication that power in the workshops meant the overthrow of the state was pure self-delusion, as Gramsci was to admit just one month later. For Fiat did not command the physical power of armies. It was only a commercial company, so the councils were not engaged in a situation of dual power by their fight for control of the factories.

The confusion surrounding the Turin councils was illustrated in another way. The ultimate test of any state is the degree to which it can coerce its class enemies. That coercion can only come through centralisation of power. The Turin movement never achieved this, remaining at the *factory council level.* There were other more centralised organs of authority under its influence but none held the power of the collective workforce in its hands. First there was the PSI branch, still very much a minority force; second the **Ordine Nuovo**, a bi-weekly journal which, for all its theoretical prowess, was not a means of intervention (whenever a major struggle arose the paper shut down because its editors felt they could be more useful elsewhere); third a 'Factory Council Study Committee' which, as its title implied, spent most of its time on constitutional details; and finally the FIOM branch which had authority only among trade unionists. Compare this to Russian or German workers' councils, which not only spanned whole countries, but had a degree of armed force to back them up.

The process of centralising power from the point of production is possible only with a growing fusion between immediate struggles at work and political action at the level of state power. This could not come through exhortation, to which the Turin councils were increasingly reduced, but through posing strategic demands (two possibilities had been food and hours, both broad class issues), which could unite the different currents in one struggle and might give an opportunity to split the army — whose united physical power remained unchallenged as the guarantor of the existing capitalist state.

As it was, the Turin councils could only fight a partial war. Fifty years earlier, Marx had argued that

> every movement in which the working class comes out as a class against the ruling classes and tries to coerce them by pressure from without is a political movement. For instance, the attempt in a

particular factory or even a particular trade to force a shorter working
day out of individual capitalists by strikes etc is a purely economic
movement. On the other hand the movement to force an eight-hour
law is a *political* movement.[12]

According to this definition the factory councils never attained a
political level. They remained geographically and industrially
limited. This inescapable fact continually dragged them away from
their intended challenge to the Italian state. No amount of rank-
and-file democracy could overcome this fundamental problem.

The councils had taken the labour movement by storm, combining the abilities of Turin's organised militants with the restless
dynamism of the masses. This was no mean achievement. But to
acquire political significance they had to tie in with the immediate
concerns of the *entire* working class. It was not as though the
commissars feared such a development. Between July 1919 and
March 1920 they repeatedly called for an all-Italy Congress of
Councils.[13] However holding such a meeting pre-supposed a
nationwide movement of socialised production units, with shopfloor organisation and class consciousness to match. This simply
did not exist outside Turin.

Why had the factory councils fallen short of the aims set by
Ordine Nuovo? Gramsci believed that workshop organisation was
the 'natural' form of workers' power (in that it democratically
involved all workers regardless of political or union affiliations,
along the lines of their productive units). At the same time he saw
the role of the revolutionary party as being little more than a ginger
group, inspiring activity but standing aside from active leadership.

The experience of Turin showed that the 'natural' factory
council form could indeed mirror productive relations (departments, workshops, factories, and so on), but its failure to spread
much beyond its local engineering base indicated how capitalist
production could divide workers from one another as much as it
united them. Gramsci suggested workers 'adopt a conscious structure in accordance with the position they occupy in the process of
production and exchange', but this only reproduced the conditions
of class subordination where metalworker is separated from miner,
miner from textile worker and so on.

Of course, achieving the maximum combination inside the
collective industrial units created by capitalism makes possible
further organisation binding the whole class. But under mass

reformism this next stage has to be consciously prepared. There is nothing 'normal' or 'natural' about a mass struggle for power, as Gramsci often argued. It is the very negation of capitalist normality. A meaningful revolutionary strategy could not depend on factory councils alone but had to address itself to the question of leadership for workers in a host of different industries and regions.

The weakness of the movement in this sphere was brought into relief by the centrist and reformist counter-attacks of December 1919 and January 1920. Not only had the councils been halted on the national scale; in Turin itself they did not live up to their revolutionary pretensions. It was clear a fresh direction was needed.

A bitter debate among the *ordinovisti* led to an important breakthrough in socialist theory. Two key documents announced an exciting new turn which dissipated the confusion of the recent past. One was by Gramsci and entitled 'First: Renew the Party'; the other he wrote in conjunction with Bordiga's small group of supporters in Turin and was titled 'The Action Programme of Turin Socialist Branch'. Both appeared in the last week of January.

These articles admitted the limitations of the council movement on two levels: firstly that the isolation of the factory movement could not be broken by the commissars alone. 'Communist' forces acting outside the immediate framework of the shopfloor would have to take action within the national organisations of labour to try and win the many good revolutionaries they contained. The second strand dealt with reviving the Turin movement internally. Gramsci and the local supporters of Bordiga such as Boero now insisted that workshop organisations were only a stage towards much broader Workers' and Peasant Soviets, whose first enemy was the *state*. The 'Action Programme' sought to build upon the achievements of the previous months but take them further:

> In Turin, the factory councils have by now established strong bonds of proletarian discipline among the working masses. Now the [socialist branch] must use this solid basis to promote the establishment of a workers' council for the city . . . In the transition period, the council will have to operate both as an organ of constant criticism of parliament and the bourgeois state and as an organ for direct control of the municipalities.

Once the limitations of internal factory struggle were recognised, it was clear that political questions had to be deliberately raised by the independent action of revolutionaries:

In order to give the revolutionary movement full autonomy and freedom of manoeuvre, the [socialist branch] must . . . set about forming communist groups on a permanent basis in every league and union. These groups will carry out revolutionary propaganda within the organisation and constantly criticise and block any opportunist or reformist degeneration.[14]

These ideas were clarified by Boero and Gramsci in the **Avanti!** of 16 March:

all party members within the organs of class struggle (factory councils, trade unions, cooperatives, Mutual Societies) . . . will form a group and elect a representative to keep contact with the Executive Committee [of the socialist branch]. The factory groups will be assembled in industrial sections to form party fractions within the unions. They will 'supervise' the general activity of the members and will try in all factory meetings to win the party's position.

Without discarding the foundations of council organisation, the new perspective tackled the need for a movement which could unite the mass of exploited Italians to physically overthrow the state, with as its immediate tasks:

1. solving the problem of arming the proletariat;
2. arousing through the province a powerful class movement of poor peasants and small-holders in solidarity with the industrial movement.[15]

While Gramsci and the local Bordigists retained their own emphases, the conclusions drawn in their joint statements had the makings of a synthesis of their two positions, one pivoting on the dynamics of the mass movement, the other upon the leading role of the revolutionary party. The result was a model for action in which the vanguard party would be a key instrument — not the ideological icing on the factory councils' cake — but a force to intervene to determine their direction. The party needed the council as a terrain for its activity, but equally the latter needed the party's guiding strategy to carry it forward.

Gramsci brilliantly captured this interrelation of council and party, which must necessarily rest on a transformation of both:

The party must acquire its own precise and distinct character . . . the party of the revolutionary proletariat in its struggle to achieve a communist society by way of the workers' state — a homogeneous, cohesive party with a doctrine and tactics of its own, and a rigid and implacable discipline. The leadership, by keeping constantly in touch with the sections, must become the motor centre for proletarian action in all its manifestations. The sections must promote the formation of communist groups in all factories, unions, cooperatives and barracks . . . and so become the trusted elements from whom the masses will delegate to form political soviets and exercise the proletarian dictatorship. The existence of a cohesive and highly disciplined communist party . . . is the fundamental and indispensable condition for attempting any experiment with soviets.[16]

The new direction taken by Gramsci had little chance to be put into effect. The councils and party branches could not change as quickly as the theoreticians. At the same time as Gramsci was writing his path-breaking articles, the employers, exasperated by the failure of the unions to keep their house in order, were gearing up for a fight. Their preparations bore all the marks of the imperialist age of capitalism with its close integration of state and capital. Battle was to be engaged at all levels — in the factories and on the streets — using pressure from union officials and politicians as well as force from the army.

In mid-February the boss of Fiat suddenly withdrew his recognition of the workshop commissars. This action was premature and he was brought to heel by a lightning strike. A more concerted strategy would be required. The various bosses' organisations were lobbied for support, and on 7 March the national employers' association *Confindustria* pledged itself to a fight to the finish. Two weeks later the final details of the offensive were agreed with the Prefect of Turin.

The fight for the survival of Turin's independent factory councils began over a trivial issue. To the workers, the introduction of legal summer time on 21 March symbolised a return to wartime conditions. On 22 March, the council at Fiat's Industrie Metallurgiche set the factory clock hands at the old time and were sacked. The response of the workforce was an occupation, which was soon joined by Acciaierie Fiat workers. On 25 March the army drove out the occupiers.[17]

At the behest of the local FIOM executive, which they controlled, the workshop commissars from all Turin held a council of war. Here was a real test of their claims to be the highest form of workers' organisation. They decided to occupy all Turin's engin-

eering factories, and 44 were seized.[18] Although this tactic was
soon called off, the continuing strike of Turin's 50,000 metalworkers showed tremendous solidarity. But the employers were
spoiling for a fight, continually upping their demands and challenging the workers to a fundamental confrontation over the issue
of workshop organisation. The **Ordine Nuovo** later saw the strike
as

> a glorious chapter in the history, not only of the Italian, but of the
> European proletariat . . . this was the first time . . . that a proletariat
> engaged in struggle for control over production, without being driven
> into action through the privations and sacrifices involved, and carried
> the struggle through to its conclusion.[19]

On 1 April, the commissars elected a committee from their
ranks to spearhead the campaign, but its influence was short-lived.
Within days it called in Bruno Buozzi, leader of FIOM and the last
person to sympathise with factory councils. He was asked to head
negotiations for an obvious reason. Turin's metalworkers were
confronting the employers and the state. To succeed they needed
assistance on a national scale. Having failed to establish rank-and-
file organisation outside Turin, they had to fall back on the very
union officials they had been defying for so many months.

On 8 April Buozzi presented a deal to the commissars under
which the union would punish its members for their earlier in-
discipline. Buozzi was happy to use the employers' support to
smash the councils. The commissars threw out the proposals by
eight votes to five, although they agreed to put them to a mass
meeting the next day.[20] This meeting took place in the heart of
Turin and was described by a correspondent of the anarchist
Umanità Nova:

> Out of 50,000 strikers, of which probably 40,000 were present . . .
> only 11,588 voted. The rest abstained.
> Did they not understand the situation? Certainly they did. However
> the masses felt that the struggle had been engaged hesitantly, without
> audacity. There were no gestures of enthusiasm, nor intransigence,
> only weak and drawn out skirmishing.
> The workers felt the leaders had erred as much in their evaluation of
> the movement as in their methods. Many indeed voted for a return to
> work because they thought that with such a leadership they stood no
> chance of winning.

The final result was a majority of 794 for a return to work. After the vote, the commissars were unsure as to whether they should accept such a small majority as binding and there was a meeting at the *Camera*. It was very long, lasting about 17 hours. Buozzi explained it would be dangerous to disregard the vote. There was a prolonged debate . . . Eventually the idea that the commissars should resign *en masse* was rejected but individuals were left the option of quitting if they felt their workmates had no confidence in them once they were back at work.[21]

Buozzi, it seemed, had won the day. The commissars were in total disarray and this had communicated itself to the rank and file. But worse was yet to come. Scenting divisions in the enemy camp, the employers decided that only total humiliation of the workers would satisfy them. When FIOM officials arrived to sign the agreement they had already negotiated, they were suddenly presented with an additional series of demands which aimed at the total emasculation of the factory councils.

The duel now had to be accepted. On 13 April FIOM, the *Camera del Lavoro* and the Turin branch of the PSI issued a joint call for a general strike to begin the next day. The response in Piedmont was magnificent, with workers and peasants throughout the districts of Novara, Alessandria and Pavia joining Turin's industries in a vast show of strength. One eye-witness recounts that

for eleven days the life of the city and province remained completely paralysed. Tramways, railways, public services and many commercial businesses stopped work, in addition to the whole of industry. There were absolutely no blacklegs.[22]

Rural workers introduced their own specific demands, and very soon 500,000 were out on strike. An 'Agitation Committee' was formed to run things. One of its activities was to issue a daily strike paper, the **Lavoratori Avanti!** (**Workers Forward!**) to which the *ordinovisti* contributed their editorial and journalistic skills.

This should have given the *ordinovisti*'s distinctive views a prominent role in the campaign. But according to one writer, the **Ordine Nuovo** had a minimal impact on the strike movement:

There was no encouragement of political debate among the masses about what was happening, on the tactical errors committed, on the need to anticipate the enemy's next move and forestall it . . . If these discussions did take place they were not publicised, did not find expression in leaflets or placards, did not appear in the bulletin of the Agitation Committee.[23]

An actual participant and more sympathetic witness has given a more favourable picture, but even Santhia, the young Fiat engineer who worked closely with Gramsci, could not pinpoint any large scale activity by the *ordinovisti*:

> Gramsci and Togliatti called a meeting of Turin socialist branch leaders, during which, for the first time, the politically important decision to spread the action was taken . . . One comrade was sent to Milan to try to shift the position of the national political and union leaders. Two others were sent to Novara, and I and another went to Vercelli [a centre of striking rural workers].[24]

Five emissaries could not substitute for the leadership of a revolutionary party. There had been insufficient time for the ideas of the 'Action Programme' to be put into practice. Without an organisation of revolutionaries, even though it might have been a relatively small minority of the class, the *ordinovisti* were reduced to playing the part of impotent spectators. Compare this with the Bolsheviks whose organisation in 1917, though reduced to 20,000 by years of arrest and the forced exile of many of its leaders, was quickly able to move to a position where it had the ability to shape events.

Only the anarcho-syndicalists had an independent revolutionary organisation which was able to step outside the framework of union methods and propose struggle against the state. They led a number of demonstrations in the densely-packed working-class districts of Barriera di Milano during which Garino was arrested. The cavalry intervened after skirmishes in the Corso Novara and barricades went up in the Via Tripoli. In the fighting which ensued, one worker was killed.[25]

Nationally too it was the anarcho-syndicalists who sought to give practical aid to the beleagured strikers in Piedmont. **Umanità Nova** headed its front page on 21 April:

> Workers, help! help! Proletarians of Italy, railwaymen, seamen, peasants, don't be sparing with your solidarity for the Turin comrades. Don't let the army converge on Turin. Don't be accomplices to a massacre.

Syndicalists blocked the transport of the 321st infantry regiment on the railways. Troops intending to sail into Genoa were held up and eventually the whole of the port and town stopped work. Syndicalist appeals were backed by the action of railwaymen in Florence, Pisa and Lucca.[26] But the support of the anarcho-syndicalist minority was not enough to save Turin from military occupation.

On 3 April Gramsci wrote what was to be the epitaph for all those who thought workers' control and council power were possible within the confines of one factory, industry or even one city:

> Turin is a garrisoned fortress. It is said that there are 50,000 troops in the city, that artillery is drawn up on the hills, that reinforcements are waiting on the outskirts of the town and armoured cars in the city. If there was still someone in our midst who cherished illusions . . . if anyone found difficulty in making that last step to the point where *power in the factory can be seen as just one element in relation to State power* — if such doubters, such deluded people still existed, then this lesson was for them.[27]

The 'pure' council movement which saw the principle of rank-and-file organisation as an end in itself was forced to stare the realities of politics full in the face.

Only the PSI and trade unions had the power to break the encirclement of Piedmont. Although enthusiastic support for the strike was apparent on the ground, the bureaucrats were loath to act. After 24 days of struggle, FIOM ensured that its members would do no more than 'remain disciplined and await the decisions of the executive committee'.[28]

The PSI national council was the last hope for the strikers. Originally scheduled to meet in Turin, it was moved to Milan to 'avoid disruption'. Opening the meeting Serrati said that the Turin events were a purely local union issue and of no political consequence. Tasca and Terracini, the Turin socialist delegates, countered by saying 'the situation has not arisen because of one individual or local problem. It is the expression of the general crisis facing the bourgeoisie.'[29] They ridiculed the idea of treating this massive dispute as simply a union matter. But they were alone. Even Bordiga did not understand that the fight was of national significance. His lack of interest disclosed the sterile sectarian belief that internal manoeuvres in the PSI were more important than the mass action of the working class. He believed that 'the soviet of tomorrow must arise from the local branches of the

Communist Party' — which was still to be formed.[30] So as the army extended its stranglehold over Turin, Bordiga's advice went no further than theoretical nit-picking: 'It might be possible for the proletariat to establish soviets before power had been taken, but it would be premature to build them before things were truly on the boil.'[31]

Meanwhile the basis for real soviets — the independent factory councils — were being liquidated. On 24 April D'Aragona, leader of the Italian trade unions, cobbled together a compromise solution. It meant virtual capitulation to all the employers' demands and meant that the power of the factory councils would be severely circumscribed.[32] Turin's engineers accepted defeat and returned to work.

The defeat of April 1920 was not inevitable. This was the first serious offensive against the workers' movement, which was still in confident mood in many areas of Italy. Therefore the major problem confronting those who sought revolutionary strategies was not one of working-class combativity, but political leadership. When the **Ordine Nuovo** won the support of Turin's leading workers it could have combined Marxist theory with real roots in the factories and marked the beginning of clear guidance for the struggle. But the theory and practice of workers' councils was no more than one part of a complete revolutionary programme. Another essential component was an organised revolutionary party. Bordiga argued most forcefully for such a party, but his approach to building it was thoroughly sectarian and dismissive of current workers' struggles (and the emerging councils) because he saw them as limited in their aim. This was certainly true, but the mass of workers could not be won to the revolutionary overthrow of capitalism *except* through the experience of partial struggles.

If the *ordinovisti* had been part of a national organisation of revolutionaries they might have been able to integrate the struggle in Turin into a general strategy pursued on a broader scale than simply a regional strike. But they operated in the isolation of one city and Turin's workers, though the most advanced, could not win on their own.

A vanguard can only be effective if it leads forward much wider sections outside its own ranks. A revolutionary leadership, as we saw in Germany with the Obleute and Spartakists, cannot afford to be *wholly within the mass movement, nor wholly outside it* — to be purely economic and agitational or purely political and propagandist. Without this understanding of the need for a combination of a revolutionary party and intervention in the daily struggle, the political vanguard in Turin ultimately failed to give the council movement it had helped to create a leadership which brought victory.

Postscript:
From the April strike to the September factory occupations

It might seem surprising that this account of the Turin factory councils concentrates on the period before the famous 'occupation of the factories' in September 1920, but there are reasons why this is so.

As an all-Italian movement there can be no doubt that the occupations in September involved more people than the April strike. In September 1920 half a million workers, covering all of Italy's metalworking factories and several other industries besides, were in occupation, as opposed to April's strike by the inhabitants of just one city and its surrounding province. Yet several commentators suggest that the critical moment for the Italian revolutionary movement had already been passed by September. According to Togliatti:

> The high peak of the movement was reached in the spring of 1920 when there was a general strike in Turin . . . When the occupations began not only were there already signs of weariness; the socialist and militant groups were already well aware that the whole movement lacked a leadership capable of taking it to victory.[33]

The question of whether an independent revolutionary leadership with mass support could be built had been decided in Turin in April. According to Garino, when the factory councils were defeated in the April strike there began 'the decline of the Turinese workers' movement. This took place before the occupation of the factories.'[34]

Nevertheless September's occupations were on a massive scale. In some places factory councils took the task of organising within the different plants. Although they lacked the independent character shown before the April strike, the fact that many factories were actually run without management interference, by the workers alone, should silence the reformist argument that experts must run society and that the working class is incapable of doing so. By the third day of the occupations Fiat Centro was actually turning out more motor cars than for some time.

But for all its apparent strengths, the September movement had several underlying weaknesses. Unlike the April strike, which began over the issue of rank-and-file influence at the point of production, the occupations followed four months of top level negotiations and a go-slow over the new engineering wage claim. The tactic of invading the factories began after workers were locked out at the Romeo plant in Milan on 30 August. At first the occupations were basically a bargaining counter, and although the resumption of production under workers' control implied a challenge to 'managements' right to manage', the rank and file in the factories were far from controlling the dispute, as had at least been the case in the first stages of the April strike. The tactic of a 'work-in' thus appeared more radical than it actually was.

In September the passive attitude of the rank and file towards leadership allowed the following bizarre discussion to take place between the bureaucrats of the PSI and the trade unions. On 10 September, when the occupations showed no signs of abating, the Socialist Party felt constrained to make its customary militant noises. In a clever manoeuvre, D'Aragona, for the trade unions, said to the party leadership: 'You believe that this is the moment for the revolution. Very well then. You assume the responsibility.'[35] The PSI centrists sounded revolutionary but had absolutely no intention of acting on their words and simply renounced all leadership in favour of the trade unions. Italy was then treated to the ludicrous spectacle of an assembly of union bureaucrats casting block votes for or against a revolution. Unfortunately the revolution fell by 591,245 to 409,569![36]

When the occupations finally ended on 30 September the result appeared superficially to be a compromise; but in the shifting battlefronts of class war, to stand still for even a moment is to invite defeat. The occupations had goaded the capitalist system with the threat of revolution, but not finished it off. This was to drive the ruling class towards Mussolini's fascists, while disorienting the workers' movement. The 'March on Rome' in which the fascists took power was to follow just two years later.

The seeds of passivity in September 1920 were sown by the smashing of the *independent* factory councils in April. The full scale of the demoralisation after that strike was brought home in late May 1920. In a decisive confrontation Angelo Tasca overthrew the original **Ordine Nuovo** position on factory council autonomy and won the idea that the councils should henceforth be an extension of the union machine, putting them under strict official control. Gramsci opposed this line but was in a minority. Without the democratic thrust of the rank and file, the chance of independent revolutionary leadership in opposition to the bureaucrats was lost.

Chapter Eleven

CONCLUSION

THE WORKERS' council first appeared during the Russian revolution of 1905. Even at that time it aroused controversy in the Western labour movement. In 1906 Rosa Luxemburg wrote that some people 'are in the habit of denying that the lessons and the example of the Russian Revolution can be a criterion for Germany . . . [But] just as in the Russian Revolution . . . so will it be in Germany.'[1] Her opponents' reaction was one that is still familiar today: 'Those who have such a surplus of "revolutionary energy" . . . Go back to Russia.'[2]

After the First World War it was Kautsky who launched the attack on those who wished to follow the Russian party. Between the two labour movements, he argued, there could be nothing in common.[3] Since then many others have joined him in denying the relevance of the October revolution and the soviet. Even West European Communist Parties which were founded as a direct result of the 1917 revolution have done this. The British Communist Party's recent programme says, for example:

> Britain's road to socialism will be different from the Soviet road. The Soviet path of insurrection and civil war, the creation of new organs of power (the Soviets) . . . was governed by the historical conditions and background of Tsarist autocratic rule . . .[4]

Lenin's opinion was entirely different. He believed 'the Russian model reveals to all countries something — and something highly significant — of their near and inevitable future.'[5] The Communist International, founded in 1919 and the rallying point for millions of revolutionary workers in the 1920s, called 'on proletarians everywhere to follow the Russian example . . . [and to] support every Soviet republic.'[6]

The destruction of soviet democracy by Russia's prolonged

isolation and the Stalinist bureaucracy has not changed the fundamental question. Can the revolutionary struggles of the First World War and their peak of achievement — Soviet Russia — serve as a guide for socialists? The strong parallels between Russian's soviets and the workers' council movements in Germany, Italy and Britain give an affirmative answer. At the same time, the failure of the latter three to win power shows an obvious difference.

Russia — the exception or the rule?

The events of 1917 in Russia were an example of what Trotsky called 'permanent revolution'. Years before, in defiance of conventional Marxist wisdom which saw workers' power first appearing where capitalism and the industrial working class were well-established, he had predicted that the numerically tiny Russian working class would not be the last in line but 'the *initiator* of the liquidation of world capitalism'.[7]

Russia in 1917 was a peculiar mixture of modernity and backwardness. Peasants made up 80 per cent of the population. Ruling over them was an autocratic monarchy, a relic of feudalism. At the same time, there was a modern capitalist class, though small in number and politically dependent on Tsarism for survival. Capitalist expansion led to the emergence of an industrial working class, a proletariat. Though only three million strong, the concentrated growth of industry promoted a high level of unity in its ranks. This plus the crisis-ridden condition of Tsarism encouraged a degree of militancy unique in the world at that time. Even in the decade before the 1905 revolution an average of 493,000 workers went on strike each year. The equivalent figures for Germany and Britain were 84,000 and 136,000 respectively. Yet the working classes of these two countries were three and four times more numerous than that in Russia.

Tsarism was ripe for overthrow by a bourgeois revolution, but while the working class showed tremendous vigour, the bourgeoisie's fear for its property outweighed any desire to achieve political power. That was why Lenin said that the bourgeoisie suffered from such 'instability, half-heartedness and treachery' that it could never lead the fight against the autocracy.[8] This special combination of factors led Trotsky to argue that:

So far as its direct and indirect tasks are concerned, the Russian revolution is a 'bourgeois' revolution because it sets out to liberate bourgeois society from the chains and fetters of absolutism and feudal ownership. But the principal driving force of the Russian revolution is the proletariat, and that is why, so far as its method is concerned, it is a proletarian revolution.[9]

These conditions modified the character of Russian workers' struggle. Although fundamentally the same as elsewhere, insofar as its starting point was dictated by the character of collective social production, the surface manifestations of the movement were exceptional. This showed itself in several ways.

Firstly, the working class was spurred into independent action around the political demands of bourgeois democracy. Thus the mass demonstration of 9 January 1905 outside the Winter Palace placed 'at the head of everything . . . the convening of a Constituent Assembly by universal and equal suffrage.'[10] The state's answer to this demand was to massacre the demonstrators and thus begin a revolution. Later that year the Soviet emerged from a general strike whose main demand was again the Constituent Assembly. Every time workers went forward around slogans of bourgeois democracy they were forced to use methods which went far beyond parliamentarism and implied workers' power instead. The demand for a Constituent Assembly led directly to the workers' soviet. As Trotsky argued, bourgeois democracy was not

> irrelevant, *it was a necessary stage in the development of the working masses* — with the wholly important reservation that in one case this stage lasts for decades, while in another, the revolutionary situation permits the masses to emancipate themselves from the prejudices of [bourgeois] political democracy even before its institutions have been converted into reality.[11]

Secondly, the political weakness of the Russian capitalist class and its institutions was matched by the frailty of its ideological hold on the workers. In Western Europe workers had for several decades received crumbs from the table of capitalism in the form of wage rises and so on. Many enjoyed the right to organise — as long as this involved no direct threat to the system. This had accustomed them to believe in the possibility of a reformist road to socialism. Equally important, many had ceased to see any connection between economic progress and the political power of their class. This was not the case in Russia. The factory delegates to the 1905 Soviet put as their first priority *political strike action*, realising that even basic economic advance could not be achieved except by armed power. That was the significance of the slogan 'Eight hours and a gun'. In Russia this revolutionary understanding was shared by a substantial portion of the working class. In the West the proportion of revolutionaries was much smaller, and the influence of reformism that much greater.

Thirdly, the division between sectional struggle and class struggle was far less wide than in Western Europe. This difference was rooted in the pace of Russian industrialisation and the role of Tsarism. Marx saw Britain as the classic case of capitalist development. Its industrial technology and organisation developed gradually over a period. This meant that in the 1850s certain groups such as engineering workers were able to form 'model unions' based on exclusive control of craft knowledge. Restricted entry into the trade kept their skills at a premium and extracted concessions from employers. Sectional organisation was thus of immediate advantage to the group Engels called 'the labour aristocracy'. To a slightly lesser degree the same pattern applied to countries which industrialised hard on the heels of Britain.[12]

So in the West the extra bargaining power derived from craft knowledge was an important factor in shaping workers' organisation. It was sometimes the only lever by which workers could build permanent collective organisation. But the result was often a sectional attitude, a conservative refusal to support other workers in struggle. This was not the case in Russia.[13] As Trotsky wrote:

> Capitalist industry arose in our country under the direct and immediate pressure of European capital. It took possession of a soil essentially virginal, primitive, without encountering any resistance from craft culture . . . It gathered around itself the army of the industrial proletariat and prevented the rise and development of crafts. As a result of this process there appeared among us as the main force in the towns, at the moment of the bourgeois revolution, an industrial proletariat of an extremely highly developed social type.[14]

In addition the Russian state was indiscriminate in the way it battered all groups of workers and effectively barred them from even sectional organisation. This was not so in the West.

This led to a fourth difference. In Russia the soviet, a political body, was the *first* serious collective organisation of the industrial working class. In 1905 and 1917 it *preceded* the creation of sectional, economic institutions — the trade unions and shopfloor organisations (factory committees, shop stewards and so on). The latter led major economic battles which followed in the wake of the political challenge and deepened it, but except for a brief period in mid-1917 the soviet had no rivals for the allegiance of the class. Even right-wing reformists promoted its formation since they lacked any other means of influencing the masses. This was not the case in Western Europe, where there were already reformist-controlled trade unions in existence. These used their tremendous influence and powerful apparatuses to hinder the growth of council organisation and challenge it for authority.

Thus the sequence of events in the West was the reverse of the Russian. In the West the councils did not begin as organs of political power which opened the way to economic organisation. They grew up in opposition to the trade union bureaucracy, and as the statement of the Clyde Workers' Committee suggested, defined themselves in relation to this bureaucracy, fighting its influence in the unions. The political meaning of working-class struggle during capitalist crisis only became explicit later on and only to a minority of Western workers.

In Russia the battle against reformist leaders was fought out *within* the soviet. With its system of instant recall they were easily replaced, the major struggle against mass reformism being compressed into a few brief months. In the West developments tended to be far slower, with reformist leaders entrenched in bureaucratically-controlled union machines.

These were not the only differences. A most important factor in Russia was the existence of a tempered revolutionary party, something singularly lacking in the West. This is not the place to discuss how much the Bolsheviks owed to the peculiarities of Russian historical development,[15] but without minimising the ability and dedication of its members, it must be admitted that the conditions of permanent revolution certainly assisted the party's development. The weakness of conventional reformism meant that even in times of reaction the body of support for revolutionary ideas (even if it could be organised with only the greatest difficulty) remained large. Thus the Bolsheviks won a majority of Petrograd workers' votes in elections to the War Industries Committees as early as September 1915, even before the revolution had begun to transform the consciousness of many. While the Mensheviks and

Social Revolutionaries (SRs) benefitted most from the euphoria of
the February 1917 revolution, the Bolsheviks won control of the
Petrograd factory committees and unions after just three months.
The principal Russian soviets did not have Bolshevik majorities
until at least September 1917, but this delay was mainly due to the
predominance of soldiers' delegates, not lack of workers' support.

Although numerous, the peculiarities of Russian development
must not obscure the fundamental connection between the working classes of all countries — the struggle against capitalism.
Internationalism — the belief that workers everywhere have a
single collective interest — is more than a theory. This was proved
in the First World War when workers, though separated by barbed
wire and trenches, found themselves confronting the same class
enemy and adopted identical forms of combat organisation in
response. The metalworker at Putilov was no different from the
wage slave at Berlin's DMV, Glasgow's Parkhead Forge or Turin's
Fiat Centro. Centres of council organisation as far apart as Petrograd and Turin were linked. As Marx predicted in 1848:

> the need for a constantly expanding market chases the bourgeois over
> the whole surface of the globe. It must nestle everywhere, settle
> everywhere, establish connections everywhere . . . [and] draw all,
> even the most barbarous nations into civilisation.[16]

However the contrast between Russia and the West had an
important influence on the manner in which struggles developed.
In 1924, Trotsky, considering 'The Lessons of October' in the
light of past defeats and the new Communist International wrote:

> It must not be forgotten that in our country the soviets grew up in the
> 'democratic' stage of the revolution, becoming legalised, as it were, at
> that stage, and subsequently inherited and utilised by us. This will
> not be repeated in the proletarian revolutions of the West. There, in
> most cases, the soviets will be created as the direct organs of proletarian
> insurrection . . . Most likely, it will be possible to create the soviets
> only in the very last days as the direct organs of the insurgent masses.
> Finally it is quite probable that such circumstances will arise as will
> make the soviets emerge either after the insurrection has passed its
> critical stage, or even in its closing stages as organs of the new state
> power.[17]

Such successful soviets, alas, were not to appear during Trotsky's
lifetime. Of those that preceded the formation of mass Communist

Parties in the 1920s only the German workers' and soldiers' councils briefly attained the level of soviets — armed authority which directly challenged the bourgeois state for power.

Nevertheless the past sixty years have seen a number of occasions in which workers' council organisation has reappeared in one form or another. This should dispel any notion that it is somehow a Russian phenomenon, or that it can only appear during world war.

The mass movement in Barcelona in 1936 was occasioned by a right-wing coup which sought to topple an elected government. In this case the chief reason for the failure of the armed workers' movement was the anarchists' refusal to centralise the undoubted power of the workers into an authoritative state form. The Trotskyist left was far too weak to accomplish this task and in the vacuum an unholy alliance of Stalinists and bourgeoisie destroyed the elements of workers' councils that did develop. Another council movement unconnected with international war grew up in Hungary in 1956. Here the origin lay in divisions within the state capitalist ruling class. Centralised workers' councils were created only to be physically smashed by Russian soldiers.

Other recent examples include Portugal in 1974 where failure in colonial wars split the army and opened the way for workers' self-organisation. In this case the weakness of the revolutionary current meant that Stalinism and Social Democracy were able to stem the growth of independent organisation almost before it got off the ground. The Solidarity movement in Poland was more than a trade union but less than a soviet, though it was clear in the months preceding martial law that Solidarity could have moved in the direction of dual power if it had had a clear leadership.

All of these examples should warn us against a rigid understanding of what constitutes the objective condition for a workers' council and the particular organisational form it must take. A striking feature of all such forms of mass self-organisation is their great flexibility.

The workers' councils which grew up in the West developed under conditions of reformism in which the stranglehold of bureaucracy necessitated rank-and-file movements in the trade union field. Such organisations, though capable, given the right circumstances, of growing into soviets, should *not* be confused with them. The soviet can arise only during a situation of dual power. Rank-and-file movements can exist in non-revolutionary periods as they do not constitute an immediate challenge to the bourgeois monopoly of armed force. Nevertheless, as the war years showed, the Western rank-and-file movements were very important in preparing the way for soviets.

Capitalism has never been closer to destruction on an international scale than in the period following the Russian revolution. The reason for this was the existence of mass organisations which, though in various stages of development, were clearly capable of providing an alternative authority not only to the bourgeois state machine but to the apparatus of reformism within the working class. The defeat of the post-war wave of revolution was not due to the weakness or lack of courage of rank-and-file workers, nor to the insufficiency of the workers' council as a form of organisation. The tremendous battles fought under the banner of workers' councils and the self-sacrifice of hundreds of thousands of workers East and West are ample testimony to this. The origins of failure were to be found in a lack of revolutionary leadership and the strength of reformism.

The problem of reformism

The importance of ruling-class influence not so much as an external coercive power but as an ideology *within* the working-class movement cannot be overstated. As Trotsky puts it:

> The ruling class forces *its* ends upon society and habituates it into considering all those means which contradict its ends as immoral . . . Such a regime could not endure for even a week through force alone.[18]

Reformism is the form taken by ruling-class influence inside the working class. Reformist organisations grow out of working-class struggles that are shaped and limited by a relatively stable capitalist environment. Thus trade unions resolve immediate problems such as relative levels of wages, the establishment of a certain standard of working conditions and so on, while in the political sphere reformist parties seek to win advantages for the working class; both operate within the framework of capitalism. When the system is not in crisis it is possible by such methods to win some short-term benefits and sustain the illusion that socialism can be won in the long term by gradual means.

Both trade unions and reformist parties are clearly marked by the society in which they were born. Trade unions are often sectionally organised, with miners divided from engineers, rail-

waymen from teachers and so on. They also tend to separate their
economic function from political aims and are dominated by a
bureaucracy (a reflection of the subjective weakness felt by the
rank and file who elevate union leaders to the position of a semi-
autonomous power). Reformist parties bear equal signs of capitalist influence. They openly accept the bourgeois state as their
allotted field of activity, with all the limitations that this implies.
They conform to the national aims of 'their' state. They comply
with the decisions of 'their' unelected judges, accept the need to
defend 'their' (capitalist) economy from foreign competitors and
workers at home, and so on.

The right of capital to dominance is not challenged, only the
terms of that dominance are negotiated. By channelling workers'
activity in safe directions and at the same time accepting capitalist
ends as their own they reinforce capitalism, whatever the intentions
of their rank-and-file supporters.

Yet in one sense these sorts of reformist organisations are a
tremendous positive gain for the workers. On many occasions the
freedom of the ruling class is to an extent curtailed by the resistance
such organisations can mount (even though this resistance is frequently in spite of the activity of the bureaucrats who lead them).

However, what is a gain in periods of capitalist stability
becomes a serious obstacle in times of revolution. At such points in
history reformist ideas and organisation do not disappear, leaving
the ground free for new institutions suited to all-out class warfare.
Even though reformism can no longer offer any progress, nor even
protect the working class from the ravages of a society in decline, if
no credible revolutionary alternative is available, masses of workers
will cling to reformist ideas for want of anything better.

In Western Europe after the First World War reformist organisations, through their leaders, acted as a buffer between capital
and labour, obscuring the real character of the crisis which was one
of exploiter versus exploited. The advance of the working class was
thus weakened and the opportunity to finish capitalism once and
for all was missed. In Germany reformists went even further,
physically attacking and murdering the most advanced sections of
the working class.

The net result of such tactics was to give international capitalism time to regroup its forces. It won a certain room for manoeuvre
which allowed it to survive even in desperate revolutionary situ-
ations such as that in Germany. By giving employers and the state

the chance to make minor concessions, and by maintaining an ideology of 'co-operation' between workers and employers, reformism hid the fundamental antagonism between capital and labour — allowing capital the possibility of a temporary retreat. In Russia, by contrast, capital was dependent on Tsarism and the political crudity of its repressive state machine. In the high point of class struggle that came in 1917 the antagonism between capital and labour was far clearer to workers in Russia than in Western Europe, where the established reformist tradition was to fudge the real issues, so weakening and dividing the movement towards workers' councils and workers' power.

It can be seen from the above account of reformism that it has a dual nature — it is a means to basic workers' organisation but one that limits further advance. It creates defensive barriers against the naked exploitation of capitalism but gives great influence to leaders who, as a bureaucracy, serve the ends of class collaboration, which are different from the interests of their rank-and-file followers. The dual nature of reformism was one of the problems which revolutionaries in Western Europe had to come to terms with when building workers' councils in the first place and within the councils once these were established.

The overcoming of this problem was a prolonged and painful process, for it was as much through the experience of failure as success that post-war revolutionaries were to learn how to operate under conditions of reformism. On the one hand they found they had to relate to the mass of reformist-thinking workers who through struggle for immediate ends could, in the midst of crisis, be brought to draw revolutionary conclusions. They had therefore, for example, to be in the mass reformist organisations of the trade union movement. On the other hand, revolutionaries discovered the need to wage an implacable war on the ideas of reformism and the bureaucratic leaders who used their influence to sabotage workers' offensives. Though operating within the trade unions they could not afford to forget that the chief weapon in this ideological war was the revolutionary party, which had to pursue a policy that kept in view the connection between immediate issues and socialist aims at all times.

These were the theoretical lessons which were won in the early 1920s. They were the result of hard years of practical struggle in Russia and Western Europe in the period of the war and immediately after. One of the most prominent features of this struggle was the workers' council. But it was not the only one. Councils were merely the leading edge of a much broader revolt that took a multitude of forms. The ferment was extremely uneven, both politically and geographically. Although workers the world over faced fundamentally the same enemy in capitalism, in Western Europe, for example, several decades of social stratification had created differences inside the working class between skilled, un-skilled and so on. Equally the various histories of Europe's national states led to variations in the degree to which reformism held sway from one country to another and from one industry to another.

The main area of activity for some workers in the years 1915–20 was within the workers' council movement. Others were satis-fied with the achievement of bourgeois democracy through the overthrow of the monarchy, such as in Germany or Austro-Hungary. Even as sections fought for working-class dictatorship others were casting their votes in parliamentary elections or joining unions for the very first time. Thus in Germany the rise of workers' councils was paralleled by an eightfold expansion of the SPD-controlled Free Trade Unions. After the war women in Britain were granted the vote, as were Italian peasants. Mass activity of the most diverse kind continued to roll across Europe for many years.

Yet in the myriad of workers' struggles, certain places stood out as the most advanced. For the sake of convenience we shall call these centres of workers' council activity 'revolutionary capitals' in the sense that in each country they led on the road towards revolu-tion (even though in the case of Glasgow and Turin the destination was never reached). Though distinct activity in these areas was not separate from struggles elsewhere, since

> if the capital plays as dominating a role in a revolution as though it
> concentrated in itself the will of the nation, that is simply because the
> capital expresses most clearly and thoroughly the fundamental ten-
> dencies of the new society. The provinces accept the steps taken by
> the capital as their own intentions already materialised. In the initi-
> atory role of the centres there is no violation of democracy but rather
> its dynamic realisation.[19]

Trotsky's description of Petrograd showed the potential of Turin, Glasgow or Berlin. The origin of these key centres of workers' council organisation can be traced back to the imperialist crisis on the one hand, and the subjective response of labour on the other.

Building the councils — the objective conditions

The world-wide system of capitalism creates chains of domination wherever it goes. But some links in the chain are weaker than others. The centres of council organisation were an example. Though ruled by states ranging from semi-feudal to bourgeois democratic, they were all areas which had experienced a period of turbulent social development which upset traditional patterns. The influx of immigrants, often unused to modern industrial conditions, brought a fresh view of life under capitalism, a perspective less clouded by established ideology and procedures.

Though of less importance in Russia, where Tsarism repressed all workers with an equal ferocity, the growth of engineering proved a major factor in the development of Western council strongholds. There was nothing inherently radicalising about handling metal products. It was the capitalist context in which the industry was set that opened the path to revolution. A combination of industrial concentration and technological dynamism compelled those who worked in engineering continually to reconsider their position and fight to maintain their ground. Today engineering has been joined by a number of mass production industries and by vast national and international companies in which the collective power of the class can be even greater. And now even those in white-collar jobs are threatened by new technology, as was the engineer of 1914. As both white-collar and manual workers possess collective strength, the shift away from traditional industries in recent years has not diminished the potential for socialism, but in many ways enhanced it.

In 1914 there was one factor that seemed peculiar to engineering, however. Its technological character had attracted a high proportion of skilled workers, who now had a strong bargaining position. This allowed them to build a level of shopfloor organisation which was only accessible with difficulty to the unskilled. When skilled workers were threatened by the new methods of production, they began to fight back. Until its transformation during the war, engineering militancy did not hit the headlines. Yet the daily round of sectional disputes within factories and the need to generalise activity during wartime created a wide network of self-confident rank-and-file leaders.

The battle to defend the advantages conferred by skill did not have to make engineers a qualitatively separate group. It was merely one front in the common war between capital and labour. Nevertheless it was an important one. Capitalism is always changing its production techniques. While these changes bring individual capitalists a temporary advantage, they can also threaten their collective downfall. As Marx put it:

> The bourgeoisie cannot exist without constantly revolutionising the instruments of production, and thereby the relations of production, and with them the whole relations of society . . . uninterrupted disturbance of all social conditions, everlasting uncertainty and agitation distinguish the bourgeois epoch from all earlier ones. All fixed, fast-frozen relations, with their train of ancient and venerable prejudices and opinions are swept away . . . and man is at last compelled to face with sober senses, his real conditions of life, and his relations with his kind.[20]

Capitalist relations of *production* ensured the creation of a collective class of workers and drove them into struggle. Capitalist relations of *destruction* reinforced the tendency. In the imperialist crisis all the warring states adopted repressive policies identical to those of their enemies, while protesting that war was necessary to prevent the rule of alien methods from abroad. Here too the tactics of the ruling class could be turned against them. The example set by the integrated wartime economies was dangerous. The system showed just how productive industry could be once competition was abolished within the national unit. Yet the competitive driving force had not been suppressed. It merely re-emerged as an external military struggle whose senseless slaughter further encouraged workers to fight.

But before this upturn in struggle came about, the workers' movement suffered a major attack. First came the co-option of the parties of the Second International and the trade union bureaucracies into the war effort of each national state. This paralysed the working class and left it leaderless. Second came the construction of state capitalist machines which took the coercive power of the state into every workshop. Strikes became illegal and punishable by prison, or worse by despatch to the trenches. And the contradiction Engels noted between the social nature of factory production and capitalist use of its product was felt all the more sharply by munitions workers.

To combat the bosses' offensive workers had to develop a new leadership, one that could centralise broad struggles while responding flexibly to rapid changes in the situation. Grassroots democracy was a brilliant solution to this problem. By building from the workplace upwards, the new leaderships could be sure of their support, just as the rank and file would be safe from bureaucratic sell-outs. The principle of instant recall reinforced the links between the masses and their representatives by ensuring that at any one moment the leadership was the genuine expression of the base.

The second prong of the ruling class offensive — state capitalism — also shaped working-class struggle. The sustained expansion of the system between 1870 and 1914 had separated politics and economics in workers' minds, leaving them ill-equipped to confront the class enemy. The depth of the capitalist crisis stripped away the false division which capitalism normally projects between the economic and political, forcing the use of the state to control directly the economic relations of society, and thus also forcing workers to respond at a political level. When strikes were illegal and the foreman had police, courts, prisons and the army unashamedly supporting him, it was possible to demonstrate that the rank and file could not afford to limit its fight to one factory or to trade union methods. It was not easy to win workers to such new ideas, for they ran against methods of organised activity that had been operating with moderate success for years. But now at least, the crisis had helped clarify the problem.

The workers' council was the logical answer and one which suggested itself in many different countries. Though its particular form and stage of development varied from place to place, it was sufficiently consistent in method and structure for one to say that it was the developed version of workers' power that Marx had glimpsed in the Paris Commune and called: 'the political form . . . under which to work out the economical emancipation of labour.'[21]

Building the councils — the subjective conditions

There were many potential 'revolutionary capitals' in war-torn Europe, many areas combining recent population influx with expansion in engineering. Although the objective conditions of crisis were widespread, it was the subjective response of the local labour movement that proved decisive in creating such capitals. Though the war forced many into action, whether this took revolutionary form was conditioned by the conscious activity of often tiny groups of individuals. Where these were present the seeds of the workers' council movement could grow despite reformist influence. Nevertheless reformism did have a damaging effect, for these key initiating groups tended to be divided into separate political and militant vanguards. The word vanguard is appropriate here because it was too early to talk of such solid forms as revolutionary parties or soviet leaderships, though each was a step in those directions.

Before the war, Clydeside's militants had painstakingly built workplace organisation over years of now hidden, now open struggle, almost as much in defiance of union headquarters as the bosses. Similarly the Obleute fought for democracy in the DMV and established a tradition of factory leadership. This preparatory work was done before 1914. It did not concentrate on grandiose questions but challenged the employers over day-to-day issues. Without such apparently unimportant spadework a strategy of workers' council building would have been much harder.

The idea that soviets could spring up spontaneously might have fitted Russia, where even economic agitation was outlawed, but it was wrong in Western Europe where an entrenched reformist leadership had to be countered by building shopfloor organisation which could act independently given the right circumstances. This early work was done under the protective umbrella of the official trade union movement. Shop stewards originated as an arm of the union machine inside the workshop, although, as later developments showed, they could also act as autonomous rank-and-file leaders. The fact that the militant vanguard was *within* the official movement but able to be *independent* of it was important. Before the war some socialists attempted to transform class struggle from the top down by capturing senior union positions. Others formed alternative revolutionary unions (this was the aim of the British SLP, Germany's 'Lokalisten' and the Italian anarcho-syndicalists) but they had all failed. No pretence at mass support could replace genuine roots in the workplaces.

Nonetheless the degree of formal organisation achieved at shopfloor level should not be exaggerated. Only on the Clyde did it have a fairly independent and structured basis in the ASE Vigilance Committee. In Berlin and Turin the connections were far looser. But vital in all three cases was the network of rank-and-file leaders who had won support through the daily round of class struggle. This alone made them able to withstand wartime pressures.

The second essential element in a revolutionary capital was the political vanguard. In 1914 there were no other groups comparable to the Bolsheviks. Nevertheless those who politically shaped the workers' council movements were revolutionary socialists who shared a commitment to internationalism and fought to overcome the separation of politics and economics. The political vanguard faced a problem that did not apply to factory militants. To use Gramsci's definition, the latter operated around workers' 'natural' organisation. This derived its strength from rank-and-file support and so depended on the rhythm of class militancy. Though the ground for truly independent organisation and action in the factories could be prepared, it could not be artificially created but had to await the rise of mass struggle. Thus factory militants could only lead *in spite of* the officials when conditions forced workers to take action and abandon 'normal' trade union practices.

In contrast, the political vanguard needed to be organised independently from the beginning. It was a 'voluntary' grouping whose only attraction was its revolutionary ideas. These had to be spelled out clearly and effectively. In short, revolutionaries could not afford to wait for the mass movement to arise before clarifying their position both organisationally and politically. Though a minority under capitalism, to be effective they had to be formed into an interventionist force — a party. At the outbreak of the war, with the iron bonds of emergency legislation enclosing them, it was exceedingly difficult to start building such parties.

Nonetheless, the importance of the political element should not be underestimated. At great personal cost these handfuls of individuals helped transform the struggles of the revolutionary capitals. Their task was not helped by the inheritance of pre-war socialism. The political vanguard found itself distanced from the industrial militants who alone had the ability to mobilise the collective power of the class.

The distinction between political revolutionaries and factory militants was not rigid. Often the same person considered himself or herself a revolutionary socialist *and* a good workplace activist. But this did not mean that their activity within each sphere was connected. Until the council experience, most socialists lacked a method of linking their two sorts of agitation *in practice*.

Despite these problems, the arguments of revolutionary socialists were essential to guide the workers' council movements. To stand any chance of developing in wartime conditions, rank-and-file struggles needed political ideas. Without them how could reformist calls for social peace be combatted or strikes in different factories and industries connected? If John Maclean had not been urging the Clyde Workers' Committee forward, it would not have attempted to expose capitalist war aims through its strategy against dilution; nor would it have been the leading agitational centre against conscription in January 1918. In Germany Liebknecht's daring made possible the first major strike of the Obleute, and the politics of Spartakism opened the way for mass anti-war activity. The Turin *ordinovisti* were a tiny group, but their gathering of the different strands in the labour movement gave a powerful impetus towards factory councils.

These vanguards encouraged another less visible, but not less important phenomenon. This was the beginning of a socialist practice which bridged the gap between politics and economics. The origins of the workers' councils were to be found where socialists strove to make their ideas relevant to the workplace, just as the concerns of the workplace were brought into the life of the workers' political organisations.

Councils were neither planned nor spontaneous. The vanguards could not decide to set them up, but neither would they have emerged to challenge the existing reformist alternatives without their conscious intervention. It took the inspired initiatives of those who had earned the right to lead the rank and file.

These then were the elements of the revolutionary capitals. They cannot be recreated in exactly the same form again, but we can be sure that both capitalist crisis and workers' resistance *will* recur. While one cannot choose the objective circumstances of any future struggle, there are lessons to be learnt from the subjective response of the workers' movement in past struggles. The efforts of past revolutionaries were necessarily fumbling and confused for they were not guided by prior experience. Yet within a few years, and in the face of overwhelming odds, they created real possibilities of overturning capitalism. If the barely-organised revolutionary groups and networks of militants can be replaced by solid organisations tempered by a knowledge of past successes and failures, how much more powerful might they be?

Workers' democracy in action

Workers' councils were not invented. Even the nineteenth-century utopian socialists, who indulged in social fantasy, could never have visualised anything so firmly rooted in the present and yet so liberating in potential. Yet even the Russian soviet did not offer socialism on a plate. There would have to be a period of international struggle, and of reconstruction to repair the devastation of capitalist crisis and further develop the forces of production. Only then could humanity be rid of the scourge of material shortage and social exploitation. But the workers' council showed how this new society might be achieved, for it released the creative power of the proletariat.

The working class could not hope to radically change society by any other means than creating its own state. This would differ greatly from the parliamentary version. Bourgeois democracy guarantees the domination of big business all the more effectively because it wins a passive acceptance of capitalism through disguising its rule in egalitarian clothing. This is done in several ways:

Political equality hiding economic inequality:

All electors are supposedly equal because they have one vote each. But there is a vast difference between the small group of wealthy people who regulate the movement of capital, can bankrupt whole countries or devastate industrial regions by withholding investment; and the great majority whose only leverage is their ability to sell their labour power.

Constituency voting:

Parliamentary elections are based on geographical constituencies. These encourage workers to see themselves as individual 'citizens' rather than people with a collective class interest. As isolated atoms within their own homes, workers are easily influenced by the capitalist media and notions of 'national interest'. In contrast, at work the real conflict of interest is visibly not nation against nation but capital versus labour.

Lack of control over representatives:

Since constituencies are purely arbitrary units which cut across the real divisions in society, they cannot be the focus for collective decision-making. Therefore members of parliament are not subject to day-to-day control. What passes for political life is outside the reach of the masses who are *spoken for* by experts who are called to account only once every few years. This prevents any effective mass influence inside parliament. Elections are at best no more than an occasional commentary on decisions already made, and certainly no means of deciding the future.

Removal of politics from daily life:

The net result of these factors is that whether consciously or not, the mass of people feel they can do nothing to shape their lives in the way they want through parliament. Politics are seen as boring or irrelevant. Behind the parliamentary debates, 'questions in the House' and so on, lies a vast bureaucracy of unelected civil servants and judges. In the crucial area of coercion — the police, prisons and army, there is never even the pretence of democracy. Police chiefs and generals have always served the interests of the capitalist class from which they are recruited. The key forces of the capitalist state are organised *outside* and *against* the mass of the population.

The role of bourgeois democracy is thus to give the mass of workers an illusion of control, so leaving the *real* control of the capitalist class to continue out of view. The immediate experience of workers in the factories and offices suggests to them that only by collective organisation such as trade unions can workers win even a small say in what goes on at work, but the effect of parliamentary democracy is to counter this impression and foster the illusion of a 'free country' in which laws are made for and by the majority, and so on. Behind this facade capital enjoys all the real freedom and dictates the general shape of law-making and state action.

The workers' council, in its highest form as the soviet, is the complete negation of parliamentarism. As political power ultimately rests on control of social wealth, the soviet is based directly on mass organisation in the factories. The strength of the movement grows from the control which the working class exercises over the forces of production as well as its ability to paralyse and dismantle the old state machine. The Western councils emphasised that shopfloor organisation and workers' control are therefore inseparable elements of the movement for political power.

Vastly outnumbering the capitalists, the working class has no need to disguise the means through which it rules. The basis of its organisation is not a fictional unit such as the constituency, but the productive units given by the very development of society. Collective will is expressed through discussion in the factories and offices. Policy is based on common experience and debate. Only where workers meet collectively every day can they maintain the constant level of debate and scrutiny that makes democratic election a reality. A natural result of the workplace basis of workers' councils is mass involvement and the right of instant recall. The workplace, unlike the ballot box, is a permanent focus of human activity, which means delegates elected to the councils can be replaced as soon as they cease to be representative. The right to recall is not written into any fixed constitution. It arises from the life and struggles of workers who in shaping their lives can accept no five-year gap between elections.

Another danger has to be countered. Instant recall and the like mean nothing if the decisions taken have no effect. The bourgeoisie defends itself most directly by means of army, police and prisons. Only in Russia, and to a lesser extent in Germany, was the soviet able to reverse the position in which armed force is directed against the majority. Its method was simple. The masses were given arms. Workers' militias and democratic soldiers' councils were not ruled from above, but like the soviets of which they were but an extension, grew up from the rank and file. In a soviet state, power is utterly transformed. Hitherto the state had existed to protect property from people. The workers' council state exists to protect people from the power of property. The state no longer stands above the masses, it *is* the masses.

However power consists of more than just physical force. After all, Western capitalists have only had to resort to repressive violence during periods of open challenge, while the 'normal' method of rule is altogether more subtle. Under the present system decisions are dictated by economic forces which seem to impose inexorable laws of profitability. Such 'laws' have never been passed, let alone discussed in parliament. Yet the blind operations of competition subordinate all capitalist governments to their will. Clearly the notion that there can be democracy without control over economic power is a nonsense.

The workers' council takes full account of this. Whereas capitalism pretends that the political superstructure of society can operate freely of the economic base, the soviet recognises the real relationship within its own structure. The power of the producers in the factories is mobilised and organised into a political state. Economic and political power become one and the same thing.

This fusion is no accidental phenomenon. In Western Europe it grew with the development of working-class consciousness. As workers gained the confidence to fight independently of the union bureaucracy and to beat the employer at the point of production, so they won the confidence to seize state power. Bukharin explained the content of workers' council power when it had attained its full soviet form:

If the state power of the proletariat is a means of economic revolution, then clearly 'economics' and 'politics' should merge into one. We also get such a merger under the dictatorship of finance capital in its classical final form, that of state capitalism. But the dictatorship of the proletariat turns all the relations of the old world upside down — in other words, the *political* dictatorship of the working class must inevitably entail its economic dictatorship too.[22]

The geographically-based, alienating capitalist state *cannot* be adapted to the needs of workers' power. Despite the different nuances that reactionaries or reformists give to their policies, the parliamentary system enshrines the interests of the capitalist class. By contrast the workers' council is the organised expression of the working class. And just as the interests of the exploiters cannot be reconciled with those of the exploited, so parliament cannot be reconciled with the workers' council. Only the latter fulfils Lenin's three criteria for proletarian democracy:

first . . . the electors are the working and exploited people; the bourgeoisie is excluded. Secondly . . . all bureaucratic formalities and restrictions of elections are abolished; the people themselves determine the order and time of elections, and are completely free to recall any elected person. Thirdly . . . a start is made by the *entire* population in learning the art of administration, and in beginning to administer.[23]

This fundamental antagonism of bourgeois and proletarian forms of class rule has been obscured by centrists. In 1917 the Mensheviks hoped the Provisional Government and soviets might peacefully co-exist. But years of civil war in which the remnant of the Provisional Government sided with the most reactionary generals, such as Kornilov, in their attempt to smash the workers' state of October 1917 showed beyond doubt that the choice was either 'all power to the soviets' or the drowning of the Russian workers' movement in blood.

The same centrist ideas concerning the equal validity of parliamentary and extra-parliamentary action and organisation reappeared in Germany. During the first weeks of the German revolution Kautsky wrote: 'The National Assembly [the bourgeois parliament] *and* workers' and soldiers' councils are equally necessary, but each of these two institutions has its own tasks . . .'[24] In the unstable conditions of dual power prevailing at the time, both parliamentary forms and workers' councils could *temporarily* function side by side. But soon German capitalism called upon their own version of Kornilov, the right-wing Social Democrat Noske. He had more success than his Russian counterpart in crushing workers' revolt. The culmination of his reactionary offensive came in March 1919 when two million Germans, following Kautsky's mistaken faith in a blend of workers' councils and parliament, went on strike to force the government to 'incorporate the workers' and soldiers' councils' into the constitution. They were met with murderous gunfire and hundreds killed. Five months earlier, Lenin had predicted just such a tragedy arising from Kautsky's position:

> To say to the soviets: fight but don't take all state power into your hands, don't become state organisations — is tantamount to preaching class collaboration and 'social peace' between the proletariat and the bourgeoisie. It is ridiculous even to think that such a position in the midst of fierce struggle could lead to anything but ignominious failure. [25]

Workers' power can be built only by smashing the political power of the capitalist class in both its military and parliamentary forms. There can be no truce between workers' power in the councils and parliament.

Councils, parties and unions

Workers' councils are *organs of direct mass struggle*. They are composed of delegates chosen in the workplaces to answer an immediate problem. These delegates meet together in order to widen solidarity and give a united lead to workers of an area.

Such rank-and-file bodies are different from the two other typical forms of workers' organisation — parties and trade unions. As organs of mass struggle workers' councils arise only in periods of social crisis, when workers are forced to go beyond their traditional organisations and embrace revolutionary methods of action. Accordingly, they cannot be created at will or to a pre-arranged formula. They can only be encouraged when the *mass* of workers feel the need to solve their specific problems in a new way. By contrast, parties and trade unions, at least under bourgeois democracy, can exist during periods of downturn or capitalist stability.

The workers' council should not be confused with the party. The latter is a voluntary grouping based on political ideas. Workers' council structure follows the contours of the productive unit, not the political beliefs of the individuals it contains. With the weight of reformism against them, the Western councils tended to begin with specific problems and in the struggle broaden out to political questions. Just as parliament is the forum for parties to debate how to solve the problems of capitalism, so the workers' council becomes the forum for a solution of workers' needs, when it becomes clear that the old methods of solving problems are no longer effective.

The trade union too is a 'natural' form in that it too mirrors the outlines of the capitalist organisation of the economy. But unions are limited in crucial ways. They are founded on different sections of workers. Some may organise at workplace level rather than geographically, but each union caters for only sectional needs. The unions are tied to the economic struggles of workers and rarely progress beyond this limit.

Trade unions often develop over a long period of time and therefore take permanent shape when class struggle is not at the point of revolutionary upheaval.[26] In Western Europe they have worked within a more or less stable capitalism to try to improve wages and conditions. They employ experts whose precise duty is to negotiate the price of labour with management, but certainly not abolish its sale. (If the latter were done the function of the union bureaucrat would simply disappear.)

The workers' council, on the other hand, can arise only when negotiation within the system is virtually ruled out, and when the working class can win nothing unless it unites on *as broad a basis as possible*. Thus it bursts through the barriers of sectionalism and economics to lead the fight of all workers. As a *class* organisation in a period of crisis, the council can take on the question of political and social power, laying the basis for a soviet state.

In Russia, even before the October revolution, the soviets took over the maintenance of transport, food supplies and public order. In Germany these, plus the pressing problem of demobilisation, had to be solved. Even the embryonic council movements in Britain and Italy considered issues which took them far beyond the trade union sphere to questions of war and peace, workers' control and so on.

There is, of course, an overlap between party, union and workers' council. The council is the arena in which different working-class parties fight for allegiance and the right to leadership. Councils use the basic network of workers' organisation established by the unions as their starting point. Thus in the First World War shop stewards played the leading role in establishing councils. Nevertheless, the basic distinction between these three bodies remains. For all their strengths, councils *cannot* succeed on their own. They are but part of the final class struggle, the other major role being played by a revolutionary party.

The October 1917 revolution was the only time workers achieved absolute state power. Their success was made possible by the action of the Bolsheviks. Although the idea of a Leninist-type party was absent from discussions in Western Europe at the time, the question of the party is clearly an essential part of any study of workers' councils. The positive experience of Russia and the failures of Western movements showed that both a revolutionary party and workers' councils are necessary to achieve a workers' state.

Berlin's struggle demonstrated the folly of a party attempting revolution *without* involving the workers' council. Turin's experience suggested the reverse, that workers' councils could not succeed without a party. In other words, *no revolutionary party can be successful without a perspective centred on achieving power through the workers' council*, just as *no workers' council can succeed unless it is led by revolutionaries organised in a mass party*.

Even during revolutions the party cannot substitute for the workers' council. This is not simply a technical problem — the need to print enough membership cards or set up branches. Revolutions are not made just by revolutionaries. In Germany for example the majority of those who overthrew the Kaiser believed in the ideas of the reformist SPD. Though the revolutionary party must be big enough to encompass the leading workers, under capitalism these are a minority. Even at the moment of insurrection the party is not flexible enough to recruit whole factories at a time, with their vast range of opinion from reactionary to revolutionary. Indeed to do so would mean to abandon its political principles. Only the workers' council can provide the vital link connecting a vanguard party and the masses.

The workers' council process

Workers' revolutionary self-organisation only becomes possible in times of crisis. It must be a dynamic force changing almost as quickly as mass consciousness, which in days of revolution can

make tremendous strides. The phases which collective mass organisation passed through in Glasgow, Berlin and Turin differed
markedly from the Russian model.

As noted above, the February revolution of 1917 saw the
almost simultaneous creation of political power, in the shape of the
soviet, and shopfloor organisation through the factory committees.
With economics and politics already linked in their minds, Russian
workers launched their attack on the economic strongholds of
capitalism within days of their assault on the state.

In the West the process of organisational development was
markedly slower and showed a progression from economic to
political struggles, in the sense that the target shifted from sectional immediate issues to the question of class power at state level.
Reformism had to be driven back by first presenting an alternative
form of mass organisation and activity at the most basic level. As
Trotsky suggested, dual power might erupt suddenly, soviets
emerging only days before or even during the final insurrection.
But the undermining of mighty reformist earthworks through
mass self-activity would obviously take longer, and be a more
prominent feature of the revolution than in Russia.

On Clydeside this process was begun when stewards linked
together the different munitions factories and fought on urgent
issues facing militant craftsmen. But they did not go very far. The
Clyde Workers' Committee organised only the skilled engineering sections and despite Maclean's hopes never took overt anti-
war action. Although more ambitious in intent, Turin's factory
council movement fared only a little better. It was true that all
workers irrespective of skill were united in its ranks. Yet still
there were serious limitations. Factory councils did not spread
much beyond the city's boundaries and the fight for workers'
control, though a step beyond the engrained sectionalism of the
Clydesiders, never really confronted the question of state power.
Only in Berlin could the scale of the movement be said to have
compared with Russia. But here too developments to the point of
dual power seemed closer to the model of Glasgow and Turin than
Petrograd. Berlin saw the pre-war establishment of a network of
union militants who in wartime were able to fight on immediate
issues, link together and move forward to mass political action.
The fact that reformism successfully prevented genuine workers'
and soldiers' councils where independent shopfloor traditions
were lacking showed that in Germany, as in Britain and Italy, the

struggle would be more difficult than in Russia.

The problems of creating workers' councils and progressing to political action in the face of reformist opposition were not insurmountable. Perhaps things would take longer in the West, but it would be quite wrong to presume that defeat was inevitable. The key problem lay not in the council movements themselves. Although they lagged behind Russia they clearly had the potential to match and even surpass its soviet state. The problem was in the leadership provided by the vanguard elements. As Russia had shown after the 'July Days', without revolutionary leadership the councils would stagnate and die. Even soviets could be destroyed by the disease of bureaucracy. Nevertheless it was still true that the workers' council alone could rapidly organise the masses into a disciplined army drawing on the collective strength of the industrial working class — but for that army to advance into battle at the right time and with the right military strategy the correct leadership was essential.

In all three Western examples that leadership was missing. In October 1917 the party, soviets and masses had been linked together in one forward movement. Trotsky compared this to a system of cogs meshing together. In the West the connections between these three forces were never to be made. Each time, the weaknesses of the workers' councils, and therefore of the wider workers' movement, could be ascribed to the failure of revolutionary leadership.

Workers' council democracy is intensely vulnerable to this problem. It reflects at every moment the changing consciousness of the masses. Although violent class struggles may precipitate a revolutionary crisis, the mass of workers do not start with a coherent socialist outlook, but are still dragged back by reformist ideas. They can only reach revolutionary socialist consciousness through the experience of their own struggles. This means that while revolutionaries may set a workers' council in motion, as it spreads in support and comes to reflect wider and wider sections of the class its democratic structure will more than likely put reformists in control, reformists who oppose everything the council stands for. It can be won back from its enemies only if revolutionaries build their influence during the crisis until such time as their ideas have majority support within the working class. To do that requires party organisation, something that was absent in Western Europe in the years 1915–20.

Weakness in leadership caused breakdowns at all the other levels. The problems manifested themselves rather differently in each of the revolutionary capitals. On Clydeside the chief difficulty facing the left was how to harness the militancy shown in the unofficial 'two-pence' strike of February 1915. To succeed even in defending their own position within engineering, the workers had to stand up to the wartime state capitalist machine. The only answer was therefore an attack on the wartime nationalism upon which it rested. The Clyde Workers' Committee's ultimate failure to take this step forward lay in the fact that while most *leaders* were convinced of the political strategy, little had been done to secure *rank-and-file* support for it. Maclean's propaganda group was far too small to achieve this, while the shop stewards had presented themselves in the workshops as no more than good trade union militants (though as revolutionary socialists outside). With the transition from economic agitation to politics unfinished the council movement had no appeal outside the core of engineering workers and ground to a halt.

In Germany the objective circumstances gave the movement a head start. The political capital of the defeated state neatly co-incided with the centre of engineering militancy and revolutionary politics. This helped council organisation to develop rapidly. But the fact that the council did become an alternative political author-ity put all the more responsibility on those who were trying to lead it towards establishing a socialist state.

On 9 November 1918 when the Kaiser was overthrown, the revolutionary action of the masses had outstripped their political consciousness. A sign of this was that the SPD won a majority on the Berlin Council Executive the very next day. Nevertheless, during the succeeding weeks the pressure of crisis forced the masses to the left and gave revolutionaries broad scope for lead-ing the councils forward. This was when the poor connection between the shop stewards and Spartakists proved disastrous. The Obleute were left without any notion of where they were going.Müller and his fellow militants veered wildly, one minute abandoning economic struggle to concentrate on securing state power, next reversing the equation, and so on. Because they proved so inept in the driving seat of the councils, a number of revolutionaries decided to abandon the vehicle altogether and strike out on their own. Only Ebert stood to gain from such impatience, for it gave his reactionary bloodhounds a golden opportunity to split the workers' movement and break its best elements.

The Berlin central workers' council had state power within reach. The process of linking shopfloor organisation to armed militias had gone far, just as economic and political struggles overlapped (despite the confusion at the top). The process of education through action was proceeding apace and in February 1919 the SPD lost control of the Berlin councils. But by then the damage had already been done — the appalling mistake of the January insurrection had cost the revolutionary left dear.

In Turin everything seemed to give way to the onward march of the factory councils. But appearances were deceptive. The organisations that emerged did not match the soviets that Gramsci had hoped for in the early months of 1919. The revised internal commissions were indeed the first stage of the council's organisational process, but development to higher and more political forms could not be achieved by an act of will, only through concrete strategies which could end the isolation of the revolutionary capital.

Three problems beset Glasgow, Berlin and Turin — the gap between economic struggle and war, accurate timing, and the unique character of each revolutionary capital. These obstacles were not insurmountable. Russia showed that with an effective leadership such difficulties could be resolved. One has only to compare the relative strengths of the revolutionary groupings to see why Bolshevism succeeded where the rest of the European left failed:

Russia: Bolshevik party with 14 years' experience; 200,000 members (October 1917); 17 daily papers with a circulation of 320,000 in July 1917.

Germany: Communist Party established one week before counter-revolution (although Spartakists had two to three years' experience); around 3,000 members; daily paper, circulation unknown.

Italy: ordinovisti, a tiny group of socialists collected over several months; fortnightly journal circulation of 5,000.

Britain: Maclean's group, a mere handful of active supporters collected over several years; monthly paper appeared three times, circulation 3,000.

The Bolsheviks were able to link economic struggle to the war through the simple slogan of 'peace, bread and land' which was broadcast in thousands of workplaces by a mass party. The slogan became a material force connecting different sections of the working class and peasantry in a common struggle.

The question of timing was acute in Russia in 1917. In the space of six months revolutionaries had to negotiate the equivalent of several centuries of political history — from Tsarist feudalism through capitalism to workers' power. Correspondingly, the Russian workers did not have to battle through the defences that a slowly-developing capitalism had erected over the centuries in Western Europe. The superb sense of timing shown by Lenin's party depended on its ability to refuse or accept challenges on its own terms. The holding operation of the 'July Days' and the forward offensive of October 1917 were made possible only by the powerful influence of a disciplined mass party within the working class.

The revolutionary capital of Petrograd might easily have been isolated from the rest of Russia by the vast geographical distances and weak growth of industry in a sea of agricultural production. Again Bolshevism was able to nurture the socialist movement in the advanced city while all the time maintaining links outside, through their land reform programme, nationalities policy and so on.

To our original question of what the Western councils needed to establish a workers' state, the verdict of history answers: *effective leadership by a revolutionary party.*

This was only the starting point, however. The Bolsheviks had always insisted that the transition to socialism depended on successful revolutions in more than one country. The absence of mass revolutionary parties in Western Europe and the consequent defeat of the workers' councils left Soviet Russia isolated. Eventually the workers' state, deprived of its class basis by war and industrial collapse, succumbed to Stalinist state capitalism.

The theoretical lessons of the Western councils

It would be easy to suggest that the initial success of Russia's Leninist party and soviet state makes them the only relevant models for study and that the Western experience, which ended in failure, was second rate, only deserving a place in the footnotes. This would be a mistake. Firstly, the workers' council movements of the West fought with efficacy against entrenched mass reformism, an enemy far stronger here than in Russia. Secondly, the

European councils highlighted important features which were either absent or barely visible in the lightning quick transformations that took place in Russia between February and October 1917. The theoretical conclusions that flow from the Western councils are therefore not unimportant.

In 1914 revolutionary socialists had to discard the rotten legacy of the Second International and approach their problems afresh. They needed a new revolutionary practice appropriate to the conditions of Western Europe. Alas, in the thick of the struggle, they had little time to write down what they discovered. The following is an attempt to sum up in theory what they were striving for in practice. The first section deals with the general nature of revolutionary change, the second narrows the focus to particular lessons for the party.

ONE: Unevenness and unity, vanguards and class

The war period demonstrated the importance of vanguards in *initiating* and directing working-class action. It also emphasised the opposite point. Generals without troops are helpless, and the class, composed of a great variety of individuals, women and men, manual and white-collar, revolutionary and reformist, had to be moulded into a single fighting force.

The workers' council showed how such a concentration is possible. It cannot arise from a formal arrangement between existing labour institutions which have adapted to 'normal' conditions of capitalism. The amalgamation of Britain's craft unions or the various German workers' parties would have possessed nothing of the power yielded by mass solidarity at the base. This could not be created passively, but through a leadership which united rank-and-file workers *in action* around commonly felt needs.

Yet the workers' council did not bring people together on the basis of the lowest common denominator, as does the Labour politician touting for votes. It recognised the difference between the skilled and unskilled (as in Britain), revolutionaries and reformists (in Germany's political parties) and unionists or non-unionists (in Italy). Because the vanguard acted in an organised way and the habits of organisation lend a certain conservatism, it occasionally lagged behind the masses. But if this inertia was overcome, it could use the strength of its strong sections — skilled strength, left politics and organised trade unionism — for the benefit of the whole movement. Division and unevenness could be turned to advantage if the advance guard could lead the rest forward.

TWO: Politics and economics

The workers' council was able to reverse the attack of wartime state capitalism by forming its own counter-force which mirrored the concentrated economic/political power of its enemy. Workplace organisation which developed in the direction of workers' councils posed a threat to capitalist *state power*, just as centralised class organisation had the potential to break the bonds of capitalism *in the factory*. This cut across pre-war thinking.

The 'politicians' of the Second International argued that only when workers came forward as a class and took state power could the economic basis of capitalism be destroyed and socialism secured. Therefore any economic struggle or fight from just one section was bound to be limited and had to be subordinated to the wider political aim of capturing the state. In practice this meant reformist leaders tried to dampen strike activity in order not to disrupt elections.

Syndicalists believed the opposite. If production is at the heart of the system and determines the rest — the nature of the state, ideology and so on — then capitalism had to be fought on the shopfloor. This meant supporting strike activity but shunning any political strategy.

The workers' council resolved this conundrum. It fought at the most basic economic level, whether wages, conditions or food provision, *and* laid claim to state power. It underlined the fact that in periods of open class war, no strike is purely economic but has political implications in terms of class confidence, the weakening of the state and so on. Similarly it stressed that politics is not a question of parliamentary elections but of workers' self-activity *against* the state.

THREE: Consciousness from within or without?

Before the war the 'politicians' insisted that only socialist *education* and the preaching of ideas could change society. The syndicalists were not concerned with theory; they trusted to *industrial struggle* to automatically transform people into revolutionaries. In its starkest form, the choice was between consciousness arising from the intervention of socialist intellectuals from outside the labour movement, or the spontaneous generation of revolutionary consciousness inside it through trade union activity.

The workers' council offered an answer to this problem. Two elements were involved: firstly, as a result of the crisis, simple economic struggle threatened to extend beyond the boundaries of one enterprise or industry, for behind every employer was the national state apparatus. Thus the sectional became generalised and the industrial struggle tended towards the class struggle. Trade union methods had to be discarded in favour of broader action. The result was a sort of consciousness 'from within'. The workers' council provided the organisational framework for this process by combining the disparate struggles of various sections under one roof. *But this did not occur automatically.* Consciousness from without was the second part of the answer. Workers did not spontaneously free themselves from reformism, although self-activity prepared the way for new ideas. The alternative ideas of revolutionary socialism had to be introduced by an organisation independent of the majority of workers, for this majority was still in the grip of reformist thinking. In this sense revolutionary ideas could be said to come 'from without'.

Though apparently contradictory — consciousness from within by spontaneous generation, or without by the intervention of independent revolutionary propaganda — a dynamic combination of both was vital.

FOUR: Organisation or politics?

The years 1915 to 1920 were a laboratory for a number of experiments. They ranged from revolutionary movements founded on pure politics and a rejection of solid organisation, to those which put their faith in structure alone.

The Spartakists were in the former category, for their real interest was in propaganda rather than the detailed work of organisation. But when put to the test in 1918–19, the politics of the German Communist Party were swamped by a mass of followers who were prey to ultra-left abstentionism and anti-trade unionism. It proved impossible to promote a serious political argument without regard to organisation.

The reverse was also true. Organisational purity was no guarantee of revolutionary potential. Many British and Italian socialists made a fetish of democratic workers' councils and trusted that the right type of thinking would follow as a result. The Clyde stewards saw formal unity as more important than internationalism. Their defeat by the state showed that workers' organisation had to take account of the general situation in which it functioned. Turin's organisationally 'pure' model could not, of itself, guarantee revolutionary consciousness either. The commissars hoped workshop organisation would form the basis of a pyramid of power that would transform society. But they barely confronted political questions and Gramsci was brought to a painful awareness of the limitations of depending entirely on organisational procedures to achieve political goals. This led him to affirm the need for independent action through a revolutionary party.

Throughout this book we have seen the fallacy of posing revolutionary change in terms of 'either/or' logic — either consciousness or organisation, immediate action or long-term preparation, party or class. Each of the polar opposites must be understood not as a fixed proposition, but constantly in motion, reflecting and at the same time changing the social universe of which it is part.

The most important relationship concerning us here was that of party and council. We have seen how the success of the workers' council, in becoming a soviet and seizing state power, depended on a mass organisation of revolutionaries. This has been further confirmed by sixty years of class struggle since then. Many councils or other forms of organised mass self-activity have emerged. Spain in 1936, Hungary in 1956, Portugal in 1974 or Poland 1980 are but a few examples. While Western Europe in 1915–20 shows that the conscious element in the building of councils was important, in the case of party building conscious and deliberate work is even more essential. The Russian soviet could be built in 24 hours, and while the Clyde Workers' Committee or Turin factory councils took longer to assemble the council form was flexible enough quickly to overcome problems.

The revolutionary party, which Trotsky called the 'brain' of the class, must draw on the lessons of history, the analytical tools of Marxism, the experience of a large body of vanguard workers, in order to synthesise this wealth of experience and use it to guide the class. This process of synthesis takes time. The Bolshevik party existed for 14 years before its triumph. The European Communist Parties were formed in the midst of mass struggle and their newness was one reason why they proved unequal to the tasks before them. Nevertheless the very fact that they were established at all at that time owed not a little to the workers' council experience. For this had been the first opportunity in decades for revolutionaries to take on the challenge of mass leadership. Some lessons useful to the building of revolutionary parties in conditions of reformism could therefore be drawn from the 1915–20 period.

Firstly, stress on a rank-and-file orientation was essential. Reformists rely on bureaucrats distanced from the direct struggle of the working class, but the revolutionary party sees the process of workers' self-emancipation beginning in the workplaces, not at union headquarters or in parliament. Concentrating on building shopfloor confidence and organisation means working inside trade unions, not to capture the apparatus, but to raise the confidence of the rank and file in their own abilities.

Secondly, the transition from sectional or economic struggle to political class struggle is not something that begins on the day of the revolution. Reformists always refuse to raise the level of economic struggle to anything higher. Sectarians always stand aside from such struggle for fear of sullying their political purity. To build a revolutionary party every workers' issue must be approached with the aim of raising the self-activity of those involved and increasing the extent to which the fight of a section is generalised and the class struggle as a whole lifted.

The interrelation of party, collective organisation and masses reached its highest point in October 1917. While we are obviously far from such a situation today, if this strategy is adopted every strike can become a training ground for socialist revolution, every strike committee the embryo of a workers' council.

Thirdly, the workers' council cannot be left as a historical curiosity, to be pulled down from the shelf for academic debates. A revolutionary party can only be built if the final view is kept firmly in sight, and present-day work directed to that goal. The aim of a workers' state tomorrow implies a certain method of operation today.

★ ★ ★ ★ ★

There is an essential continuity of workers' revolt and revolutionary self-organisation that spans this century. It arises in the most diverse forms and countries but traces its common origin in the nature of capitalism itself. At the very heart of the system is the drive to accumulate. This leads inexorably to the development of the working class, a continual disturbance of all fixed social forms and relations, and inevitably to crisis. Trench warfare and the pneumatic lathe might seem factors unique to their time. But they reappear once more in a new guise.

Today we are in the midst of a 'second industrial revolution' brought about by the microchip. Capitalism is once more in an intractable crisis. In 1914 such a crisis led to imperialist war. Now

the race to amass weapons of destruction makes the rush before the
First World War to build 'Dreadnought' battleships pale into
insignificance. However the forces which can be marshalled against
capitalism today are also much greater. Despite the exaggerated
notions of academics such as André Gorz or Eric Hobsbawm, who
write off the working class, its potential collective power far exceeds
that of 1915–20. This is easily proved. Though the proportion of
white-collar workers in Britain is rising (and many of these see
themselves as workers and join unions) the 10 million manual
workers still form a majority of the class. In engineering the
number employed exceeds the 1921 figure.[27] Today we are not
dealing with one or two mass production industries or a handful of
European cities, but a world system with a proletariat massed in
centres as far apart as Sao Paulo, Gdansk and Bangkok.

At present, as in Rosa Luxemburg's day, the fundamental
choice facing humanity is 'socialism or barbarism', but now the
alternatives are even more sharply defined. Barbarism means total
destruction through nuclear war; socialism means a society where
the miracles of modern technology could work to satisfy all material
needs and provide the basis for ending social oppression and
exploitation. Socialists today have several advantages over those
who came before, one of which is the example of the soviet and
workers' council movements after the First World War.

This means the tragic defeats need not be repeated. We do not
have to retrace the steps of European revolutionaries who discovered how to build parties *after* the capitalist crisis had reached
its highest pitch. Taken side by side with the Russian experience,
the successes and failures of the years 1915–20 in Western Europe
are a rich source of information on how modern capitalism can be
fought and defeated. Socialism can only be realised if a revolutionary
party is built. This must base itself on the workers' council tradition, which replaces the sham of parliament with the only power
that can really change society — the collective strength of workers.

NOTES

INTRODUCTION
1. Quoted in G A Williams, **Proletarian Order** (London 1975) page 214.

Chapter One: SOVIETS AND REVOLUTION IN PETROGRAD
1. R Luxemburg, **Rosa Luxemburg Speaks, a selection of her writings** (New York 1970) page 269.
2. Quoted in J Braunthal, **History of the International**, volume 2 (London 1967) pages 168–169 (note).
3. British Government Cabinet Papers, GT6 323 and 326 (13 November 1918).
4. **Die Kommunistische Internationale**, no 1 (April 1919), English translation in Braunthal, page 168 (note).
5. V I Lenin, **Collected Works** (Moscow 1965) volume 25, page 387.
6. Lenin, **Collected Works**, volume 25, page 389.
7. Lenin, **Collected Works**, volume 25, page 388.
8. Marx, Engels, Lenin, **Anarchism and Anarcho-Syndicalism** (USSR 1972) page 103.
9. Quoted from Marx, in Lenin, **Collected Works**, volume 25, page 462.
10. Lenin, **Collected Works**, volume 25, page 492.
11. For a full discussion of the class nature of Russia see T Cliff, **State Capitalism in Russia** (London 1974).
12. Lenin, **Collected Works**, volume 25, page 492.
13. Lenin, **Collected Works**, volume 29, pages 106–108.
14. Quoted in Lenin, **Collected Works**, volume 25, page 414.
15. V I Lenin, **The Proletarian Revolution and the Renegade Kautsky** (Moscow 1976) page 22.
16. L Trotsky, **1905** (London 1971) page 122.
17. Trotsky, **1905**, page 122.
18. Trotsky, **1905**, page 123.
19. Trotsky, **1905**, page 201.
20. Trotsky, **1905**, page 266.
21. Quoted in T Cliff, **Lenin**, volume 1 (London 1975) page 163.
22. Quoted in Cliff, **Lenin**, volume 1, page 166.
23. D Mandel, **The Petrograd Workers and the Fall of the Old Regime** (London 1983) page 44.

24.   S Smith, **Red Petrograd** (London 1983) page 10.
25.   Mandel, page 44.
26.   For a discussion of this point see C Goodey, 'Factory Committees and the Dictatorship of the Proletariat', in **Critique** no 3 (Autumn 1974); S Smith, **Red Petrograd**, and D Mandel, **The Petrograd Workers and the Fall of the Old Regime**.
27.   Smith, page 50.
28.   T Hasegawa, **The February Revolution in Petrograd 1917** (Seattle 1981) page 326.
29.   Some Bolsheviks were too busy fighting on the barricades and others involved in building 'party factory committees' to pay attention to these moves. See Hasegawa, page 328.
30.   N N Sukhanov, **The Russian Revolution 1917** (London 1955) page 60.
31.   Sukhanov, page 61.
32.   Trotsky, **1905**, page 267.
33.   M Ferro, **The Russian Revolution of February 1917** (London 1972) page 79 and M Ferro, **The October Revolution** (London 1980) page 183.
34.   Quoted in W H Chamberlin, **The Russian Revolution** (New York 1976) volume 1, page 101.
35.   Trotsky, **History of the Russian Revolution** (London 1977) page 224.
36.   Trotsky, **History of the Russian Revolution**, pages 212–213.
37.   Mandel, pages 91–92.
38.   Smith, page 55.
39.   Smith, page 98.
40.   R A Wade, 'Workers' Militia and Red Guards', in R Carter Elwood (editor), **Reconsiderations on the Russian Revolution** (Columbus, Ohio, 1976) page 29.
41.   Smith, pages 104 and 109.
42.   This was 2.4 per cent of the total. See J H Keep, **The Russian Revolution, A Study in Mass Mobilisation** (London 1976) page 146.
43.   Sukhanov, page 258.
44.   Translation in O Anweiler, **The Soviets** (New York 1974) page 130.
45.   Quoted in Hasegawa, page 402.
46.   Hasegawa, page 402.
47.   Mandel, page 87.
48.   Sukhanov, page 86.
49.   Lenin, **Collected Works**, volume 24, page 38.
50.   Lenin, **Collected Works**, volume 24, page 38.
51.   Lenin, **Collected Works**, volume 24, page 49.
52.   Lenin, **Collected Works**, volume 25, page 171.
53.   Quoted in Cliff, **Lenin**, volume 2, page 171.
54.   Quoted in Trotsky, **History of the Russian Revolution**, page 363.
55.   Trotsky, **History of the Russian Revolution**, page 364.
56.   'On 23 May the moderate-controlled Petrograd Soviet Executive resolved to issue procedural rules for such re-elections. They were to be held only once a quarter of the voters had demanded them and their wish had been reported to the Soviet through regular channels; an electoral commission would then be set up; the elections would not be held until seven days had elapsed, to allow all parties sufficient opportunity to campaign; the sitting deputy must be present at the poll; finally the results were to be approved by the Soviet's "credentials commission".' Keep, page 145.

57. Mandel, page 125.
58. Mandel, page 127.
59. Of course the homogeneity of the Bolshevik party can be exaggerated, and this is one of the distortions of the Stalinist era. While many recent studies have uncovered the frequent internal differences within the Bolsheviks, the fact that in general the party was able to offer consistent policies and yet was flexible enough to adapt quickly and as a whole to every shift in the masses is clear evidence of the value of democratic centralist party organisation.
60. Smith, page 149.
61. Sukhanov, page 395.
62. Sukhanov, page 418.
63. A Rabinowitch, **Prelude to Revolution** (Indiana University Press, 1968) page 114.
64. Rabinowitch, page 119.
65. Quoted in Rabinowitch, page 188.
66. Quoted in Rabinowitch, page 194.
67. Trotsky, **History of the Russian Revolution**, pages 575–576.
68. Trotsky, **History of the Russian Revolution**, page 825.
69. Lenin, **Collected Works**, volume 24, page 38.
70. Lenin, **Collected Works**, volume 25, page 189.
71. Trotsky, **History of the Russian Revolution**, page 804.
72. Trotsky, **History of the Russian Revolution**, pages 928–929.
73. Smith, page 124.
74. Smith, page 125.
75. Quoted in Smith, page 157.
76. See strike statistics for 1917 in U Brügmann, **Die russischen Gewerkschaften in Revolution und Bürgerkrieg** (Frankfurt-am-Main 1972) page 86.
77. Lenin, **Collected Works**, volume 26, pages 19–21.
78. Lenin, **Collected Works**, volume 26, page 21.
79. Lenin, **Collected Works**, volume 26, page 83.
80. Art, unlike science, allows for wide variation of method and interpretation. That insurrection was an 'art' was borne out by the wide differences that emerged between Lenin and Trotsky on the handling of the October rising. Trotsky was vindicated by the swift success of the seizure of power he organised in Petrograd. For discussion of this question see Cliff, **Lenin**, volume 2, pages 367–376.
81. Trotsky, **History of the Russian Revolution**, page 943.
82. Trotsky, **History of the Russian Revolution**, page 961.
83. Trotsky, **History of the Russian Revolution**, page 1130.
84. Trotsky, **History of the Russian Revolution**, page 1021 (my emphasis).

Chapter 2: WESTERN IMPERIALISM IN CRISIS

1. D Mitchell, **1919, Red Mirage** (London 1970) page 16.
2. D Lloyd George, **War Memoirs** (London 1938) volume 1, page 147.
3. See W Rathenau, quoted in G Feldman, **Army, Industry and Labor in Germany 1914–18** (Princeton 1966) page 49.
4. F Engels, **Anti-Dühring** (Peking 1976) page 352.
5. P Frölich, **Rosa Luxemburg** (London 1972) pages 168–9.

6.   B Buozzi, quoted in M Abrate, **La Lotta Sindicale nella Industrializzazione** (Milan 1967) page 168.

7.   J Hinton, **The First Shop Stewards' Movement** (London 1973) page 34.

8.   For the full text of the Auxiliary Service Law see Feldman, pages 535–541.

9.   Lloyd George, volume 2, page 2041; G A Williams, **Proletarian Order**, page 55; J B Drabkin, **Die Novemberrevolution 1918 in Deutschland** (Berlin 1968) page 71.

10. J M Winter, 'The Impact of the First World War on Civilian Health in Britain', **Economic History Review** (1977) pages 502–505.

11. **Avanti!** (Turin, 13 January 1918).

12. E C Schöck, **Arbeitslosigkeit und Rationalisierung** (Regensburg 1977) page 237.

13. D Horowitz, **The Italian Labour Movement** (Cambridge, Massachusetts 1963) page 75.

14. **Luxemburg Speaks**, page 261.

15. Abstract of Labour Statistics (HMSO London 1926) page 144; J Kuczynski, **Die Geschichte der Lage der Arbeiter unter dem Kapitalismus** (Berlin 1966) volume 4, page 249; Annuario Statistico Italiano, volume 4 (1925) page 512.

16. For a statistical analysis of metalworkers' strike patterns before the war in Britain and Germany see P Stearns, **Lives of Labour** (London 1975) pages 374–383. The wartime period could not have been more different. In 1918 in Germany, the number of strikers in selected industries were as follows:

	Political strikers	Economic strikers
Metals and machines	378,000	188,000
Mining	144,000	396,000
Building	27	5,000
Transport	193	3,000

(**Reichsarbeitsblatt**, 1919, no 11, pages 866–867).
In Italy metals also had a leading position, although it was temporarily surpassed by textiles:

Strikers in selected industries in Italy (thousands)

	1914	1915	1916	1917	1918	1919	1920
Metals	19	22	33	24	69	395	188
Textiles	23	57	50	98	52	195	115
Building	32	8	2	9	.3	45	70
Transport	36	22	8	2	5	82	241

(**Annuario Statistico Italiano**, 1918, page 331 and 1919–21, page 396.)

17. R Müller, **Vom Kaiserreich zur Republik**, volume 1 (Vienna 1924) page 56.

18. Müller, page 40.

19. Quoted in M Cole, **The Story of Fabian Socialism** (London 1961) page 163 (footnote).

20. Beveridge Collection on Munitions, in the British Library of Economic and Political Science, Section 5, Item 2.

21. A de Grand, 'Women under Italian Fascism' in **Historical Journal** (1976) page 948.

22. J Kocka, **Klassengesellschaft im Krieg 1914–18** (Göttingen 1973) page 12.

23. This argument is stated clearly in S Bologna, 'Class Composition and the Theory of the Party at the Origin of the Workers' Council Movement' in **Telos** (Fall 1972). It underpins the approach of K H Roth in **L'altro movimento operaio**

(Milan 1976) and is implicit in much of Hinton's book. See for example his discussion of the difference between labour aristocrats in the northern engineering centres and the sort of militancy witnessed in modern Coventry (pages 220–221).

The evidence produced by international comparison decisively refutes this idea. Metalworking experienced rapid growth and transformation in the period before the war. In Britain, where the rate of change was slowest and the labour aristocracy most entrenched, revolutionary ideas and workers' councils had the weakest hold on the mass of engineering workers.

Percentage growth of labour force in the expanding industries of the pre-war period

	Britain	Germany	Italy
	(1891–1901)	*(1895–1907)*	*(1901–1911)*
General engineering	2.4	13.4	59.3
Mining	2.7	2.7	—
Building	1.6	3.6	23.2
Chemicals	3.9	4.1	75.9
Printing	2.4	5.1	—

(Sources: Stearns, page 26, and I Barbadoro, **Storia del Sindicalismo Italiano**, volume 1 (Florence 1973) page 22.)
24. **Public Opinion** (31 August 1917).

Chapter 3: GLASGOW — LAYING THE FOUNDATIONS

1.   R H Middlemas, **The Clydesiders** (London 1965) page 19.
2.   **Municipal Glasgow** (Glasgow 1914) page 131.
3.   W Kendall, **The Revolutionary Movement in Britain** (London 1969) page 107.
4.   T Bell, **Pioneering Days** (London 1941) pages 72–73.
5.   Quoted in N Milton, **John Maclean** (London 1973) page 73.
6.   H McShane and J Smith, **Harry McShane, No Mean Fighter** (London 1978) page 59.
7.   See Hinton, pages 76–93.
8.   **Socialist Unity Conference, 30 September to 1 October 1911** (no date or place of publication given) page 18.
9.   **The Miners' Next Step** (first published 1912, reprinted London 1973) page 22.
10. **The Socialist**, paper of the SLP (March 1910).
11. Milton, page 79.
12. Hinton, page 125.
13. See for example Johnny Muir's discussion of socialism, revolution and industrial unionism reported in **The Socialist** (February 1910).
14. W Gallacher, **Revolt on the Clyde** (London 1978) page 13.
15. McShane, page 31.
16. Gallacher, pages 39–40.
17. Hinton, page 106.
18. Clyde Workers' Committee leaflet in Beveridge Collection, III, Item 15.
19. Gallacher, page 51.
20. Gallacher, page 51.
21. Hinton, page 120.
22. Hinton, page 119.

23. Clyde Workers' Committee leaflet in Beveridge Collection, III, Item 5.

24. Report of the special committee appointed by the annual conference of the Labour Party held at Manchester in January 1917 to inquire into and report upon the circumstances which resulted in the deportation, in March 1916, of David Kirkwood and other workmen employed in Munitions factories in the Clyde District (London 1917) pages 15–16.

25. J D Macdougall, quoted in Milton, page 79.

26. Milton, page 97.

27. Kendall, page 116.

28. Beveridge Collection, V, Item 6.

29. An important argument of Muir's statement was the following: dilution 'is a step in the direct line of industrial evolution. But — and this is where the present difficulties arise — its progressive character is lost to the community unless it is accompanied by a corresponding step in social evolution.' This approach avoids any traces of craftism and a defence of skilled privilege for its own sake. It is also a graphic description of the peculiar position of the engineering worker, who now saw the rapid socialisation of the labour process accompanied by the private appropriation of the wealth that this created.

30. **The Worker**, paper of the Clyde Workers' Committee (15 January 1916).

31. Hinton, page 132.

32. J T Murphy, **Preparing for Power** (London 1972) page 121.

33. **Vanguard** (December 1915).

34. **Vanguard** (October 1915).

35. Quoted in Kendall, page 116.

36. McShane, page 77.

37. This disruption was organised by Maclean's supporters rather than the committee, which published a rebuttal of the disorderly behaviour.

38. The account was printed in the **Voice of Labour** and taken from **Forward**, the ILP paper suppressed for carrying the report in January 1916.

39. Beveridge Collection, III, Item 36.

40. See Beveridge Collection, V, Item 6, and Hinton, pages 151–152.

41. J T Murphy, **New Horizons** (London 1941) page 44.

Chapter 4: THE LESSONS OF FAILURE

1. For a full account see Hinton, pages 196–212.

2. Murphy, page 153.

3. 'The Leeds Convention: a report from the Daily Herald', in **British Labour and the Russian Revolution** (Nottingham 1974) pages 29–30.

4. **British Labour and the Russian Revolution**, page 34.

5. **The Call**, paper of the BSP (28 December 1917).

6. **Glasgow Herald** (19 January 1918).

7. Gallacher, pages 183–184.

8. **Solidarity**, paper of national stewards' movement (February 1918).

9. **Forward** (11 May 1918).

10. **Glasgow Herald** (9 September 1918).

11. **Forward** (23 November 1918).

12. For full results see **Labour Leader** (2 January 1919). In fact the 'Khaki

election' was a serious defeat for the Labour Party in that its vote increased only because more candidates were fielded. The Lloyd George coalition was returned with a landslide majority. Still, the point about the relative increase in Glasgow's vote stands.

13. Milton, page 183.

14. J Leopold, 'The forty hours strike', in **We Shall Be All** (Glasgow 1978) page 34.

15. D S Morton, **The Forty Hours' Strike** (Glasgow, no date) page 12.

16. The Joint Committee which ran the strike included the Scottish TUC Parliamentary Committee, Glasgow Trades Council, district committees of the Ship and Allied Trades, the Scottish Union of Dock Labourers, the Railwaymen, the Municipal Workers' Association, the Building Trades and Electricians' representatives. Thus the Clyde Workers' Committee, which also took part, was not the decisive element in the leadership.

17. **The Worker** (28 December 1918).

18. Morton, page 6.

19. Morton, page 6.

20. Manifesto completed on 2 January 1919 and presented to SLP Conference of 11–12 January 1919, published in **The Socialist** (30 January 1919).

21. **The Socialist** (30 January 1919).

22. **The Socialist** (30 January 1919).

Chapter 5: GERMANY IN WAR

1. D Baudis and H Roth, 'Berliner Opfer der Novemberrevolution 1918/19', in **Jahrbuch für Wirtschaftsgeschichte** volume 3 (Berlin 1968) page 109.

2. A Lange, **Das Wilhelminische Berlin** (Berlin 1967) pages 89–90.

3. Report of the Berlin Chamber of Commerce for 1910, cited in **Deutsche Metallarbeiterzeitung** (DMZ) (4 February 1911).

4. For example, the 72,000 workers in 'large' machine and instrument works (with more than 50 employees) outnumbered by 19 to 1 the employees of 'small' firms (with between one and five employees) (Lange, page 11). This was at a time when *nationally* the average number of workers in engineering factories was just 5.6.

5. Baudis and Roth, page 108.

6. R Woldt, 'Gross Industrien und Gewerkschaftsarbeit' in **Die Neue Zeit**, Jahrg 31, Band 1.2, page 805.

7. J Karski, 'Neue Studien zur soziale Lage der Berliner Metallarbeiter', in **Die Neue Zeit**, Jahrg 29, Band 2.1.

8. DMZ (13 June 1914).

9. **Der DMV in Zahlen** (Berlin 1932) page 111.

10. For a discussion of the changing situation in the unions see R V Elm, 'Massen und Führer', in **Die Neue Zeit**, Jahrg 20, Band 1.2.

11. The 'middle level' consisted of 23 branch representatives, 23 district representatives, 39 full-time officials and eight honorary members.

12. P Broué, **Révolution en Allemagne** (Paris 1971) page 291.

13. **Luxemburg Speaks**, page 185.

14. A Pannekoek, 'Massen Aktionen und Revolution' in **Die Neue Zeit**, Jahrg 30, Band 2.2, pages 534–548.

15.   **Internationaler Sozialisten-Kongress zu Stuttgart, 1907** (Berlin 1907) page 106.

16.   C Harman, **The Lost Revolution** (London 1982) pages 16–17.

17.   K Kautsky, **The Road to Power** (Chicago 1909) page 50.

18.   **Luxemburg Speaks**, page 330.

19.   K Retzlaw, **Gezeiten der Revolution** (Frankfurt-a-M 1972) page 44.

20.   P van Oertzen, **Betriebsräte in der Novemberrevolution** (Düsseldorf 1961) page 74. See also the estimates of George Ledebour and Volkmann in W Tormin, **Zwischen Rätediktatur und sozialer Demokratie** (Düsseldorf 1954) page 42.

21.   Feldman, page 79.

22.   Kuczynski, volume 4, pages 256 and 269.

23.   G Bry, **Wages in Germany 1871–1945** (Princeton 1960) pages 191–192.

24.   R Müller, **Der Burgerkrieg in Deutschland** (Berlin 1925) page 86.

25.   R Müller, **Vom Kaiserreich zur Republik** (Vienna 1924) volume 1, page 125.

26.   Müller, **Vom Kaiserreich**, volume 1, pages 58–60. In fact Cohen escaped the test of election again in the November revolution by threatening to wreck the DMV apparatus if his competence was questioned. See **Freiheit** (20 November 1918).

27.   Broué, page 79.

28.   Müller, **Vom Kaiserreich**, volume 1, pages 65–66.

29.   Retzlaw, page 51.

30.   O K Flechtheim, **Die KPD in der Weimarer Republik** (Frankfurt-a-M 1966) page 103.

31.   E Kolb, **Arbeiterräte in der deutschen Innenpolitik, 1918/19** (Düsseldorf 1962) pages 52–53.

32.   Unabhängige Sozialdemokratische Partei: Protokoll über die Verhandlungen des aussenordentlichen Parteitags, in Halle vom 12 bis 17 Oktober (Berlin 1920).

33.   C Schorske, **German Social Democracy, 1907–17** (Harvard 1972) page 296.

34.   Schorske, page 296. This is Ebert's calculation.

35.   Liebknecht, speaking to the founding Congress of the Communist Party, in A and D Prudhommeaux (editors), **Spartakus et la Commune de Berlin 1918–1919** (Paris, no date) pages 40–41.

36.   Müller, **Vom Kaiserreich**, page 96.

37.   Quoted in Harman, page 33.

38.   Although it should be noted that this confusion was not entirely confined to the Obleute. The actual proposal that the SPD leaders be co-opted apparently came from a Spartakist.

39.   **Illustrierte Geschichte der Novemberrevolution in Deutschland** (Berlin 1968) page 30.

40.   **Dokumente und Materialen zur Geschichte der deutschen Arbeiter-Bewegung**, Reihe II (Berlin 1955) Band 2, page 175.

Chapter 6: THE KAISER FALLS

1.   See Harman, page 306 and Broué, pages 106–109.

2.   F C Carsten, **Reichswehr und Politik** (Köln 1964) page 19.

3.   In many military units Hindenberg's tactics paid off and officers maintained complete dominance. See U Kluge, **Soldatenräte und Revolution** (Berlin 1975) pages 158–9. In the field of workers' councils, Carsten has unearthed several bodies

euphemistically bearing this title. Landsberg, on the river Lech, had a 12-man workers' council which included a lawyer, police official, prison inspector, innkeeper, merchant, brewer and storekeeper. Another example of extremist subversion was to be found at Neumarkt, where the chairman of the so-called workers' council was a vet and the other officials a master baker and master plumber. (F C Carsten, **Revolution in Central Europe** (London 1972) page 191.)

4.   For local details see I Materna, **Der Vollzugsrat der Berliner Arbeiter- und Soldatenräte, 1918/19** (Berlin 1978) page 20; E Lucas, **Frankfurt unter der Herrschaft des Arbeiter und Soldatenrats** (Frankfurt-a-M 1969); R Comfort, **Revolutionary Hamburg** (Stanford 1966); E Kolb and K Schöhoven (editors), **Regionale und lokale Räteorganisationen in Württemberg** (Düsseldorf 1976).

5.   Reichsarchiv, **Der Weltkrieg, 1914–18** (Berlin, no date) page 31.

6.   **Der 9 November 1918** (Berlin 1958) page 28–29.

7.   P Scheidemann, **Memoirs of a Social Democrat** (London 1929) volume 2, page 567.

8.   'Die Ersten Tage der Novemberrevolution', in Berlin, **Beitrag zur Geschichte**, Sonderheft zum 50 Jahrestag der Novemberrevolution (1968) page 50.

9.   E Eichhorn, **Mein Tätigkeit im Berlin Polizeipräsidium** (Berlin 1919) page 8.

10.   **Berliner Tageblatt** (10 November 1918). English translation in S Haffner, **Failure of a Revolution, Germany 1918/1919** (London 1973) page 102.

11.   Quoted in Harman, page 46.

12.   Quoted in Carsten, **Reichswehr**, page 24.

13.   Scheidemann, page 600.

14.   For a study of this contradictory phenomenon see H E Friedlander, 'Conflict of Revolutionary Authority', in **International Review of Social History** (1963) pages 163–176.

Chapter 7: THE REVOLUTIONARY CHEMISTRY OF NOVEMBER 1918

1.   **Vorwärts** (10 November 1918).

2.   Rote Fahne (10 November 1918).

3.   **Rote Fahne** (14 December 1918). English translation in H Gruber (editor), **International Communism in the era of Lenin** (New York 1972) pages 110–112.

4.   Drabkin, page 71.

5.   D Geary, 'Radicalism and the Worker' in R Evans (editor), **Society and Politics in Wilhelmine Germany** (London 1978) page 274.

6.   W Wille, 'Als Mitglied des Neuköllner Vollzugsrates in der Novemberrevolution', bzg (Sonderheft 1968).

7.   See **Berliner Tageblatt** (10–14 November 1918).

8.   **Berliner Tageblatt** (12 November 1918).

9.   **Weltrevolution**, paper of the Neukölln council (10 November 1918).

10.   **Berliner Tageblatt** (13 November 1918).

11.   D Baudis, 'Revolution und Konterrevolution im Kampf um die Betriebe' in **Jahrbuch für Wirtschaftsgeschichte** volume 4 (Berlin 1967).

12.   Harman, page 55.

13.   **Vorwärts** (13 November 1918).

14.   **Berliner Tageblatt** (15 November 1918).

15.   Materna, page 66.

16. Materna, page 56.
17. 'Protokoll der Sitzung des Vollzugsrat der Arbeiter- und Soldatenräte am 16 November 1918' in BZG, Sonderheft, pages 138–145.
18. **Rote Fahne** (5 December 1918).
19. **Freiheit** (15 November 1918).
20. Quoted in C S Maier, **Recasting Bourgeois Europe** (Princeton 1975) page 60.
21. See, for example, **Correspondenzblatt der Generalkommission der Gewerkschaften** (20 and 27 April 1918).
22. **Berliner Tageblatt** (15 November 1918).
23. **Correspondenzblatt** (23 November 1918).
24. **Vorwärts** (25 November 1918).
25. **Freiheit** (20 November 1918).
26. **Freiheit** (30 November 1918).
27. Materna, page 90.
28. **Rote Fahne** (20 November 1918).
29. **Berliner Tageblatt** (18 November 1918).
30. **Rote Fahne** (20 November 1918).
31. **Rote Fahne** (27 November 1918).
32. Summary of bourgeois press in **Rote Fahne** (27 November 1918).
33. **Rote Fahne** (27 November 1918).
34. **Freiheit** (25 November 1918).
35. Materna, page 100.
36. **Berliner Tageblatt** (25 November 1918).
37. **Vorwärts** (28 November 1918).
38. F Bey-Heard, **Haupstadt und Staatsumwälzung Berlin 1919** (Stuttgart 1969) page 96.
39. Quoted in **Rote Fahne** (25 November 1918).
40. **Rote Fahne** (28 November 1918).
41. **Berliner Tageblatt** (27 November 1918).
42. **Freiheit** (28 November 1918).
43. **Vorwärts** (29 November 1918).

Chapter 8: REACTION VERSUS REVOLUTION

1. **Rote Fahne** (30 November 1918).
2. **Berliner Tageblatt** (3 December 1918).
3. Baudis, 'Revolution und Konterrevolution', page 155.
4. F Oeckel, **Die Revolutionäre Volkswehr 1918/19** (Berlin 1968) page 155.
5. Materna, page 23.
6. Broué, page 228.
7. **Rote Fahne** (8 December 1918).
8. **Rote Fahne** (9 December 1918).
9. **Rote Fahne** (15 December 1918).
10. R Rürup (editor), **Arbeiter- and Soldenräte im Rheinisch Westfälschen Industriegebiet** (Wuppertal 1975) page 183.
11. **Rote Fahne** (15 December 1918).
12. **Vorwärts** (12 December 1918).
13. **Vorwärts** (2 December 1918).

14. **Berliner Tageblatt** (14 December 1918).
15. **Berliner Tageblatt** (14 December 1918).
16. **Rote Fahne** (11 December 1918).
17. Appendix to **Allgemeine Kongress der Arbeiter- und Soldatenräte Deutschlands vom 16 bis 21 Dezember 1918, Illustrierte Geschichte**, pages 249–250, and Broué, page 158.
18. Eugen Leviné's report, in appendix to R Leviné-Meyer, **Leviné, The Life of a Revolutionary** (Farnborough 1973) page 189.
19. **Freiheit** (17 December 1918).
20. **Berliner Tageblatt** (24 December 1918).
21. Retzlaw, page 64.
22. **Rote Fahne** (20 December 1918).
23. **Rote Fahne** (14 and 24 December 1918).
24. F Zikelsky, **Das Gewehr in meiner Hand** (Berlin 1958) pages 156–7.
25. Unemployment stood at 88,500 in Berlin and was mounting quickly.
26. **Illustrierte Geschichte**, page 257. English translation in Harman, page 64.
27. **Berliner Tageblatt** (30 December 1918).
28. **Rote Fahne** (3 January 1919).
29. Prudhommeaux, page 50.
30. **Berliner Tageblatt** (25 February 1919).
31. **Protokoll der Sitzung der revolutionären Obleute und Vertrauensleute der Grossbetriebe am 1 Jan. 1919, BZG**, no 6 (1975) page 1009.
32. **Rote Fahne** (25 November 1918).
33. **Rote Fahne** (23 December 1918).
34. **Rote Fahne** (3 January 1919).
35. **Freiheit** (30 December 1918).
36. **Freiheit** (30 December 1918).
37. **Rote Fahne** (5 January 1919).
38. **Freiheit** (5 January 1919).
39. Quoted in **Der Sieg der Arbeiter und Matrosen im Dezember 1918** (Berlin 1958) page 24.
40. **Rote Fahne** (5 September 1920).
41. **Freiheit** and **Rote Fahne** (5 January 1919). English translation in Gruber, page 115.
42. Paul Levi, **Rote Fahne** (5 September 1920). English translation in Scheidemann, volume 2, page 609.
43. Broué, page 245.
44. **Freiheit** (11 January 1919).
45. An analysis has been made of those revolutionaries killed in the months between November 1918 and January 1919. Of the 110 about whom details are available, 93 were manual workers. Almost 60 per cent were skilled or semi-skilled. By far the largest group were metalworkers; indeed, eleven came from a single factory — the DWM.
    Study of other biographical details reveals further interesting facts. The social background of the victims suggests their fathers tended to hold jobs with higher social standing. Thus the proportion who had self-employed fathers was 24.3 per cent, while among the dead themselves only 2.7 per cent had been self-employed. It seems that rapid expansion of giant metal factories and the rapid proletarianisation of the imperialist era were therefore important.

Finally, the age structure (the 16–20 group alone made up 24 per cent of victims, while those under 30 formed 60 per cent of all deaths) and the fact that only a minority were born in Berlin itself, demonstrates the relevance of accelerated growth in city size as a factor in generating revolutionary capitals. (Baudis and Roth, 'Berliner Opfer', pages 77–105.)

46. **Rote Fahne** (9 January 1919).

47. *Public election results for the three main parties in Berlin (thousands)*

	National Assembly *(19 January 1919)*	Prussian Landtag *(26 January 1919)*	Local Government *(23 February 1919)*
SPD	405	343	249
Independents	306	275	260
Bourgeois Democrats	178	149	114

Berliner Tageblatt (25 and 26 February 1919).

48. Sources: **Rote Fahne** (25 November 1918), **Berliner Tageblatt** (14 December 1918), **Freiheit** (17 January 1919) and **Arbeiterrat** nos 5 and 9.

49. This is not just speculation. It has been discovered, for example, that the person who initiated the invasion of the **Vorwärts** building was in fact a government *agent provocateur*. See Broué, page 243 (note).

50. **Freiheit** (15 January 1919).

51. **Freiheit** (14 February 1919).

52. **Freiheit** (14 February 1919).

Chapter 9: ITALY — COUNCILS AND BEYOND

1. P Spriano, **Storia di Torino operaia e socialista** (Turin 1972) page 339.

2. M Clark, **Antonio Gramsci and the Revolution that Failed** (New Haven 1977) page 22.

3. **Gramsci, Selections from Political Writings, 1910–20**, edited by Q Hoare (London 1977) page 151, henceforth referred to as Gramsci, **Selections**.

4. B Crappone, first president of Turin's Lega Industriale, quoted in M Abrate, **La Lotta Sindicale nella Industrializzazione** (Milan 1967) page 66.

5. C Goodrich, **The Frontier of Control** (London 1975) page 32.

6. G Carretto quoted in M P Quercioli (editor), **Gramsci Vivo** (Milan 1977) page 67.

7. B Buozzi, **Scritti e discorsi** (Rome 1975) page 148.

8. G Procacci, quoted in Barbadoro, page 41.

9. **Il Grido del Popolo** (15 March 1913).

10. **Il Metallurgico** (1 May 1912).

11. E Santarelli, **Il Socialismo anarchicho in Italia** (Milan 1959) page 42.

12. The main points of the final agreement were:

1. Hours reduced from 59 in December 1913 to 57 in December 1914.

2. Workers could be five minutes late for a maximum of two days each week. Any excess would lead to dismissal.

3. A maximum of eight hours' overtime could be requested by management.

4. An arbitration committee of 20, split evenly between employers and workers, was to be established.

(**Il Grido** (15 March 1913).)

13. **Almanacco Socialista Italiano** (Milan 1919) page 255.

14.   B Santhia, **Con Gramsci all'Ordine Nuovo** (Rome 1956) page 46.
15.   B Santhia, quoted in C Pajetta (editor), **I Comunisti a Torino** (Rome 1974) page 16.
16.   **Avanti!** (Turin) (17 October 1918).
17.   **Il Grido** (15 July 1916).
18.   **Il Grido** (18 November 1916).
19.   C Ravera, **Diario di Trent'anni** (Rome 1973) page 19.
20.   M Montagnana, **Ricordi di un operaio torinese** (Rome 1952) page 69.
21.   R Romeo, **Storia della granda industria in Italia** (Milan 1961) pages 85–87.
22.   Clark, page 21.
23.   Santhia, page 51.
24.   Santhia, page 55.
25.   A Tasca in G Berti (editor), 'Un tentativo di recostruzione e di interpretazione degli anni 1914–20 negli appunti inediti di Angelo Tasca', **Annali Feltrinelli** (1966) page 42.
26.   E Soave, 'Appunti sulle origine teoriche e pratiche dei Consigli di Fabbrica a Torino' in **Rivista Storica del Socialismo**, no 21 (1964) page 13.
27.   **Avanti!** (Turin) (22 April 1918).
28.   Quoted in Spriano, **Storia di Torino**, page 46.
29.   **Avanti!** (Turin) (14 September 1918).
30.   **Avanti!** (Turin) (17 October 1918).
31.   G E Modigliani in **Critica Sociale** (1–15 December 1918). English translation in Clark, page 40.
32.   Vincenzo Riccio on 15 December 1918, quoted in C S Maier, **Recasting Bourgeois Europe** (Princeton 1975) page 89.
33.   P Spriano, **Storia del Partito comunista italiano**, volume 1 (Turin 1967) page 26.
34.   **Avanti!** (Milan) (17 January 1919).
35.   **Avanti!** (Milan) (14 December 1918).
36.   **Avanti!** (Milan) (2 October 1919).
37.   **Avanti!** (Milan) (5 July 1919).
38.   **Il Soviet** (1 January 1919).
39.   **Il Soviet** (16 February 1919).
40.   Clark, page 31.
41.   Buozzi, page 148, and Soave, pages 13–15.
42.   Clark's estimate, page 80.
43.   **Avanti!** (Turin) (22 December 1918).
44.   **Avanti!** (Turin) (26, 27 and 28 October 1918 are good examples).
45.   For progress on the eight-hour campaign see **Avanti!** (Turin) (22 February, 9 March and 1 April 1919).
46.   **Battaglia Sindicali** (8 March 1919).
47.   **Battaglia Sindicali** (8 March 1919).
48.   **Avanti!** (Turin) (17 March 1919).
49.   Buozzi, page 135.
50.   See **Avanti!** (Turin) (18 and 23 March 1919) for the role of the commission at Fiat Centro and (30 April) for action on wage rates. The ambiguous role the commission could play was illustrated when workers threatening unofficial action were forced back to work. See G Maione, **Il Biennio Rosso** (Bologna 1975) page 17.

51. Major trouble broke out at the Fiat Ferrier, Gnome, Ansaldo S Giorgio plants among others. See Maione, pages 20–21.

52. See for example quotation from C Artesani, a FIOM official, in Soave, page 13.

53. A Oberti in **Gramsci Vivo**, pages 123–124.

54. **Avanti!** (Turin) (17 March 1919).

55. **Ordine Nuovo** (1 May 1919).

56. **Ordine Nuovo** (15 May 1919).

57. English translation in Gramsci, **Political Writings**, page 65.

58. P Togliatti, 'Antonio Gramsci un capo della classe operaia', reprinted in P Togliatti, **Antonio Gramsci** (Rome 1977) page 4.

59. Quoted in P Spriano, **L'Ordine Nuovo e i Consigli di Fabbrica** (Turin 1971) page 82.

60. For details of the anarcho-syndicalist debate on this question see **Volonta** (1 September 1919) which reported the following resolution from a meeting of Piedmont anarchists on 14 July 1919:
'Having debated the question of the dictatorship of the proletariat, this convention of Piedmont anarchists reaffirms the absolute need for intransigence in anti-authoritarian principles, noting that the social revolution must institute the free community of producers, we accept the dictatorship of the proletariat as a means of struggle against the present society. However, we will prevent this dictatorship from being monopolised by any group or party at any cost. We therefore accept the principle of workers' and peasants' councils proposed by maximalist socialists, but will strive to make these no more than provisional and conform as much as possible to libertarian principles.'
Under the influence of the **Ordine Nuovo**, Piedmontese anarchists were much more favourable to the temporary dictatorship of the proletariat than were anarchists nationally. See for example the **Programme anarchico accettato dall'Union Anarchica Italiana nel Congresso di Bologna del 1–4 luglio 1920** (no place or date of publication given).

61. **Avanti!** (Turin) (1 September 1919).

62. Gramsci, **Political Writings**, page 95.

63. Gramsci, **Political Writings**, page 67.

64. Gramsci, **Political Writings**, page 95.

65. **Avanti!** (Turin) (16 October 1919).

66. Maione, page 50.

67. Gramsci, **Political Writings**, page 96.

68. **Avanti!** (Turin) (25 October 1919).

69. **Avanti!** (Turin) (25, 27 and 30 June 1919).

70. **Avanti!** (Turin) (3 November and 24 December 1919).

71. **Avanguardia** (30 November 1919).

72. Gramsci, **Political Writings**, page 114.

73. Gramsci, **Political Writings**, page 116.

74. Williams, pages 132–133.

75. **Battaglia Sindicali** (22 November 1919).

76. **Avanti!** (Milan) (4 November 1919).

77. For full details see **Avanti!** (Turin) (7 and 13 January 1920), and **Battaglia Sindicali** (31 January and 7 February 1920).

78. See discussion in **Il Comunismo** (1–15 March 1920).

79. **Il Comunismo** (15–30 October 1919) contains full details of the Congress.

80.   **Avanti!** (Milan) (2 October 1919).
81.   **Dittadura Proletaria** (10 October 1919).
82.   **Dittadura Proletaria** (5 December 1919).
83.   **Ordine Nuovo** (13 March 1920).

Chapter 10: REASSESSMENT AND CONFRONTATION

1.   **La Squilla** (2 December 1919).
2.   Gramsci, **Political Writings**, page 100.
3.   Gramsci, **Political Writings**, page 318.
4.   This judgement of the mood of many ex-combatants was confirmed by the phenomenon of the *arditi del popolo*, a mass movement of ex-servicemen which emerged spontaneously in 1921 to combat fascist terror. But for want of political leadership it disappeared as quickly as it had grown.
5.   **Avanti!** (Turin) (6 February 1920).
6.   Maione, page 116.
7.   Gramsci, **Political Writings**, page 121.
8.   **Il Corriere della Sera** (9 March 1920) quoted in Spriano, **Storia del PCI**, page 51.
9.   Gramsci, **Political Writings**, pages 145–146.
10.   A Leonetti in **Compagni** (16 February 1920), reprinted in A Leonetti, **Caminno di un Ordinovista** (Bari 1978) page 45.
11.   **Ordine Nuovo** (27 March 1920).
12.   Marx to F Bolte (23 November 1871) in Marx, Engels, Lenin, **Anarchism and Anarcho-syndicalism**, page 57.
13.   **Avanti!** (Turin) (3 July and 25 October 1919); **La Squilla** (2 December 1919).
14.   Gramsci, **Political Writings**, pages 159–160.
15.   Gramsci, **Political Writings**, page 161.
16.   Gramsci, **Political Writings**, pages 194–195.
17.   **Avanti!** (Turin) (25 March 1920).
18.   **Avanti!** (Turin) (28 March 1920).
19.   See Maione, pages 125–129. Nominally the dispute was over the rights of the factory council executives (which were still called by the old name of internal commissions), rather than the structure of commissars which underpinned them.
20.   Maione, pages 131–132.
21.   **Umanità Nova** (14 April 1920).
22.   Quoted in Williams, page 205.
23.   Maione, page 138.
24.   Santhia, pages 79–80.
25.   **Umanità Nova** (15 April 1920).
26.   P C Masini, **Anarchici e Comunisti nel movimento di Consigli** (Turin 1951) page 20.
27.   Gramsci, **Political Writings**, page 182.
28.   **Lavoratori Avanti!** (17 April 1920).
29.   **Avanti!** (Milan) (20 April 1920).
30.   See Gramsci, **Political Writings**, page 205.
31.   **Avanti!** (Milan) (20 April 1920).
32.   See Clark, pages 108–109.
33.   Quoted in Spriano, **Occupation of the Factories**, page 134.

34. **Gramsci Vivo**, page 95.
35. Quoted in Spriano, **Occupation of the Factories**, page 90.
36. Spriano, **Occupation of the Factories**, page 92.

Chapter 11: CONCLUSION
1.   **Luxemburg Speaks**, pages 205–207.
2.   Quoted in Schorske, page 41.
3.   See for example, K Kautsky, **Bolshevism at a Deadlock** (London 1931) pages 102–141.
4.   Quoted in A Callinicos, 'Soviet Power', in **International Socialism** no 103 (November 1977).
5.   V I Lenin, **Left-Wing Communism, An Infantile Disorder** (Moscow 1968) page 6.
6.   **Theses and Manifestoes of the First Four Congresses of the Third International** (London 1980) page 124.
7.   My emphasis. L Trotsky, **The Permanent Revolution, and Results and Prospects** (London 1962) page 240.
8.   Lenin, **Selected Works**, volume 3, page 40.
9.   Trotsky, **1905**, page 66.
10. Trotsky, **1905**, page 90.
11. Trotsky, **Permanent Revolution**, page 119.
12. In Germany, for example, 500,000 engineers in this skilled industry had won union recognition by 1912. The equally massive coal industry, to which workers had virtually unrestricted access, had only 77 miners with union recognition. Northern Italy industrialised rather later, when technology had reduced the skill content of many jobs. Here the gap between the skilled and unskilled was rather narrower than in Britain and closer to the Russian situation.
13. Trotsky, **Permanent Revolution**, page 92.
14. Trotsky, **Permanent Revolution**, page 92.
15. For a discussion of this question see my article, 'The Missing Party', in **International Socialism** (new series) no 22 (Winter 1984) and A Callinicos, 'Party and class before 1917' in **International Socialism** (new series) no 24 (Summer 1984).
16. Marx, **Communist Manifesto**, in **Revolutions of 1848**, edited D Fernbach (Harmondsworth 1973) page 71.
17. Trotsky, **Lessons of October** (London 1973) page 58.
18. L Trotsky, **Their Morals and Ours** (London 1968) page 12.
19. Trotsky, **History of the Russian Revolution**, page 159.
20. Marx, **Communist Manifesto**, pages 70–71.
21. K Marx, **The Civil War in France**, in **The First International and After**, edited D Fernbach (Harmondsworth 1974) page 212.
22. N Bukharin, **The Politics and Economics of the Transition Period** (London 1979) page 48.
23. Lenin, **Collected Works**, volume 27, page 271.
24. **Freiheit** (5 December 1918).
25. Lenin, **The Proletarian REvolution and the Renegade Kautsky**, page 39.
26. Lenin, **Collected Works**, volume 10, page 19.
27. C Harman, in **Socialist Worker** (16 April 1983).

INDEX

BOOKMARKS is London's leading socialist bookshop, where you'll find
two floors of books on socialism, internationalism, trade unions, workers'
history, economics, women's issues, socialist novels and much more.
We're just round the corner from Finsbury Park tube station. If you live
too far away to call in, we also run a large socialist mail order service,
sending books all over the world. Just drop us a line and ask for our latest
booklist.
BOOKMARKS, 265 Seven Sisters Road, Finsbury Park, London
N4 2DE, England.